to be returned on or bef
the last date below

McKenzie 4H

^ckenzie. 4.H.

Melita M. Neal

Dunstable College

New Metric Edition

BLACKIE AND SON LIMITED

Bishopbriggs Glasgow G64 2NZ
5 Fitzhardinge Street London W1H 0DL

First published 1961
New Metric Edition 1975

ISBN 0 216 89960 5

Printed in Great Britain by
Robert MacLehose and Company Limited
Printers to the University of Glasgow

PREFACE

Cookery for Schools is intended as a class book of information on the theory and methods necessary for passing examinations in cookery or food and nutrition, especially at O level.

First published in 1961, it was completely revised, metricated and re-issued in 1975 so it is virtually a new book based on a tried and tested favourite, to use a cooking term.

Much practice is given in compiling nutritional and attractive dishes for varying types of people but it is not a recipe book, as recipes can be found in my own recipe book for schools, in the hundreds of others on the market, or can be evolved and tested by the pupils themselves following suggestions in the book.

A feature of the book was always its pointers to further study and this edition has considerably more suggestions for research and development of critical appraisal and observation. It also gives indications of how this may be combined with work in a science laboratory to clarify the information given, or to make further discoveries.

New sets of questions, some in the popular 'matching' form have been added to each chapter. For many of these, acknowledgment is due to the General Certificate of Education Boards of the University of Cambridge, the Associated Examining Board and the City and Guilds of London Institute.

I should like to acknowledge the generous assistance of my colleague, Jeanne Pitkin, in checking the revision.

M.M.N.

CONTENTS

1

THE KITCHEN

ARRANGEMENT

PLANNING

The kitchen has been described as 'the heart of the home' and indeed it is the living centre of the household, in which the housewife spends a large proportion of her working hours. Even if she does not have the good fortune to be able to design her own kitchen from the beginning it is not long before she has stamped her own taste and personality upon the room. The present wide variety of bright and attractive paints and finishing materials gives her plenty of scope in creating a cheerful, efficient and attractive working environment which the whole family can enjoy.

Smooth wall surfaces are desirable for ease of cleaning but plain paint can be replaced with or augmented by other washable surfaces such as plastic-coated paper, coloured tiles (vinyl ones are less expensive than ceramics; plain white ceramic tiles may be covered at intervals by self-adhesive coloured and patterned plastic squares), wood strips (real or simulated) or laminated panels.

Plain white-painted ceilings give light to any room but many do-it-yourself home decorators find the repainting of a large surface awkward and laborious. Many ceilings are covered with stick-on polystyrene tiles which are easier to manage. Some concern has been expressed about the fire risk involved, polystyrene being highly inflammable. It is possible, however, to obtain a special paint for use on these surfaces which reduces their flammability, and thorough adhesion, which prevents the trapping of air between the ceiling and the tile, is also advisable.

The variety of designs of floor coverings is almost as large as that offered for walls, ready to be laid upon the wooden boards or cement flooring installed by the builder. Quiet, easy-to-clean coverings are provided by vinyl tiles, vinyl asbestos, felt-backed vinyl sheets, non-backed vinyl sheets, lino tiles, cork (which must be sealed to be suitable for kitchen use) and cork bonded with vinyl. It is important that no toe-catching irregularities in the floor covering are tolerated, for obvious safety reasons. Care must also be taken not to allow vinyl surfaces to become wet in patches—they can be very slippery.

The furnishings and fittings of the kitchen should be so arranged that free, unhampered movement is possible, while at the same time economizing in necessary movement. The sink, working-tops and the cooker should be arranged in sequence in order to minimize the number of steps required to move from one to another, and it may be that 'pier' or 'island' fittings are more convenient than wall furnishings. Hot plates and ovens can be fitted side by side to suit individual kitchen arrangements instead of one above the other; although more expensive than conventional cookers, these 'split' models do mean less stooping for the cook. The spaces below, like those under the sink and draining board, should be used for cupboards, increasing storage space and reducing difficult cleaning areas.

Most kitchen units are available in sizes which make them easily assembled to fit the space to be furnished. The most efficient arrangement is usually to combine storage units at the same level and a convenient height so that their tops form a continuous working surface. In a small room sliding doors are often more convenient than swing ones which, if unavoidable, should be arranged so that they do not clash against each other when more than one is open. The top sections of high wall-fitments should be kept for the less-often-used goods, and care must be taken that the fastening can be easily reached. Refrigerators and washing machines can be purchased in sizes convenient for fitting below the working surfaces if space is limited.

The position of the sink is generally limited by the necessity for plumbing it to an outside wall whenever possible. This usually allows a window to be immediately above the sink unit. If this looks out over the garden or onto any view but a blank wall, the minimum of curtaining is required and the worker at the sink has a pleasant or, at least, interesting outlook. (See p. 3 for choice and care of sinks.)

Modern kitchens often have a dining-area incorporated into their plans but some families prefer a separate dining-room. Many steps may be saved if it is possible for a hatch to be opened in the common wall between the dining-room and the kitchen. A working-top or table immediately below it is useful.

It is essential that the kitchen should be quickly aired and freed from cooking smells. Windows should open easily, in sections if possible, to regulate the air flow. Good window space also makes the kitchen a pleasant room in which to work. If it is closely overlooked by another house, the windows can be of frosted or patterned glass. If ventilation is limited, extractor fans fitted into a small window or an outside wall or door can be very helpful. An increasingly popular aid to ventilation is a cooker hood; this can be either fan-operated and ducted through an outside wall, or the ductless type which draws in stale air through a filter and purifies it before re-circulation.

Once the kitchen is in use it is important that the cook should not have to work in her own light, as is often the case in the evening when there is only a central pendant light. Hanging lights can be replaced by fluorescent tubes which cast little shadow, or by a small light which can be fixed over the sink and/or cooker. Extra lights in deep cupboards can also be very useful.

EQUIPPING

Having planned an attractive and efficient kitchen, the housewife must consider the equipment which she needs to install and the number of small items which she will require for carrying out her cooking.

Whatever piece of equipment is purchased, there are a number of general rules which should be followed:

1 Buy the best quality which can be afforded. Although the initial cost of good quality equipment may be greater, the frequency with which cheaper products must be replaced counteracts this disadvantage.

2 Choose items of suitable sizes for the requirements of the family.

3 Choose equipment for its efficiency rather than for its attractive appearance.

4 Be guided by guarantees and the British Standards Kite Marks; these are only awarded to products which have been tested by experts and passed as efficient for the work for which they have been designed. There are also several associations which guide the public in their choice of branded goods; one in particular compares the value of specific items sold under different names.

5 Choose colours and finishes which blend with the general colour scheme of the kitchen.

CHOOSING AND CARING FOR KITCHEN EQUIPMENT

Cookers
Refrigerators } See 'Gas in the Kitchen' (p. 17) and
Water Heaters 'Electricity in the Kitchen' (p. 24).

SINKS

Choosing

Choose the best sink which can be afforded, preferably in a unit utilizing the spaces below the sink and the draining board as cupboards.

Choose an easily cleaned surface:

a plastic, which is attractive and wears well but which becomes roughened in time, and progressively more difficult to keep clean

b porcelain, which is easy to clean but can become scratched and chipped with age and rough usage

c stainless steel, which is expensive but very durable and easily cleaned.

Make sure that the sink is fitted at a convenient height for its chief user to be able to stand at it comfortably, without stooping.

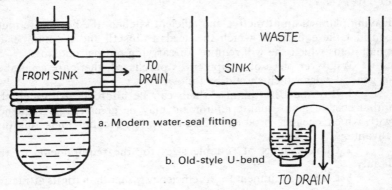

a. Modern water-seal fitting

b. Old-style U-bend

Choose a plastic seal-pipe fitting rather than the older U-bend type. Although a screw at the bottom of the U-bend will allow access to the pipe for cleaning should it become blocked, the newer plastic screw-cup type is much easier to manage.

Note It is possible to purchase a sink fitted with a waste-disposal unit. The sink must be made of steel and it must be specifically ordered for use with the unit, as the outlet must be 8·75 cm in diameter. These sinks are particularly useful in flats where refuse is difficult to dispose of. The unit must, of course, be attached to the electrical circuit.

Using
Do

1 use a plastic sink basket (or sink-tidy) to catch small pieces of refuse, or use a crumb strainer waste-pipe cover.

2 use a plastic bowl inside the sink to save running sufficient water to fill the entire sink when only small quantities are necessary.

3 rinse the sink after every use, flushing it well with clean water each time dirty water is emptied down. This will ensure that there is always clean water in the water-seal and smells will not travel up the waste-pipe.

4 clean thoroughly at least once a day, usually when clearing up after the main meal.

5 use a disinfectant rinse weekly to keep the pipes and drains free from germs and smells (add sufficient disinfectant to a sink full of water to make the water cloudy).

Do not

1 allow gritty substances to collect between the bowl (if used) and the sink. The friction which is caused may scratch the surface of the sink, but can be avoided by using a plastic mat between the bottom of the sink and the bowl.

2 force any waste matter (vegetable pieces, coffee grounds, etc.) down the waste-pipe. These will collect in the water-seal or U-bend and cause a blockage. All scraps should be removed from the top of the waste-pipe as soon as they collect.

3 pour liquid fat down the waste-pipe. It will solidify as it cools, or when cold water is flushed down, and will cause a blockage.

Cleaning

1 Remove any scraps from the top of the waste-pipe.

2 Wash with hot, soapy water.

3 Rinse.

4 Remove stains if necessary:

a from stainless steel—use stainless steel cleaner on a soft pad. Do not bleach.

b from other surfaces—use nylon scourer, with a mild scouring powder if necessary. Bleach obstinate stains.

5 Rinse.

6 Dry off stainless steel with a soft cloth.

Unblocking

1 Try the easiest methods first—create a suction.

a Place the heel of the hand or a folded cloth over the top of the waste-pipe to seal it completely, wait a few seconds and then remove it quickly. Repeat several times.

b Use a rubber sink plunger.

c Place the plug in position and fill the sink with water until it flows down the over-flow pipe. Keep the tap running, wait a few seconds and then remove the plug quickly.

2 Use a flexible coiled wire (a curtain wire will do if a commercially-prepared one is not available) which can be pushed down the waste-pipe and will curve into the U-bend or water-seal.

3 If the blockage is caused by congealed grease, place a large lump of soda on the waste-pipe grid and pour a stream of boiling water slowly over it.

4 Place a bucket underneath the U-bend or water-seal pipe and undo the bottom nut or section. Clear the pipe in both directions, using

a flexible wire or strong bottle brush. Replace the nut or cup and flush the pipe with hot water. Rinse with cold water.

Draining Boards/Drainers

These should always be set at an angle which allows waste water to run downwards to the sink without being so steep that crockery and cutlery slide downwards as well.

Few wooden drainers are fitted nowadays but if one is already installed it should be rinsed with cold water and wiped as dry as possible after each use. The grooves must not be allowed to become filled with waste matter. If stained, it should be scrubbed with warm water and hard soap, working the brush in small circles along the grain of the wood. Plastic or stainless steel drainers should be wiped dry after use. A drying rack for crockery and cutlery will prevent scratching and facilitate draining. Stainless steel can be polished with a dry cloth after use.

TABLES

Many modern kitchens do not need a conventional table as they are fitted with working surfaces and pier units. If a small eating area is part of the kitchen, however, a separate table and chairs, stools or benches may be required.

Choosing

Plain frames with laminated surfaces on tables and plastic covered seats for chairs make for easy cleaning and attractive appearance.

Care

1 Keep surfaces wiped clean and ledges dusted. Laminated surfaces (such as Formica, Warerite, Arborite) can be kept smooth and shiny with an aerosol polish.

2 Protect laminated surfaces from heat. They are not completely heat-resistant and hot containers should be placed on pan stands, asbestos mats or more decorative table mats at meal times if necessary. A folded, dry dish cloth or a pad of newspaper may be used during cooking operations if a pan-stand is not available.

3 Protect surfaces from scratches. Chop or slice onto a chopping board: if it is not plastic-coated it will be made of hard wood and the grain is not easily damaged.

REFUSE BINS

Dustbins

The conventional galvanized iron or thick plastic bin is being replaced by lift-off bins lined with disposable plastic bags or stout paper sacks supported on a metal frame with a hinged lid. Care is reduced to a minimum for the housewife, but she must remember not to allow sharp surfaces or hot ashes to damage either kind of sack.

Binettes

Choose a model with a well-fitting lid, raised by a pedal. These are usually made of coloured plastic and can blend with the scheme of decoration.

Care

1 Use the bin as far as possible for dry refuse only; wrap peelings and other damp scraps in newspaper if they cannot be placed on a compost heap or garden incinerator.

2 Empty frequently: the most convenient time is usually when cleaning-up after the main meal.

3 Clean regularly: wash with hot, soapy water containing a little disinfectant. Dry thoroughly.

4 Line with newspaper before re-use, or use a commercial bin-liner. These are very convenient but, of course, more expensive.

SMALL EQUIPMENT

Choosing Pans

Buy the best quality that can be afforded. Buy reasonably thick-walled pans with flat bases, particularly if they are to be used on electric cookers. When choosing, place the pan on the counter and test it to make sure that it does not wobble at all.

Note The walls of a thick pan hold heat (known as residual heat) and therefore the temperature of the contents will continue to rise *after* the pan has been removed from the heat. Allowance must be made for this particularly in the heating of milk, which will boil over even after the pan has been removed from the cooker.

Consider the amount of use and the size of the family for which the pan is required and gauge the size accordingly.

Try the handle and make sure that it is comfortable to hold and firmly attached to the pan. It must be sufficiently strong to support the weight of the pan *when full*. Very large pans should have a second grip opposite the handle to allow it to be supported safely.

Make sure that the handle and lid-knob are made of heat-resisting material.

Try the lid on the pan and make sure that it fits snugly.

See that the surface can be easily cleaned and that there is no sharp angle between the bottom and side of the pan.

Non-stick Cookware

Some pots, pans and baking tins are coated with a special lining containing chemicals to which food particles are unable to cling.

They are particularly useful for

a heating milk, scrambled eggs and starch mixtures which can be difficult to wash from untreated vessels

b 'frying' without fat for anyone having to follow a fat-free diet

c easy release of cakes and pastries after cooking.

When using, remember

a to wash and rinse the pan before using it for the first time. Dry thoroughly and brush it lightly with oil to 'precondition' the lining.

b to avoid extreme heat—this could affect the appearance and the efficiency of the cooking.

c to wash it in hot, soapy water after use. Use a nylon brush or rubber scraper to remove stubborn patches if necessary.

d that unless guaranteed 'hardbase', metal utensils should not be used for stirring, etc.

e that large cake tins do not need protective paper linings.

Care

Do

1 use them only on the cooker for which they were intended.

2 store them in a dry, well-ventilated place. Turn them upside-down on shelves to prevent dust on the inside, or stand them right way up with the lid not quite on. (Pans may smell musty if left for long with a tightly-fitting lid in position.)

3 dry saucepans thoroughly before putting them away, to avoid rusting. (Chips on enamelled pans quickly show red rust and aluminium ones become covered with a white, powdery deposit which is aluminium rust, almost impossible to remove.)

Do not

1 use knives or metal spoons with sharp edges for stirring and mixing. This practice damages the surface of the pan, particularly of non-stick linings, besides being very noisy. Stir with wooden or plastic spoons or spatulas.

2 bend the pan out of shape by leaning heavily on it while cleaning it, particularly when it is turned on its side.

Cleaning Pans

1 Remove all scraps of food.

2 Fill the pan with cold water immediately it has been emptied of food. This is particularly necessary in the case of a milk pan, on which the lactalbumen sets if treated with warm water.

3 If necessary, steep burnt pans. Fill them with cold water and add a handful of cooking salt.

4 Clean according to the surface of the pan, using the simplest methods first—*a*. washing, *b*. mild abrasive, *c*. coarse abrasive. Do not use abrasives on pans with non-stick linings.

5 Repeat the cleaning on the outside.
6 Rinse in clean water.
7 Dry thoroughly.
Note Pay particular attention to the angle of the pan and to the rim of the lid when cleaning.

BAKING TINS

Choosing Baking Tins

Choose the best which can be afforded: cheap tins bend easily, very often have uncomfortably sharp edges and the surface very quickly wears.

Buy tins of a convenient size for the use required and for the oven in which they are used. They should not be so large that the edges come above the burners of the oven. When this happens the food either at the back or the sides of the tin will cook very quickly and burn while the rest is cooking.

See also 'Non-stick Cookware' (p. 7).

When Using Baking Tins
Do

1 store them carefully so that they are not forced against each other and bent out of shape.

2 allow tins to cool before filling with cold water for soaking, *or* fill hot tins with hot water. Very sudden changes of temperature may cause the tins to warp by quick and uneven contraction.

3 dry thoroughly after washing, to avoid rusting.
Do not

1 allow jam or any other fillings to boil over and burn the baking tin.

2 lean on tins while cleaning them, thus bending them out of shape.

3 bend or dent tins by dropping them.

Cleaning Tins

1 Remove as much adhering food as possible while the tin is still hot (use a *round*-bladed knife, unless the tin is lined with a non-stick finish, when soaking will usually be sufficient).

2 Soak the tins if necessary, using hot soda water for greasy tins and cold salt water for burnt ones.

3 Wash them in hot soapy water, using an abrasive (steel wool is useful, but try salt or a nylon scourer first) if necessary.

4 Rinse in clean water.

5 Dry thoroughly (place in hot oven if available).

6 Store carefully.

CASSEROLES

There is a large variety of most attractive ware available in a wide range of prices, and materials used include heat-resistant glass, stoneware (glazed and unglazed), enamelled iron, cast iron and 'pyroceram' (e.g. 'Pyrosil'). Bearing in mind the fact that success depends upon the long, slow, combined stewing and steaming of the contents, it is obvious that the vessels must be thick-walled and have well-fitting lids. When choosing, it must be remembered that a weighty casserole dish will be even heavier when full and it is essential that the dish can be conveniently handled.

As an oven-to-table dish, the choice of such a utensil serves a double purpose and this fact offsets a little the initial cost. Moreover, such a method of cooking does cut down the labour of oven-cleaning.

Heat-resistant Glassware
Care must be taken
    a not to place hot glass upon cold surfaces *or* to fill hot dishes with cold water to soak
    b not to scour glass with a coarse abrasive which can scratch the surface
    c never to place any but 'Pyrosil' type glass directly over heat.

LABOUR-SAVERS

There is an extremely large and somewhat bewildering variety of cooking utensils and so-called labour-saving gadgets for the housewife to choose from. Some take more time to assemble before, and to clean after use than their actual performance justifies, and these should be looked upon as luxuries rather than necessities.

The following items are those which form a good basis of equipment for most cooking processes and in choosing them the rules noted on p. 3 should be followed.

1 *An electric mixer*, which can be fitted with attachments for blending, chopping, liquidizing and kneading, saves a great deal of time and effort and, if the initial cost can be afforded, is a most valuable piece of equipment. A smaller, hand-held model is cheaper but its versatility is not as great as that of the table model.

The usual care of electrical equipment must be observed and the beaters must be kept very clean.

Note If an electric mixer is available, several of the following items may not be required.

2 *Mincer* This is not an essential piece of equipment but is very useful when making réchauffé dishes. Mincers may be obtained in colours to match the kitchen decoration and may be fixed to the working-top by suction caps at the bottom of the 'feet'.

3 *Food chopper* Like the mincer, this is not a necessity but saves much labour in preparing vegetables for soups, foods for réchauffé dishes, nuts for decoration, etc.

4 *Whisk* Balloon-type wire whisks are particularly efficient for beating egg-whites, but the rotary type requires less effort. Both types must be washed carefully after use, dried thoroughly in a warm place and stored so that there is no likelihood of the wires or beaters becoming bent. The safest way is to hang it on a rack or hook.

5 *Chopping board* Slicing and chopping should always be carried out on a hard board rather than on a working surface. The surface of the board may be plastic covered and require only washing. If the surface of the wood is exposed, it should be scrubbed regularly, particularly when used for strongly-flavoured foods. It is advisable to reverse the board after such use if it is required again immediately.

6 *Mixing bowl/basins* One large mixing bowl and a minimum of one large and one small basin are required and these may be of heat-resistant glass or china as required.

7 *Rolling pin* A wooden or glass rolling pin may be chosen.

8 *Sieves* One large and one small meshed sieve are desirable, made from either wire or nylon and fitted with handles. These should be scrubbed clean after each use and dried thoroughly.

9 *Flour/sugar dredger* Plastic containers with pierced tops may be used for either purpose as required.

10 *Scales* A pair of balance scales and weights give longer service than the more up-to-date spring-balance type, but these are usually more expensive. Wall-mounted spring-balance scales are neat and attractive. Scale pans must be kept clean and the balance used gently to maintain its efficiency.

11 *Grater* There are a number of different types of grater available, the most useful, efficient and easily cleaned being the metal, four-sided type which stands firmly on the working surface while in use. Each side grates to a different degree of fineness. After use, all food residue must be scrubbed away and the grater dried thoroughly in a warm place before storing.

12 *Measuring jug* A glass or plastic jug marked in fluid capacity makes the measurement of liquids consistent and accurate.

13 *Colander* This may be of metal or plastic, care being taken not to bend or dent metal or to damage plastic with excess heat.

14 *Lemon squeezer* This is the most efficient, quickest aid to removing juice from citrus fruit and may be made of glass, metal or plastic.

15 *Masher* A perforated metal vegetable masher for use on cooked foods will last a lifetime and is easy to use and to clean.

16 *Can opener* A wall-mounted can opener is more convenient and safer to use than the hand-operated type. It may be obtained in a number of gay colours and can be fitted with a magnetic disc which

prevents lids from dropping into the contents of the cans as they are opened.

The cutting wheel should be wiped after every use, and it is advisable to keep the opener covered when not in use. A plastic bag used as a 'hood' and secured with a rubber band is an easy and convenient method of doing so.

17 *Scissors*   A pair of kitchen scissors, preferably those especially made for such use, is a handy tool for a number of uses. The scissors should not be used for other purposes in the household.

18 *Knives*   One palette knife, one large cook's knife, one vegetable knife and a general-purpose round-bladed knife give the service required.

All knives should be sharpened regularly and stored carefully in a drawer compartment, not mixed with other utensils, to avoid fingers being cut while searching for them.

A vegetable peeler may be preferred for use in preparing root vegetables, apples, etc. This may be obtained to suit either a right or left-handed person.

19 *Forks*   A carving fork (with a protection guard) and a general-purposes large fork are the minimum requirements.

20 *Spoons*   One wooden spoon is desirable; a second, square-ended one is useful but not essential. A flexible plastic spatula makes the cleaning out of mixing bowls easy, and one each of tea, dessert and table-sized spoons are useful, especially for measuring. Although plastic ones are available, these are limited in their use in very hot fluids and the metal type is preferable.

HOMELY MEASURES

2 teaspoonfuls are equivalent to 1 dessertspoonful
2 dessertspoonfuls are equivalent to 1 tablespoonful
Powders, e.g. flour, icing sugar, fine cereals:

1 rounded tablespoonful	= 20 g
1 level tablespoonful	= 10 g
1 rounded dessertspoonful	= 10 g
1 level dessertspoonful	= 5 g

Dried fruit, coarse cereals, sugar:

1 rounded tablespoonful	= 40 g
1 level tablespoonful	= 20 g
1 rounded dessertspoonful	= 20 g
1 level dessertspoonful	= 10 g

Syrup:

1 tablespoonful 2 dessertspoonfuls }	= 30 g
3 dessertspoonfuls	= 50 g
3 tablespoonfuls	= 100 g

Liquids:
> 1 tablespoonful   = 20 ml
> 1 dessertspoonful = 10 ml
> 1 teaspoonful   = 5 ml

Note 'Rounded' means that there is as much above the bowl of the spoon as is contained in the bowl.

KITCHEN CLOTHS

Choosing Cloths

Buy the best quality that can be afforded. Most kitchen cloths are subjected to very hard wear and frequent replacement of cheap cloths make little difference in the over-all expense.

Choose cloths of a suitable texture for the use they are to receive.

Fabrics chosen should be easily laundered. Most kitchen cloths are made of cotton which is hard-wearing, absorbent, cheap and may be boiled. Tea-towels made of linen are excellent for drying and glass-polishing purposes but are expensive. *Cheap* cotton tea-towels very soon become soaked and leave fluff on dried surfaces.

The latest kitchen 'cloths' are made of paper which is at the same time tough, soft and absorbent. These last a surprisingly long time and are hygienic to use and very reasonably priced.

Using Cloths

Do

> 1 use the cloth *only* for its own particular purpose.
> 2 clean thoroughly after every use. Steep, in soda water if necessary, to remove grease. Then wash out in hot, soapy water and hang in the air to dry.
> 3 prolong the life of tea-towels which have worn very thin by stitching them together one over another.

Do not

> 1 use wet cloths to hold saucepan handles or to remove dishes from the oven. (Use oven gloves for these purposes.)
> 2 leave dirty or wet cloths lying in heaps. They develop smells if stale water is left in them.

KITCHEN ROUTINE

Use of Storage Units

Organize units so that each section is used for one type of content. All shelves should be painted or covered with adhesive plastic to make cleaning easier.

China cupboards   Plates and saucers should be sorted in piles. Plastic-covered wire racks are very useful fittings in which these can be stored in small piles or on edge. Cups and jugs may be hung from a series of hooks underneath shelves where space permits.

Saucepan cupboards   Pans should preferably be stored upside down on shelves but if this is not possible they may be stacked one inside another. A convenient way of storing lids is to slip them under thin rods or flexible wires fixed across the back of the cupboard doors.

Food cupboards   A good deal of space can easily be wasted here if the use of space is not well organized. Plastic-coated wire 'space-savers' or 'slide-on baskets' are useful for utilizing the spaces between shelves by almost doubling the storage areas; shallow shelves or racks can be fixed between two deep ones and smaller intermediate ones can be arranged on the backs of cupboard doors for tiny bottles and jars, containing herbs, spices, essences, etc.

There is a large variety of attractive, hard-wearing, easily cleaned light canisters on the market which are suitable for the storage of dry goods. Transparent containers are useful because it is obvious when their contents become depleted, and screw-top glass jars emptied of their normal contents are economical but, of course, heavier to use than plastic ones. All containers should be labelled.

MANAGEMENT OF STORES

All goods should be replenished before the last portion is used. New packets, jars and tins should be placed at the back of the storage section and not opened until the last of the old stock is used.

Keep all shelves tidily arranged and wiped clean. Use high shelves for goods which are not in frequent use.

STORAGE OF FOODS

1 Store perishable foods in the refrigerator (see p. 36). If a refrigerator is not available

a place open packets of fat, bacon slices, pieces of meat and fish on separate plates covered with foil, polythene or muslin. Do not allow these to accumulate.

b keep milk in the bottle in as cool a place as possible, if necessary in a bowl of cold water with muslin draped over the bottle into the water.

c store cheese, unwrapped, in a dish with a perforated lid, or wrap lightly and store in a cool place on a plate.

2 Empty packeted goods into appropriate containers as soon as they are opened. Group these together according to their kind.

3 Sort tinned goods according to their contents and stack them in sequence of use.

4 Store cakes and biscuits in separate airtight tins: if placed together the biscuits absorb moisture from the cake and become soft.

5 Store bread in a ventilated bread bin. This piece of equipment is usually sufficiently decorative to be on view in the kitchen.

6 Remove fruit and vegetables from their wrappings and place in a vegetable rack in a well-ventilated position.

7 Transfer 'left-overs' to smaller containers and use for réchauffé dishes as soon as possible.

WASHING-UP

This operation need never be an unpleasant chore and, like most household tasks, depends largely on good organization for success.

The essentials are: a good supply of hot water
powdered or liquid soap/washing-up liquid
a washing-up cloth and/or mop
a scourer
a tea-towel.

Preparation

1 Scrape food scraps on to newspaper and dispose of them. Empty slops (not tea leaves) down sink.

2 Fill dirty saucepans with water, cold if pan has been used for starchy or milky foods; hot, with a little soda, if pans are greasy. Add salt to the water used for soaking burnt pans. Leave to stand.

3 Stack plates and saucers in piles; group cups and glasses separately.

4 Sort knives, spoons and forks separately.

5 If knives have bone or other non-metallic handles, stand them in a jug of hot water deep enough to cover the blades.

Washing-up

1 Fill the bowl with water hot enough for the hands to bear comfortably.

2 Add sufficient soap or washing-up liquid to make a slight lather.

3 Wash glasses first. Rinse under hot running water if possible. Stand them upside down on the drainer.

4 Wash cups and stand them upside down to drain (after rinsing if possible).

5 Wash the cleanest remaining crockery and continue until the most soiled items are washed last. As each item is washed and rinsed, stack overlapping on drainer supported by cups (not glasses). If a drying rack is available, stand each plate on edge in one of the grooves.

6 If water is soiled, change it for a fresh supply of hot water and washing-up liquid.

7 Wash, rinse and drain spoons and forks.

8 Wash, rinse and drain any cooking utensils.

9 Wash, rinse and drain saucepans and baking tins, starting with the least soiled and finishing with the dirtiest (see 'Pans', p. 8).

Drying-up
1 If a drying rack is used, crockery may be left in it to dry completely before being put away. Glasses must be polished with a dry cloth.
2 If no drying rack is used: dry and polish glasses
dry and polish silver cutlery
dry plates, saucers, cups
dry cooking utensils
dry pans and baking tins.

Clearing-up
1 Empty away dirty water.
2 Wash out tea-towel and hang to dry.
3 Clean sink and washing-up bowl. Wipe sink surround.
4 Wash out washing-up cloth and hang to dry.
5 Put away all washed items.

FURTHER STUDY

THINGS TO DO

1 Collect pictures and prices of a complete set of saucepans and baking dishes suitable for an ordinary household.

2 Collect pictures and prices of two different makes of the same household utensils. Choose six pieces and compare them, giving your preference and your reasons.

3 Collect pictures and prices of a complete set of cooking utensils other than pans and baking dishes. Mount these and under each write the reasons for your choice.

4 Find illustrations and prices of sink units made by three different firms. State which you would choose and why.

5 Collect as many illustrations as you can of materials available which add to the cleanliness, efficiency and attractiveness of the kitchen.

6 Find out what is used to coat pans to make them non-stick. Compare the effects of cooking *a.* scrambled eggs, *b.* fried eggs, *c.* pancakes, *d.* white sauce, *e.* hot milk, in a non-stick pan and in an uncoated one.

7 Make up the following mixtures and cook exactly half of each in a standard tin and the other half in a non-stick tin:
a jam or lemon-curd tarts
b small cakes
c a large cake.
Compare
a the effect on the tins
b the browning of the cooked mixtures

c the texture of the cooked mixtures

d cooking times.

8 Plan your ideal kitchen, giving details of colours and materials used. Illustrate wherever possible and give a ground plan of the arrangement of the large equipment.

QUESTIONS TO ANSWER

1 What points would influence you in the purchase of

a a milk saucepan for use on an electric cooker

b a refrigerator

c an oven casserole

d a hand whisk?

What special care would you give to ensure maximum efficiency of the equipment? (A.E.B.)

2 Write notes on the following:

a oven-to-table ware

b non-stick cooking pans and tins

c laminated plastic surfaces.

3 You have won a prize of £50 worth of kitchen equipment of your choice. Describe the items you wish for, give reasons for your decision and state the special care they would require.

4 Make a list of household cloths required for general use in the house. What materials would you choose for the various cloths mentioned and what steps would you take to keep them in good condition?

5 List the basic cleaning stores you need in order to keep your new equipment in good order and say how and when you would use *three* items from your list.

6 What items are available to the contemporary housewife which enable her to organize her food storage efficiently, hygienically and economically even if she does not possess a refrigerator?

7 How would you ensure that your kitchen could always be described as hygienic?

GAS IN THE KITCHEN

Gas-heated appliances in the kitchen include

a cookers

b water heaters

c refrigerators.

GAS COOKERS

There are four basic types of gas cooker

a table-top cookers: with one or two boiling rings sometimes combined with a grill and an oven, usually used in caravans or bed-sitters *b* vertical cookers: the conventional type in which the oven, hot plate and grill are placed one over the other. These vary slightly in height and width

c range cookers: with two ovens next to each other, four hot plate burners and a grill

d split-level cookers: the oven and the hot plate and grill are separate; these are particularly useful for fitting into kitchen units and for eliminating bending.

Continental cookers may be found to have slight differences from those manufactured in this country:

a different markings are used

b the grill is nearly always inside the oven

c the hot plate can be covered with a shut-down lid when it is not in use

d the burner heating the oven is *outside* it.

Construction

The present British oven consists of a steel box, heated from the bottom by a single burner across the back providing a series of small gas jets inside the oven. The walls are double and are packed with a layer of glass fibre and foil to prevent the escape of heat. These are coated with vitreous enamel which is easy to clean and attractive in appearance.

The shelves are made of nickel-coated steel rungs which are strong enough to support heavy dishes but are sufficiently widely-spaced to allow unimpeded circulation of heated air.

Air is drawn in from an aperture at the bottom of the oven; when this is heated it rises and sets up convection currents within the oven. The thermostat regulates the temperature to the heat required and there is a flue at the back of the cooker to carry away the burnt gases.

Special features of cookers include

a pilot jets or spark igniters to light any of the hot plate burners as required. The oven burner and grill can be ignited by a pilot, a spark or by pushing a button which activates an electric current and causes an igniter to glow. The current for the igniter and spark can come directly from the mains or from a battery.

b removable roof linings which can be lifted out completely for cleaning.

c a special 'continuous-cleaning' lining which cleans itself as it is heated, owing to a catalyst incorporated into the oven lining of vitreous enamel.

d oven doors which open downwards and will lift off completely to allow easy access to the oven for cleaning. These doors make useful 'shelves' for use when basting or turning food during cooking.

e glass panels in the door which allow cooking progress to be watched, and lights in ovens, which make it easier to see the food cooking.

f rôtisserie spits worked by electricity: these may be fixed under the grill or in the oven.

g a thermostatically-controlled burner which will keep a pan and its contents at a constant temperature, particularly useful for deep-fat frying.

h automatic controls to turn the oven on and off so that food can be left in the oven and the cooker programmed to begin heating at a specific time for whatever length of cooking time is required. This is a tremendous asset to the working housewife.

Choosing a Cooker

When buying a cooker, give careful consideration to the following points and decide which model most closely fits the particular circumstances and habits:

1 *Size* Choose a model suitable for *a*. the size of the kitchen, *b*. the position of the cooker, e.g. if the kitchen is narrow, do not choose one with a drop-down door, and *c*. the amount of cooking to be carried out and the possible desirability of an automatic model.

2 *Burners* The size and position of these must be convenient for the type and amount of cooking usually required; the smaller ones are best for long, slow cooking, larger ones for quick-cooking purposes. The grids covering the burners should be easily removed for cleaning. Some hot plates are sealed and this also has its advantages.

3 *Price* It is cheaper, as with most items of equipment, to buy the cooker outright, but all models can be bought by instalments if desired. The more sophisticated models are more expensive.

4 *Position of grill* This is largely a matter of individual preference, but in a household which includes small children an eye-level grill may be safer.

Note All cookers should have the British Gas Standards Seal of Approval.

A 'marriage' has recently taken place between gas hot plate and electric fan-assisted ovens, as a result of research which showed that gas rings are generally preferred for boiling and simmering while electric

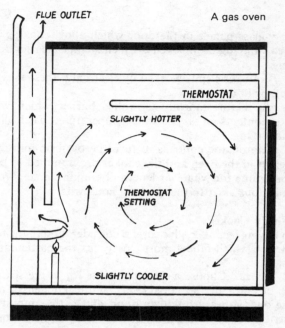

FLUE OUTLET

A gas oven

THERMOSTAT

SLIGHTLY HOTTER

THERMOSTAT SETTING

SLIGHTLY COOLER

Diagram of a thermostat

The thermostat works on the principle of the unequal expansion of different metals on heating. As it becomes hot, the brass tube (B) expands more than the steel rod (A), which consequently draws the valve head (C) closer to its seating (D). This reduces the flow of gas to the burner. As the heat in the oven lessens, so the tube cools and contracts a little. This moves valve (C) slightly away from its seating (D) so allowing more gas to reach the oven, which begins to heat up again. The by-pass allows sufficient gas to flow to keep the burner alight continuously.

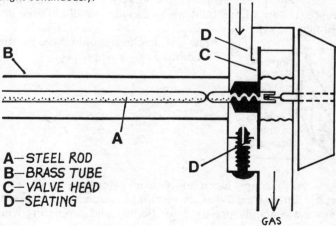

A — STEEL ROD
B — BRASS TUBE
C — VALVE HEAD
D — SEATING

GAS

ovens are more popular than gas-heated ones. The ovens are finished with a 'continuous-cleaning' lining. It is also possible to purchase combined gas/electric hobs for fitting into units.

Using the Cooker
The oven

1 The hottest part of the oven is at the top. If this is fully understood it will be possible to cook dishes requiring various heats in the same oven at the same time. For instance, a milk pudding requiring long, slow cooking may be safely placed at the bottom of an oven in which a joint of meat is being roasted in the middle and a pastry dish is successfully baked and browned on the top shelf (see diagram, p. 20).

2 The temperature of the oven should be regulated solely by using the thermostat. The oven tap should be turned full on, whatever the heat required.

3 Baking trays must not be allowed to overlap the jets, as they will become overheated and burn the outside of the food they contain.

The hot plate

1 Use the smaller burners for long, slow cooking and the larger ones for quicker boiling.

2 Do not allow the flame to come up outside the pan it is supposed to be heating. The heat of the flame is in the tip and this should lick the bottom of the pan.

Economy in the use of gas

1 ⎫
2 ⎬   see 1 and 2 above

3 Use the oven to its fullest capacity; do as much baking as possible at one time. Try to avoid lighting and heating the oven for one dish only.

4 Keep the kitchen free from draughts so that the air being drawn into the oven is not too cold and so that the flames from the burners do not flicker.

5 Use tiered steamers or a pressure cooker for cooking several items on one burner. (Complete meals are a possibility.)

6 Use pans which are not buckled or dirty.

7 Use pans of suitable sizes for the foods being cooked and do not boil more water than is required for use.

Cleaning a Cooker
Everyday cleaning

1 Wipe off splashes before they can be burned on to the surface.

2 Wipe over the inside of the oven while it is still warm. Cover joints of meat or game with foil or specially prepared plastic bags which allow the contents to brown without splashing the oven as this reduces the need for cleaning.

Occasional cleaning

1 Remove all detachable parts.

2 Wipe any very greasy parts with kitchen paper.

3 Soak bars and hot plate burners in hot, soapy water. Wash and rinse. Use fine steel-wool pads if necessary, except on 'continuous-cleaning' oven linings. Dry.

4 Brush oven burners and grill frets and burners. Clear the holes if necessary, using a cocktail stick.

5 Clean all enamel parts, inside and out, using a mild abrasive if necessary. If the oven is *very* soiled, use an aerosol cleaner according to the instructions.

6 Reassemble the cooker and light the burners to check their positioning and to ensure complete drying.

Note Do *not* allow cleaning agents to come in contact with the pilots, or with 'continuous-cleaning' oven linings.

Natural Gas

Household gas used to be manufactured at the Gas Works by the burning of coal and the incidental production of coke and coal tar. This is now referred to as Town Gas.

Natural gas comes from beneath the earth's surface, at present mainly from under the North Sea or from the Sahara. It is more economical in use than town gas, does not pollute the atmosphere, is safe to use and is not poisonous (it does not contain the carbon monoxide which is present in town gas). The smell is the same as that of town gas, because it is added artificially to natural gas. Although not toxic, it can still form an explosive mixture with air and it is essential that its presence is indicated.

Old appliances must be converted to burn natural gas and this *must* be carried out officially by the British Gas Corporation.

WATER HEATERS

Instantaneous

Cold water flows in at the bottom of the heater and the pressure causes a valve to open, letting gas flow up the inlet pipe. It is ignited by the pilot. The cold water is heated by the finned heat exchanger and can flow out through the hot tap when it is turned on. When the tap is closed, the water ceases to flow and the valve closes, cutting off the gas supply.

Storage Heaters

As in the circulation of air in an oven, cold water rises as it is heated. (This is known as a convection current.) Therefore storage tanks are fed with cold water entering through a pipe which runs from the top nearly to the bottom of the tank and the hot water is drawn off from the

Gas storage water heater

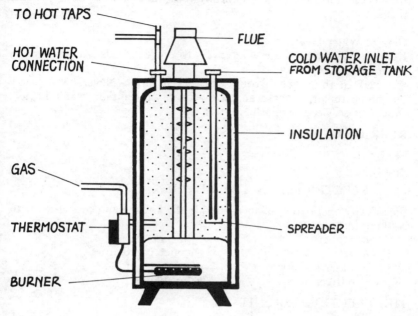

TO HOT TAPS

FLUE

HOT WATER CONNECTION

COLD WATER INLET FROM STORAGE TANK

INSULATION

GAS

THERMOSTAT

SPREADER

BURNER

Instantaneous gas water heater

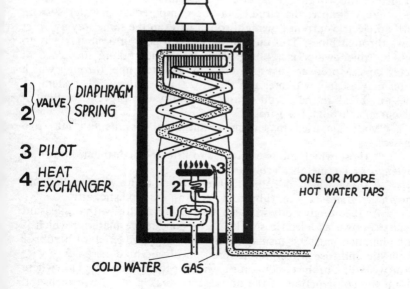

1 } VALVE { DIAPHRAGM
2 }   { SPRING

3 PILOT

4 HEAT EXCHANGER

ONE OR MORE HOT WATER TAPS

COLD WATER   GAS

top. These tanks are thermostatically controlled and lagged to insulate them.

Care of Water Heaters

Keep the flues clear—use wire covers to prevent birds from nesting in the outside flue pipe.

If anything goes wrong, call the gas fitter. Never try to carry out home repairs in case an escape of gas is caused. Water heaters should be serviced regularly.

REFRIGERATORS

See p. 31.

ELECTRICITY IN THE KITCHEN

Electrically operated appliances used in the kitchen and concerned with cooking include

a cookers
b kettles
c water heaters
d refrigerators

e mixers
f coffee percolators
g toasters
h hot plates.

THE ELECTRIC CIRCUIT

To understand the working of these appliances it is necessary to have an idea of the working of an electrical circuit.

Very simply, the circuit may be compared to a water system, with an electric current flowing through wires in the same way as water flows through pipes. This current can be 'tapped' in a similar way to that in which water is tapped, electric switches taking the place of water taps. Moreover, just as a crack in a water pipe, through which water may escape, will interrupt the flow through the whole system, so does any break in the circuit of an electrical system prevent the flow of the current through the wires.

Materials used in setting up electrical circuits fall into two classes:

a those which allow electricity to flow through them, known as *conductors*—i.e. metals, carbon, water

b those which do not allow electricity to flow through them, known as *insulators*—i.e. rubber, porcelain, glass, plastic, air.

As the human body will also act as a conductor, with unpleasant results (known as 'electric shocks'), any conductive material which is to be handled must be insulated—flex wires are covered with rubber or plastic and fuse wires are mounted on plastic holders. (A fuse wire is the weak link of the circuit—if the wires become overheated anywhere within the construction of the house, this weak portion will melt and the circuit will break. As it is in an accessible position it can be mended quite easily, whereas a normal portion of wiring may be quite unreachable. Frequent 'blowing' of fuses should be regarded as a danger signal and a qualified electrician should then be consulted.)

GENERAL CARE OF ALL ELECTRICAL EQUIPMENT

Three general, important points apply to *all* electrical equipment, whenever it is used in the home:

 a Buy reputable goods, preferably those bearing the B.E.A.B. (British Electrical Approvals Board for Domestic Appliances) symbol. If the appliance is second-hand, always have it checked by an expert before using it.

b If you suspect that something is wrong, switch off immediately.

c Never try to repair faults yourself. Always call an electrician, preferably one recommended by the Electricity Board as a member of the N.I.C.E.I.C. (National Inspection Council for Electrical Installation Contracting).

Other important safety measures are:

1 *Plugs*
a Replace cracked or chipped plugs immediately.
b If plugs become warm in use have them checked.

2 *Flexes*
a Use short flexes to avoid trailing them dangerously. Never join them.
b Replace frayed flexes at once; do not repair them with insulating tape.
c Do not run flexes under floor coverings.
d Never use three-core flex on a two-pin plug.

3 *Switches*
a Replace damaged switches immediately.
b If switches become warm in use have them checked.

4 *Sockets*
a Use as few adaptors as possible; whenever possible use *one* plug in one socket.
b Never use a three-pin plug in a two-pin adaptor.

5 *Handling*   Never handle plugs or switches with wet hands.

RE-WIRING AN ELECTRIC PLUG

Although it is not generally recommended that a non-skilled person should attempt to carry out electrical repairs, it is not difficult to re-wire a plug. Time and money can be saved if the housewife is able to do this. It can be done very easily if she follows the instructions carefully.

Wires inside flexes are being standardized throughout Europe under the new Government regulations but, as some old flexes will still be in use, it is advisable to learn the old and new equivalents.

Wire	Old Colours	New Colours
1 Earth	Green	Green and yellow stripes
2 Live	Red	Brown
3 Neutral	Black	Light blue

If the plug is fused, which is now commonly the case, it is essential that the correct size of fuse is used for the appliance to which the plug is attached:

3 Amp fuse (blue) is suitable for appliances requiring less than 750 watts

13 Amp fuse (brown is) suitable for all others

Method of Re-wiring

1 Disconnect the plug from the wall socket and the flex from the appliance.

2 Loosen the screws holding the plug sections together and remove the cover section.

3 Loosen the three exposed screws and pull out the wires they are/were holding.

4 Loosen the clamp screws and pull out the flex.

5 If the wires are broken or frayed, strip a small portion from the flex cover to expose a further length of wires and strip sufficient of the wire covers to leave just over 1 cm of bare wire free. (A special stripping tool is available which will cut the wire cover without damaging the wires as scissors all too easily do.) Trim the ends of the wires, bearing in mind that the earth wire (green or green/yellow striped) must be longer than the other two.

6 Twist the exposed wires gently to make them easier to handle and curve them to fit round the stem of the screws.

7 Pass the flex under the loosened clamp and fit the ends of each of the three wires snugly round the appropriate screws:

the earth wire (green or striped) to the top screw, marked E or with the small symbol on the diagram.

the live wire (red or brown) to the one marked R (for red) or L (for live),

the neutral wire (black or light blue) to the one marked B (for black) or N (for neutral). (See diagram.)

Make sure that there are no bare wires or whiskers of wire left exposed and screw each one down firmly, using a screwdriver.

Wiring an electric plug

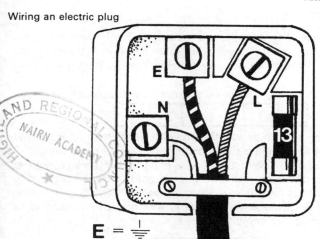

$$E = \frac{1}{\overline{\equiv}}$$

8 Screw down the clamp over the flex near the entrance to the plug.

9 Replace the cover and screw into place. Shake the plug to make sure that it does not rattle.

10 Reconnect the appliance to the electric circuit and test its performance.

Changing a Fuse

If the wiring is of the old type, i.e. where the plugs themselves do not contain fuses, the fuse must be changed at the fuse box which is usually situated near the meter. This is another simple operation which the housewife should be able to perform, and which is made simpler if a torch, a screwdriver and a card of fuse wire are always kept beside the fuse box.

1 Switch off the electricity at the main and remove the cover of the fuse box.

2 Remove each fuse in turn and inspect the wire. It will usually be obvious by the scorch marks round the carrier which one has 'blown'.

3 Replace the wire with a new piece of the correct grade.

4 Put back the fuse, close the box and switch on the main current.

Note If the fuse is of the cartridge type, test with the torch:

a Switch on the torch and unscrew the bottom cap (the light will go out).

b Place the fuse with one end touching the bottom of the battery and the other the inside of the torch case or connecting strip.

c If the light comes on again try each fuse in turn until the 'dud' is discovered.

READING METERS

Both gas and electricity supplies are passed through meters as they enter the domestic circuit, so each householder pays for exactly the amount used. It is therefore possible to calculate the number of units used over a period.

Some meters show a complete figure as a succession of digits:

6	7	5	8	0	0

it is only necessary then to deduct the previous meter reading from that shown at present to calculate the consumption of fuel since then.

Most meters, however, still show a panel of dials which register consumption and these are quite simple to read once the method is explained. Gas meters have four dials to be read, electricity meters five, but the principle is the same in each case, whether it be cubic feet or kilowatt hours which are being measured.

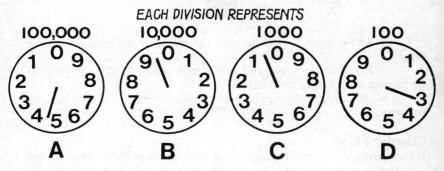

EACH DIVISION REPRESENTS
100,000   10,000   1000   100

A   B   C   D

Starting from A, read the figure on the dial which the pointer has just passed, nought being less than one but more than nine. Thus, the figure shown above should read: 490,300.

An electric meter would show divisions representing A 10,000, B 1000, C 100, D 10, E 1, but the method of reading is exactly the same.

ELECTRIC COOKERS

Electric cookers can be obtained as
    a table models: hot plate, hot plate and grill, or oven
    b vertical cookers with one or two main ovens or one main and one smaller which also acts as a grill compartment
    c split-level cookers: see p. 29.

Construction
The oven consists of a double-walled steel box with each exposed surface finished with hard vitreous enamel for easy cleaning. The lining of the

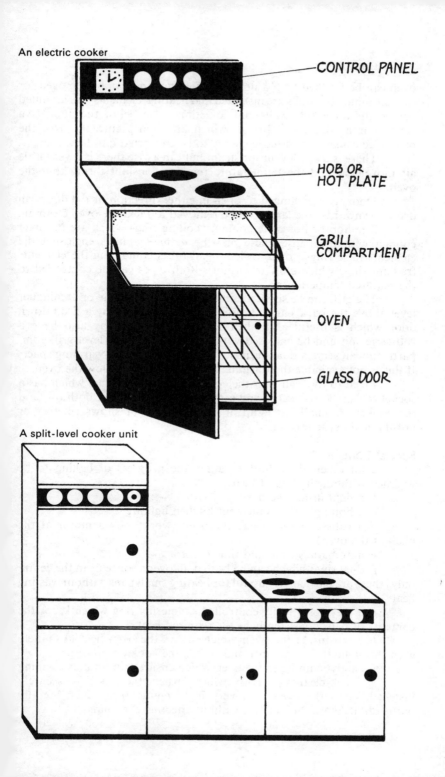

An electric cooker

CONTROL PANEL

HOB OR
HOT PLATE

GRILL
COMPARTMENT

OVEN

GLASS DOOR

A split-level cooker unit

oven can be finished with a non-stick coating, and can be removed for easy cleaning. The walls are insulated and heating 'elements' are mounted behind the inner side walls and sometimes also below the floor. (An element is a wire coil, through which an electric current flows, the resistance causing the electric energy to be converted into heat energy.)

There is a small vent for steam but otherwise there is a very little air movement and the temperature remains constant throughout the oven.

Doors can be hinged to open in either direction or the door can drop downwards; the latter can be removed to facilitate oven cleaning.

The hob or hot plate contains boiling rings which are in direct contact with the pans. These may be *a.* metal plates enclosing the elements (disc rings), or *b.* coiled metal tubes containing the elements (radiant rings which glow when hot). Both types can be controlled to the required temperature.

The grill can be situated either below the hot plate or at a higher level above the back panel. Lower ones are enclosed by a drop-down door which is useful as a shelf. The higher ones may also have a rôtisserie spit and be enclosed with a door. The lower-level grill compartment can serve a dual purpose, being used also as a warming space. If this is not available the warming space is a drawer below the oven.

Fixed to the wall near the cooker is a control panel which has a socket for an electric kettle and a main switch to control both this and the cooker. A small red lamp or similar indicator shows whether or not the main switch is on.

Special Features

a an inner glass door to allow the progress of baking to be watched without the loss of heat

b a light inside the oven

c a hob light to supplement kitchen lighting

d a rôtisserie spit inside the oven (worked by a motor at the back of the oven)

e automatic switch and time control

f dual rings which can be heated all over at once or in the centre only; these are particularly useful for heating small pans without wasting heat

g a thermostatically controlled simmering ring which keeps the contents of pans consistently at the required heat

h a fan inside the oven which makes the oven heat absolutely even throughout the chamber and speeds the cooking process

i catalytic lining to the oven which ensures continuous cleaning

j a self-cleaning device which, when the door is securely fastened, heats the oven to a very high temperature which literally burns off all the soiling matter without affecting the lining.

Choosing an Electric Cooker
    1 See points 1–4 of 'Choosing a Cooker' (p. 19).
    2 Make sure that the cooker bears the Mark of Safety of the British Electrical Approvals Board (see p. 25).

Cleaning the Electric Cooker
    1 Wipe off splashes on the enamelled surfaces as they are made; anything spilt onto boiling rings quickly chars and can be easily brushed off.
    2 Pull out and wipe the spillage tray or lift the hinged hob and wipe the tray beneath.
    3 Wipe over the inside of the oven with a damp cloth. Remove lining if necessary and use a mild abrasive on more obstinate stains. Clean shelf bars with fine steel wool.
Note Always turn off the main cooker switch before cleaning. 'Continuous-cleaning' ovens should not be cleaned at all.

WATER HEATERS

An immersion heater consists of an electrical element enclosed in a hollow tube inserted into a tank containing cold water which enters the tank from the bottom. As the water is warmed by the heated element it rises to the top of the tank and is drawn off from there when hot taps in the kitchen or bathroom are opened. As the hot water is drawn off, cold water enters to take its place; if none is taken, the entire tank becomes full of hot water. The thermostat controlling the element causes it to be switched off when a certain temperature is reached and on again if the water cools.

ELECTRIC KETTLES

These function in a similar manner to that of water heaters, a circular element at the bottom of the kettle (inside) heating the water by convection. They should never be switched on unless there is enough water in the kettle to cover the element.
    Up-to-date kettles are fitted with a safety device which causes them to switch themselves off when the water reaches boiling point.

REFRIGERATORS

It has been recognized for hundreds of years that food will remain safe for consumption for a much greater length of time when it is kept very cold than when it is exposed to normal temperatures.
    This is due to micro-organisms, minute living bacteria, having their reproduction retarded by low temperatures, and by enzymes also being inactivated. In normal conditions, and especially in moist warmth, enzyme action and bacterial growth continue to such an extent that

between midday and tea-time each micro-organism may multiply nearly 33,000 times on a warm day. It is a common experience to find food 'going off' in an ordinary larder or food cupboard very much more quickly in warm weather than in cold.

Actual freezing is not necessary to prolong the freshness of most foods, but the colder it is kept the longer it will remain edible. Below 10°C foods may be kept safely in warm kitchens and in hot weather, and a refrigerator can maintain this temperature without difficulty if properly used.

The advantages of using a refrigerator as a food store (except for tinned and dry goods) are:

a food can be kept safely without fear of food poisoning

b wastage is considerably reduced; cooked foods can be kept until another day; milk does not become sour; butter does not become rancid

c shopping can be reduced as foods can be kept for several days after purchase

d meals can be planned and prepared in advance

e chilled drinks, sweets and fruit are very pleasant to eat in hot weather.

Note A refrigerator is as important during the winter as in the summer, as kitchens are often kept as warm if not warmer by central heating in colder weather than they become on hot days when ventilation is increased.

See also 'Home Freezing', p. 165.

HOW A REFRIGERATOR WORKS

A refrigerator may be run by gas or by electricity but in both cases the underlying principle is similar, dependent upon the fact that as gases and liquids change their states heat is either absorbed or lost.

(To demonstrate the cooling effect of evaporation, rub the skin on the forehead or the inner wrist with solid perfume or methylated spirit. Notice the feeling of coolness on the skin as the warmth of the body causes the liquid to evaporate.)

A GAS REFRIGERATOR

The cabinet consists of a double-walled metal box, insulated between the layers to prevent the entrance of atmospheric warmth. The outside is finished with enamel and the inner lining can be enamelled metal or plastic-coated. It is tightly closed with an insulated door. The pipes and containers which constitute 'the works' are situated at the back of the cabinet and are quite invisible from inside.

The diagram on p. 34 shows that a small tank of ammonia solution is heated by a small gas burner, the heat thus provided driving off the ammonia as a gas. This is condensed into liquid ammonia as the thin metal plates of the condenser conduct heat away (the heat from these can be felt by placing the hand above them) and this liquid trickles into the evaporator inside the cabinet where it meets the hydrogen circuit. This meeting causes the liquid ammonia to evaporate and the change of state requires the absorption of heat. (This is why the interior of the cabinet becomes cold; the greater the rate of absorption the greater the loss of heat in the cabinet.) The mixture of gases then travels to the absorber where the ammonia gas is absorbed into the weak liquid which trickles into it from the boiler. The hydrogen, being a light gas, is not absorbed and rises back into the closed hydrogen circuit. The strong liquid ammonia returns to the boiler and any remaining hydrogen is returned to the evaporator as it does so. So the cycle is completed and can begin all over again. The thermostat which controls the temperature does so by regulating the gas flame to heat more or less rapidly, causing the whole process to take place more slowly or more quickly.

The evaporator is found at the top of the inside of the cabinet and it is here that the air is coolest. Cold air is heavy and therefore falls to the bottom of the cabinet, cooling the contents as it does so. As it thus becomes less cold it rises again, to be cooled and made heavier once more. Not only does the temperature change but moisture can be absorbed and this condenses round the evaporator and is deposited as a layer of frost or ice. These facts must be borne in mind in the use and care of a refrigerator (see p. 35).

Note There are no moving parts in a gas-operated refrigerator and therefore it is quite silent. There is no danger of parts becoming worn out and there is no chemical reason why the cycle should not continue indefinitely.

AN ELECTRIC REFRIGERATOR

The principle of heat absorption resulting from the evaporation of a liquid also applies to the electric refrigerator. In this case, however, evaporation is brought about by different means.

A refrigerant (arcton or freon, the American equivalent) enters the compressor as a gas at high pressure and therefore at high temperature (remember how hot the bottom of the metal type of bicycle pump becomes when air is being pumped into a tyre). The gas passes through the tubes of the condenser losing pressure as it does so, and therefore losing heat as it does so. The heat is conducted away by thin metal fins and the refrigerant becomes a liquid. When it reaches the expansion valve, temperature and pressure are reduced and the volume increases. A familiar example of this process is experienced if the edge of the thumb catches a part of the spray forced from an aerosol container—it becomes extremely cold! The thermostat knob is attached to the expansion valve and reduces or increases the amount of expansion,

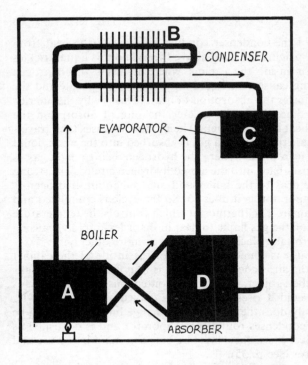

A gas refrigerator (absorption model)

A Ammonia in water, heated. Ammonia gas driven off rises to

B Ammonia gas gives up heat (through condenser fins) and changes into liquid ammonia. Trickles into

C where it meets hydrogen gas, and is converted back into gas, taking up heat from chamber as it does so. Ammonia and hydrogen gases return to

D the absorber, where ammonia gas is absorbed into the liquid and the mixture is returned to

A Hydrogen, being lighter, rises into the closed hydrogen circuit.

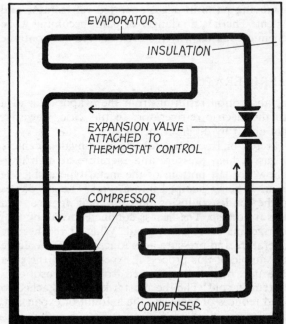

Compression refrigerator

as required. In the evaporator, to which the refrigerant now flows, heat, which always travels into cold, not vice versa, is absorbed from the contents of the cabinet. The addition of heat to the refrigerant converts it into a gas again, it returns to the compressor and the whole cycle begins again. The type described as a gas refrigerator is called an absorption model and this type can also be obtained in small sizes operated by electricity.

Choosing a Refrigerator

1 Take into consideration the fact that absorption-type models have no moving parts. It must be remembered, however, that this type is gradually being replaced by compressor models.

2 Choose a cabinet with sufficient storage space for the amount of use required by the family. Remember that the capacity of the cabinet is less than the overall size suggests.

3 Test the efficiency of the door fastening. It is essential that the door should fit closely and tightly. Nylon is often used for hinges and these never need oiling. Most models have no actual catches and are closed by the attraction of a metal and a magnetic strip.

4 Choose a model with a flat working-level top to avoid waste of space in the kitchen. Most types can be fitted into standard kitchen units. A tall, slim model should be chosen if floor space is valuable.

5 See that the rungs of shelves are well spaced to allow good air circulation, but not so wide apart that small containers cannot be stored.

6 Choose a model with a compartment for storing frozen foods for long enough to be convenient for the expected use. Remember that the 'star rating' indicates the safe storage time of the model:

✳ up to 1 week; ✳✳ up to 1 month; ✳✳✳ up to 3 months.

Useful (but not essential) Accessories
Interior light, automatically operated
Egg rack in door
Automatic defroster
Compartment for keeping butter
Frozen food compartment ⎫ these are becoming standard fittings in all
Drawer for vegetables ⎭ models

Using a Refrigerator

1 Have the cabinet installed in such a position that there is a good circulation of air all round it, and where it is not directly in contact with boilers or radiators. It is particularly essential that there should be free circulation of air over the evaporator fins of an absorption-type model.

2 Keep the door closed as much as possible to prevent the entrance of warm air from the kitchen.

3 Keep the cabinet clean and defrost as soon as necessary.

4 Cool all food before placing inside the cabinet. Hot items will raise the temperature of air circulating throughout the chamber and reduce its cooling efficiency.

5 Pack the chamber in such a way that air can circulate freely round all the items.

6 Cover liquids to reduce the amount of water vapour in the atmosphere inside the cabinet.

7 Store frozen foods in the section provided for this purpose, according to the 'star rating' shown. Use these in rotation, latest stored last used.

8 Remember that foods which have been stored in the refrigerator will deteriorate quickly once they have been brought to room temperature. Therefore

a avoid repetition of this process

b use food as soon as possible after removal.

9 Avoid storing strong-smelling fruit such as pineapples, melons and strawberries for any length of time. If chilling is desired for serving, cover or wrap and place in the cabinet for a short time only.

10 Remember that the loss of heat may also mean loss of moisture and foods can become dried out unless covered. The use of plastic film, greaseproof paper or foil can save space if food can be wrapped instead of being placed in containers. It is uneconomic use of the storage space to use it for tinned goods unless they require chilling immediately before use—they are already in a state of preservation and do not need further protection.

11 **Storage of Specific Foods**

milk: Wipe the bottles or cartons with a damp cloth and place them on the deep shelf provided for the purpose or in the rack on the door.

butter: Wrap in greaseproof paper (if the packing paper has been removed) or place in a polythene bag or plastic container and store on an upper shelf or in the compartment provided for the purpose.

cheese: Leave in the pack as bought or treat as for butter and store on a lower shelf.

meat: Wipe and wrap in polythene or paper and store in the coolest part of the cabinet.

fish: Wipe and wrap. Store as meat but keep as far as possible from milk and dairy products which easily absorb flavours.

eggs: Place in an open bowl or in the door rack provided (preferably not on a level with the freezing unit).

vegetables: Clean and trim off any inedible parts (to save space). Place in polythene bags near the bottom of the cabinet or in the drawer provided for the purpose.

Packing a refrigerator cabinet

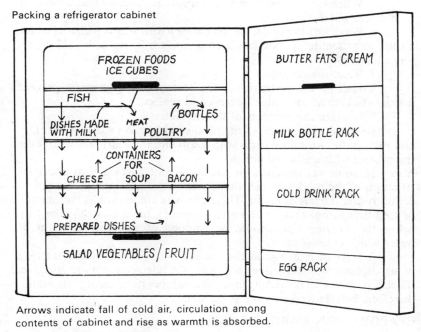

Arrows indicate fall of cold air, circulation among contents of cabinet and rise as warmth is absorbed.

fruits: Place citrus fruits in polythene bags so that their smell is not transmitted. Cover soft fruit. Avoid prolonged storage of pineapples, melons and strawberries. Do not store bananas in the refrigerator—they turn black.

12 Remember that the refrigerator can be used for storing reserve mixtures, e.g. sauces, salad dressings, pastry, bread dough, etc.

Cleaning and Defrosting the Refrigerator
Daily
Wipe off splashes from the inside or outside of the cabinet as they occur.
Occasionally

1*a* in push-button defrosting models: press the special button.

b in non-automatic defrosting models: set the dial to 'off' or 'defrost'. Allow the temperature to rise while the rest of the process is carried out.

2 Empty the refrigerator completely.

3 Wrap frozen foods in newspaper to minimize thawing-out until replaced.

4 Place a bowl of hot water on a shelf to speed up the melting of the ice. Allow the ice to melt naturally and do not attempt to chip it off.

5 When the ice has all melted, remove the shelves and wash over with warm water. Dry.

6 Wash out the inside of the cabinet with warm water in which a little bicarbonate of soda has been dissolved. Rinse with cold water. Dry thoroughly.

7 Reset the controls.

8 Half-fill the ice-trays, dry the bottom of each tray (to prevent it from sticking as the water freezes) and replace.

9 Replace the contents of the cabinet.

10 Wash the outside of the cabinet with warm soapy water. Dry and rub up the chromium trims with a soft cloth. Occasionally rub over the cabinet with a silicone polish.

Note In some refrigerators defrosting is not necessary as the construction of the model is such that a deposit of ice is never allowed to collect round the freezing unit. These cabinets are known as 'automatic' or 'self-defrosting' and all the attention they require is that the tray below the freezing unit should be emptied of the small amount of water which collects there.

A layer of frost round the cooling unit, caused by the freezing of atmospheric moisture, does not make the refrigerator more effective. Indeed, it acts as an insulating layer and reduces its efficiency. It should, therefore, be removed as soon as possible.

EVAPORATION CABINETS

When a refrigerator cannot be afforded, a useful substitute is one of the proprietary evaporation cabinets. They work on the same principle as earthenware milk coolers, i.e. a porous cabinet is soaked with cold water which, as it evaporates, absorbs heat from inside the cabinet. It is essential, however, that the walls are kept continuously damp and, in very hot weather, its efficiency is dependent upon very frequent attention.

FURTHER STUDY

THINGS TO DO

1 Find out

a the unit of measurement of gas

b the price per unit of gas in the district

c the differences between natural and town gas.

2 Visit your local coal-gas works and discover how the gas is produced. What are the by-products of gas production?

3 What is a North Sea 'rig'? Where can these be found? Indicate on a map of the British Isles which areas are served by these installations.

4 On p. 34 there are simplified versions of the process of refrigeration. Explain each step in the cycle with reference to the laws of physics, including Dalton's Law of Partial Pressures and Boyle's Law.

5 Draw the outline of a refrigerator (open), showing the shelves and cooling unit. 'Pack' the shelves with the types of food stored in a normal household and describe any special precautions you would take in doing so. Give your reasons.

6 Find out

a the unit of measurement of electricity

b the price of electricity in the area

c which use more units, power appliances or heating fittings

d what is meant by 'flat rate'

e about off-peak tariffs.

QUESTIONS TO ANSWER

1 Write out the following statements, and complete them, using only the words in the right-hand column to fill in the blanks.

a Food cooked under a grill is cooked by	conduction
b The heat from an oven does not escape because of its	evaporation
c Water in a kettle becomes hot, when placed over a gas or electric ring, by	arcton
d The unprotected handles of saucepans can become very hot by	evaporation
e Refrigerator cabinets are cooled by the .... of liquids.	ammonia
f Gases are converted into liquids by	methane
g Liquids are converted into gases by	radiation
h The liquid used in a gas refrigerator is	condensation
i The gas used in an electric refrigerator is	insulation
j The main constituent of natural gas is	convection

2 What is the meaning of 'conduction', 'convection', 'radiation' and 'insulation'? Give examples.

3 How would you ensure the best service from *either* an electric cooker *or* a gas cooker?

4 What advice would you give to a new housewife on choosing a refrigerator? Show by means of a sketch how she should arrange the contents.

2

THE VALUE OF FOOD

The human body can be compared to an ingenious, beautifully constructed, economically run engine and, like all good engines, it requires high-quality constructive materials, efficient repair and adequate fuel if it is to do its work satisfactorily. These needs are supplied by the food we eat.

So it it can be stated safely that a food is any substance (liquid or solid) which can provide the body with

a materials for growth and repair

b heat and energy

c the regulation of its functions—what is commonly called 'good health'.

The study of the processes of growth, repair and maintenance of the living body resulting from the intake of food is called *nutrition*, and the substances contained in a food which can be used by the body for any of these functions are called *nutrients*.

Food can therefore be divided into classes according to the nutrients which it contains. By eating some food from each of these classes every day the body is provided with all its needs for normal working:

Body-builders
These foods build up cell tissue and repair it because they contain a nutrient called *protein*. Under some circumstances they provide energy, but this is a secondary function and a wasteful use of these foods.

Warmers and Energizers
These foods contain *carbohydrates*, the name given to starches and sugars; they provide the body with heat and energy and any excessive amounts can be converted into body fat.

Protectors
These are the foods which keep all the processes of the body in good

Classes of Foods

Class	Function	Foodstuff	Nutrient	Sources	Recommended Daily Intake
Body-builders	a to build up and repair body tissues b to supply energy	Protein—Complete and Incomplete	Amino Acids (essential and non-essential)	Complete: meat, fish, eggs, milk and cheese Incomplete: pulses—peas, beans, lentils, nuts	boys: 20–75 g girls: 20–58 g men: 68–90 g women: 55–68 g
Warmers and Energizers	a to provide heat b to provide energy	Fats Carbohydrates (starches, sugars)	Fatty Acids Glucose	butter, oils, margarine, lard, oily fish, milk, cheese, olives cakes, biscuits, potatoes, sugar, jam, syrup, oatmeal	boys: 3·3–12·6 MJ girls: 3·3– 9·6 MJ men: 11·3–15·1 MJ women: 9·2–10·9 MJ
Protectors	to regulate all body processes and reduce the danger of infection see tables on pp. 55, 58	Vitamins Mineral Elements	A B complex C D E K Calcium Iron Phosphorus Potassium Sodium Magnesium	liver (meat and fish), dairy produce, cheese, margarine yeast, bacon, wholemeal bread, oatmeal, liver, cheese, meat blackcurrants, green vegetables, citrus fruits, potatoes, rose-hip syrup oily fish, fish liver oils, margarine vegetable oils, wheat germ, margarine, eggs green vegetables milk, fruit, green vegetables, other vegetables, meat, liver, wholemeal bread	450–750 µg Thiamine 0·5–1·5 mg Riboflavine 0·6–1·7 mg Nicotinic acid 7–18 mg 20–30 mg 2·5 µg (5 years +) incalculable average: 500 mg average: 10–15 mg no chance of deficiency 2–4 g 4 g no chance of deficiency

Note These figures are based on those published by the Department of Health and Social Security (1969). (The range of figures shown indicates the needs of boys, girls, men and women from 1 year to the adult age of maximum activity: after 55 (women) and 65 (men) it is assumed that energy requirements will decrease. Needs of women in pregnancy are not shown. For details see p. 141.)

working order and safeguard it against infection. The nutrients that they contain are:

vitamins, *mineral elements* and *water*.

Roughage may also be included in this class although it has only a mechanical value in the body and is not a true nutrient.

(All foods must be *absorbed* into the body before they can become nutrients; therefore roughage, which is not absorbed but passes through the digestive system and, in doing so, helps it to get rid of waste products, is not a nutrient.)

If the body is deprived of food from any one of these classes it will not die but will suffer from a condition known as *malnutrition*—i.e. it will be badly nourished, or fed on the wrong types of food.

If insufficient food from all these classes is given the body will be *under*-nourished (in a state of *under*-nutrition), and this state carried to extreme is known as *starvation*.

PROTEINS

The body uses proteins

    a mainly for growth and repair of body cells

    b in a lesser degree to provide heat and energy.

Protein is essential for the building of animal and plant tissue and must therefore also be used in its repair. All young animals, including babies, are formed from older animals and are therefore 'constructed' from animal materials. The best sources of protein are therefore animal products.

Protein foods

These proteins are known as *Complete* (formerly referred to as *First Class*) and are obtained from such foods as meat, poultry, fish, milk, cheese and eggs.

Incomplete or *Partially complete* proteins (which were formerly known as *Second Class*) are able to keep the body alive but do not provide for growth. These are found in pulses (peas, beans, lentils), nuts, and a little in some other vegetables.

Animal protein is very similar to human protein, i.e. it can very easily be converted into the type of protein which the body needs (see p. 45). Vegetable protein is much less akin to human protein and can less easily be used by the body. Therefore, more vegetable protein is required than animal protein. (In humans, protein is flesh, in animals, 'lean meat'.)

Adequate supplies of protein are essential in the diet of everyone, although most is required by growing children and by expectant and nursing mothers.

After the body has used what it needs of its supply of proteins for growth and repair there is usually some left over—it is very seldom that anyone eats *exactly* the amount he requires. The excess is then used to provide warmth and energy, but this is an expensive way of obtaining what can be provided by much cheaper foods. The protein's function as a body-builder cannot be taken over by any other nutrient.

The Digestion of Protein
To appreciate the value to the body of each nutrient it is necessary to understand which parts of the body are concerned in its digestion. The accompanying diagram shows a simplified outline of the digestive tract.

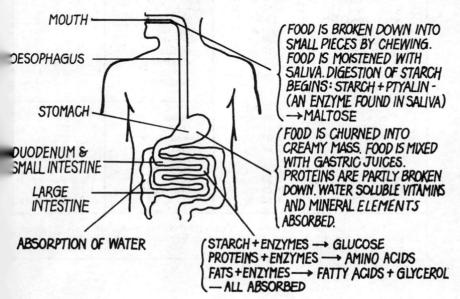

MOUTH

OESOPHAGUS

STOMACH

DUODENUM & SMALL INTESTINE

LARGE INTESTINE

ABSORPTION OF WATER

FOOD IS BROKEN DOWN INTO SMALL PIECES BY CHEWING. FOOD IS MOISTENED WITH SALIVA. DIGESTION OF STARCH BEGINS: STARCH + PTYALIN - (AN ENZYME FOUND IN SALIVA) → MALTOSE

FOOD IS CHURNED INTO CREAMY MASS. FOOD IS MIXED WITH GASTRIC JUICES. PROTEINS ARE PARTLY BROKEN DOWN. WATER SOLUBLE VITAMINS AND MINERAL ELEMENTS ABSORBED.

STARCH + ENZYMES → GLUCOSE
PROTEINS + ENZYMES → AMINO ACIDS
FATS + ENZYMES → FATTY ACIDS + GLYCEROL
— ALL ABSORBED

Main Sources of Nutrients in Normal Diet: Amount Present

Sources	Amount in 100 g	Sources	Amount in 100 g
Protein		**Nicotinic Acid**	
Complete		cornflakes	7·0 mg
cheese	25·4 g	meat	5·0 mg
meat	14·8 g	flour	1·8 mg
eggs	11·9 g	bread	1·4 mg
milk	3·3 g	vegetables	0·4–4 mg
Incomplete		fruit	0·1–1 mg
flour	10·0 g	milk	0·1 mg
bread	8·3 g		
Fats		**Vitamin C**	
oil, cooking/salad	99·9 g	brussels sprouts	100 mg
lard	99.3 g		(35 mg cooked)
margarine	85·3 g	cabbage	60 mg
butter	82·5 g		(20 mg cooked)
cheese	34·5 g	watercress	60 mg
eggs	12·3 g	oranges	50 mg
milk	3·8 g	lemons	50 mg
		grapefruit	40 mg
Carbohydrate		potatoes	20 mg
(as monosaccharide)			
sugar	105·0 g		
cornflakes	88·0 g	**Vitamin D**	
rice	86·8 g	fatty fish	12–22 μg
flour (white)	80·0 g	margarine	8·00 μg
bread	54·6 g	eggs	1·50 μg
potatoes	18·0 g	butter	1·25 μg
Vitamin A			
carrots	12,000 (c)	**Iron**	
liver	6000 μg	meat	4·0 mg
green vegetables	300–	eggs	2·5 mg
	3000 (c)	flour	1·9 mg
margarine	900 μg	bread	1·8 mg
butter	710 μg	watercress	1·6 mg
[(c) as carotene]		cabbage	1·0 mg
			(0·5 mg cooked)
		potatoes	0·7 mg
Vitamin B complex			
Thiamine			
flour	0·28 mg	**Calcium**	
bread	0·18 mg	cheese	810 mg
potatoes	0·11 mg	watercress	222 mg
meat	0·07–1 mg	milk	120 mg
milk	0·04 mg	bread	100 mg
Riboflavine		cabbage	65 mg
liver	3·00 mg		(58 mg cooked)
eggs	0·35 mg	brussels sprouts	29 mg
meat	0·20 mg		(27 mg cooked)
milk	0·15 mg		

Note The best sources of nutrient are not always those from which they are obtained in the normal diet, e.g. brewers' yeast is an excellent source of B complex but plays an uncertain rôle in the diet.

All foods have to be broken down into very simple forms before they can be absorbed into the bloodstream and do their work as nutrients. It is as if the digestive system has to sort out the individual nutrients from the complicated mass of foodstuffs (proteins, carbo-hydrates, fats) presented to it as food. It is aided in this work by *enzymes* which are juices excreted by most parts of the digestive system. Each enzyme has its own specific job to do and cannot fulfil any other function.

Proteins are composed of carbon, hydrogen, oxygen, nitrogen and sulphur. *Nitrogen* is the essential ingredient which gives proteins their value, because no cell tissue can be created without it.

These constituents arrange themselves in various combinations to form *amino acids* and one protein may contain more than twenty different acids. Although there are twenty-two acids which the body requires, it can convert some of these which it does not need into different ones which it does. Ten of these, however, cannot be manu-factured (or synthesized) by the body, and have to be provided in food. They are known as *essential amino acids*. Those which can be converted are referred to as *non-essential*.

Children require ten different essential acids for adequate growth and repair, and adults need eight.

Most animal proteins contain all the essential amino acids and are therefore called complete proteins; vegetable proteins contain only some of them, however, and are called incomplete proteins. A mixture of animal and vegetable proteins in the diet is quite satisfactory, *but* the body cannot store amino acids, so some protein food must be eaten every day.

The digestion of protein does not begin until the chewed and moistened food has passed down the oesophagus into the stomach. Here it is partly broken down and then passed into the small intestine where it is completely divided up into its amino acids. In this form it can be absorbed into the bloodstream, which carries it to the liver. From here it may be sent on to any part of the body's tissue which requires it for growth or repair; but this happens only when protein food has been accompanied by other foodstuffs. If no carbohydrate has been eaten with it it is used to provide the body with warmth and energy.

The Place of Protein in the Diet
1 Protein foods are essential to life.
2 Protein foods are, in general, the most expensive ones in the diet and their use, therefore, should be spread evenly throughout a week's meals. (See 'Planning Meals', p. 140).
3 Protein foods, being the 'core' of a meal, are usually used as the main dish of most meals.

4 Some protein food should be served every day. Incomplete proteins should be served in larger quantities than complete ones, but a mixture of both is most satisfactory, as one supplements the other.

5 Protein foods may be cooked by many different methods.

The Effect of Cooking on Protein

1 Heat *coagulates* protein, i.e. the protein sets, becoming solid and opaque. (This is very clearly seen when the fluid, semi-transparent white of an egg is heated.)

2 Protein shrinks when heated. (This is apparent when a joint is roasted, particularly when a bone is present and much more is exposed after cooking than before. Some of this shrinkage, however, is due to the evaporation of water from the tissues.)

3 If over-cooked, protein becomes less easily digested.

CARBOHYDRATES

A carbohydrate is a nutrient which provides the body with energy and which *can* be converted into stored fat. Energy is required for

a maintaining the process of living—the beating of the heart, circulation, breathing, digestion, the maintenance of body temperature —known as basal metabolism

b everyday activity—standing, eating, moving, etc.

c muscular work.

Therefore the amount of energy required by individuals—and the amount of nutrient from which it is obtained—will vary according to

a The size of the person: the larger the body the more energy is required to maintain vital processes. In general, men are larger than women and require more energy.

b The work of the person: mental activity involves the expenditure of very little body energy, whereas manual work requires a great deal.

c The age of the person: the amount of energy required increases up to adolescence and gradually decreases from early middle age to old age.

The amount of energy produced by any food is measured in joules, kilojoules and megajoules (1 kJ = 1000 J; 1 MJ = 1000 kJ or 1,000,000 J). Previously energy value was measured in kilocalories.

1 g of carbohydrate produces approx. 16 kJ when used by the body
1 g of fat   produces approx. 38 kJ when used by the body
1 g of protein   produces approx. 17 kJ when used by the body

Examples

Cooking fat or lard produces 3746 kJ per 100 g
Butter   produces 3122 kJ per 100 g
Sugar   produces 1651 kJ per 100 g

Foods containing carbohydrates

White bread   produces 1060 kJ per 100 g
Potatoes   produce   318 kJ per 100 g
Apples   produce   193 kJ per 100 g

The number of megajoules required by various types of people per day varies as follows:

Type	*Megajoules required*
Sedentary worker: man	— 10·9–11·3
Sedentary worker: woman	— 8·0– 9·2
Active worker: man	— 12·6–15·1
Active worker: woman	— 10·5
Pregnant woman	— 10·0
Boy: 12–15 years old	— 11·7
Girl: 12–15 years old	— 9·6

If more food is eaten than is required to supply the amount of energy expended, the nutrient no longer used for energy is converted into subcutaneous (i.e. under the skin) fat. 'Fattening' foods, therefore, are those which contain most kilojoules and 'slimming' can be achieved not so much by eating *less* food as by choosing carefully the *type* of food eaten.

Carbohydrates consist of compounds of carbon, hydrogen and oxygen, and include

a starches

b sugars

c cellulose.

The main sources of carbohydrates in the diet, therefore, are any foods containing flour or sugar, e.g. bread and biscuits, together with some vegetables and fruits, e.g. potatoes and bananas.

STARCHES

Most of the carbohydrate in food consists of starch, the form in which plants store their reserve food supplies.

The Digestion of Starch

Starch in food appears in the form of granules enclosed within walls consisting of cellulose, and this means that the starch cannot be easily digested. It is not until the starch is moistened, causing the granules to swell and burst, that it is made available to the body.

When starchy foods are chewed they become well moistened and mixed with saliva, the first digestive juice with which any food comes in contact. Saliva contains an enzyme called *ptyalin* and this acts upon starch to convert it into sugar (maltose—see p. 49). This change can be appreciated if a small piece of bread (white) is held in the mouth for a few minutes after it has been chewed. The slightly sweet taste which develops indicates that digestion of the starch has begun. All carbohydrates must be changed into *glucose* before they can become nutrients, glucose being the simplest form of sugar. Maltose is a more complex form of glucose and the breaking down of maltose into glucose is continued in the small intestine. Here it is absorbed into the bloodstream and carried to the liver, where it is stored in the form of *glycogen*. When energy is required by the body for any kind of physical effort, supplies of glycogen are drawn from the liver, converted back into glucose and used up by the muscles. Strenuous muscular effort can completely exhaust the glycogen reserves and the body makes it known by feeling 'tired' that fresh supplies are required. It is a common experience, for instance, to feel the need of some starchy food after swimming. Athletes, too, are often given glucose sweets (barley sugar) immediately before races, to provide readily available energy.

Gelatinization of starch

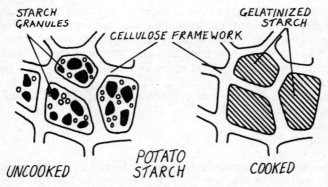

STARCH GRANULES   CELLULOSE FRAMEWORK   GELATINIZED STARCH

UNCOOKED   POTATO STARCH   COOKED

The Cooking of Starch

Starch is not soluble in cold water but it will form a thickened paste if mixed with liquid and then heated. This is obvious when starch is made for laundering purposes. When mixed with cold water a thin white (therefore undissolved) mixture is formed, but when boiling water is poured on this liquid it clears and thickens. This change is called the *gelatinization* of starch and is a similar process to its digestion.

If dry starch is heated it becomes *dextrin*, as happens when bread is toasted. Dextrin is more soluble than starch, which is the reason why thin toast is often found to be more easily digested than untoasted bread.

SUGARS

All sugars are sweet to taste and soluble in water. Sweetness, although pleasant, has no food value in itself—the value lies in the nutrient *glucose*, a simple sugar into which all more complex sugars can be broken down.

Principal Simple Sugars

Glucose is found in fruit and plant juices, and in the blood of living animals. It is also formed by the breaking down of starch and the more complex sugars in the process of digestion.

Fructose is the sweetest of the sugars and is found in plant juices, fruit (hence its name), and honey. It can also be changed into glucose, although it is itself a simple sugar.

Principal Complex Sugars

Lactose is found in milk. It is a combination of glucose and another sugar, galactose.

Maltose is composed of two different forms of glucose, and is found in germinating grain.

Sucrose is the most commonly appreciated sugar and is found in sugar cane and beet sugar. It is present in sweet fruits and root vegetables (carrots often taste slightly sweet, especially when young), and is composed of glucose and fructose.

The Digestion of Sugars

Once the complex sugars have been broken down into glucose in the small intestine, digestion continues and absorption takes place as has already been described for starches.

Effect of Cooking on Sugar

1 Sugar will very easily form a solution in most liquids, which will become syrups as the liquid evaporates.

2 If cooked without liquid it will melt and very quickly become brown in colour. It is then said to have *caramelized*. If over-heated it will char and develop a very bitter, unpleasant flavour.

CELLULOSE

Cellulose forms the framework of all fruit and vegetable cells. In vegetables this cellulose is tender and soft when young and becomes hard and woody as it becomes old, whereas in fruit young cellulose is tough and old cellulose is soft.

Cellulose is not absorbed by the body and is therefore not a nutrient. It is essential to the body, however, for its mechanical action. It acts as *roughage*, undigested bulk which assists in the movement of food through the intestines and so aids excretion. It might be called a broom, sweeping the passages of the digestive system.

Another form of carbohydrate which has no nutritive value is *pectin*, the substance in fruit which causes jam to set.

The Value of Carbohydrates in the Diet

1 Carbohydrate foods are, on the whole, the cheapest foods available and they therefore tend to be eaten in larger quantities than is necessary or advisable. Malnutrition, especially among poor people, is usually due to a diet overloaded with starchy foods.

2 These foods provide plenty of bulk and are useful to satisfy hunger.

3 They provide energy and warmth fairly quickly.

4 Carbohydrates are used as accompaniments to other foodstuffs to create balanced meals.

5 They may be cooked in many different ways to provide variety in the diet.

FATS

The fats which are eaten in the normal diet are meat fats, butter, and animal and vegetable oils.

Animals store fat for energy in the same way as plants store starch as their reserve, but fat is a more concentrated form of food supply.

Plants are able to form fat from carbohydrate, their fat content increasing as the starch decreases. Seeds which store oil in this way are used in the production of margarine. Oils are fats which remain liquid at normal atmospheric temperature but may solidify when cooled. Cooking oils and dripping (without 'jelly') are almost 100 per cent pure fat; butter is a mixture of fat and water.

Fat-supplying foods

Other Sources of Fats

1 'Oily' fish, such as herrings, mackerel, salmon, sardines, pilchards and eels, contain fat, the amount of which varies according to the time of the year.

2 'White' fish, such as cod, whiting, haddock, sole, contain little in their flesh, but cod and halibut provide valuable liver oil.

3 Olives, nuts and soya beans contain some fat but most fruit and vegetables do not.

4 With the exception of oatmeal, flour and cereals contain no fat.

The Digestion of Fat

Fats consist of *fatty acids* and *glycerol*, combined together. Before they can become nutrients they must be divided up again into their constituents, and this process is called *saponification*. An alkali is required to bring about this result and this is supplied in the small intestine, where digestion of fats takes place. In order to make this chemical change easier, the fat is first *emulsified*, or broken up into very fine particles which are evenly distributed throughout the mass of food. In the process of saponification 'soap' is formed which, being soluble in water, can readily be absorbed into the bloodstream.

Saponification: fats+alkali → soap (fatty acids+alkali)+glycerol.

Note It is a similar process, breaking down fats into fatty acids and supplying alkali with which they combine, which produces our household and toilet soaps.

More than half of the absorbed nutrient is laid down as body fat and the rest is carried by the bloodstream to the liver, where it is stored for the production of energy. (This fat is not necessarily that which causes flabbiness and overweight—many of the delicate internal organs are protected by a wrapping of fat and this is most essential to the well-being of the body).

Mineral oils, e.g. liquid paraffin, cannot be saponified and therefore cannot be absorbed. These should not, then, be used as substitutes for animal fats for they cannot be regarded as foods.

The warmth-giving property of fats will be appreciated when it is realized that a large proportion of the diet of Eskimos consists of seal and whale blubber.

The Effects of Cooking on Fat

1 Cooking has little effect on the food value of fats.

2 Most fats melt when heated and, when included in starch mixtures, help to break down the starch granules.

The Place of Fats in the Diet

1 They supply warmth and energy.

2 They may be eaten cooked or uncooked.

3 Only small amounts are required and are usually found to be most easily digested when accompanied by some carbohydrate food.

4 Fats are digested more slowly than other foodstuffs and will therefore slow down the digestion of foods in which fat is included. The lengthened activity of the digestive juices means that the feeling of 'being satisfied' is prolonged and hunger is not felt again so quickly as when no fat is present in a meal.

5 Fatty foods lubricate the digestive system to a certain extent but should not be eaten with this object in view. Satisfactory movement of food through the intestines depends upon muscular activity and this should not be discouraged.

6 Fats may be used as ingredients of mixtures, particularly as 'shortening' in starch mixtures, as accompaniments to other foodstuffs (e.g. salad oil and green salad vegetables, bread and butter), or as the medium for cooking, as in frying.

VITAMINS

As their name suggests, vitamins are *vital* to health. Only very small quantities of each are required but they are absolutely essential. Each vitamin has its specific function and lack of any one has characteristic effects.

There are two kinds of vitamins: *a.* those soluble in water, known as 'water-soluble'; *b.* those soluble in fat, known as 'fat-soluble'.

The water-soluble vitamins are: B, C (these are measured in milligrams).

The fat-soluble vitamins are: A, D, E, K (these are measured in micrograms—written as μg).

Vitamin foods

VITAMIN A   (*Fat-soluble*)

Vitamin A (chemically known as *retinol*) is necessary for
  a the satisfactory growth of children
  b the satisfactory perception of light
  c the health of all the mucous membranes.

Deficiency of this vitamin will result in generally impaired health; *but*, if more Vitamin A is taken than is actually required, it does *not* mean a corresponding degree of increased health. Indeed, recent research indicates that overdoses can be responsible for definitely unpleasant symptoms of impaired fitness.

The body is able to store supplies of Vitamin A in the liver so that reserves built up at one time (e.g. the summer) can be used up at another time when foods containing the vitamin are less available (e.g. in the winter). This fact accounts for part of the very high food value of liver.

Vitamin A is found in:
  1 Fish liver oils, liver, butter, cheese, eggs, sardines, meat.
  2 Carrots, spinach and green vegetables. (These contain Vitamin A in the form of a yellow pigment called carotene, which when converted into retinol and absorbed is only $\frac{1}{6}$ of the value of Vitamin A found in animal foods.)
  3 Margarine, which has synthetic Vitamin A added during manufacture.

VITAMIN D (*Fat-soluble*)

Vitamin D (chemically known as *cholecalciferol*) can be manufactured by the action of sunlight upon the fats under the human skin, and is therefore sometimes known as the 'sunshine vitamin'.

It is essential to the body because without it calcium cannot do its work of forming strong and healthy bone structures. Deficiency in children's diets causes rickets and in adults' diets it causes a similar disease called osteomalacia.

It is necessary to all adults for the maintenance of healthy bones, but is particularly essential to nursing and expectant mothers. Children, of course, require the greatest amounts, although it is now thought possible that overdoses can actually retard their growth.

Vitamin D is found in animal products, particularly fish oils and margarine.

VITAMIN E (*Fat-soluble*)

This vitamin is concerned with muscular activity and is found in plants, seeds, milk, vegetable oils and egg yolk.

VITAMIN K (*Fat-soluble*)

This vitamin is necessary for the clotting of blood. It is found in green vegetables, cereals and eggs.

VITAMIN B (*Water-soluble*)

This is really a group of vitamins, rather than an individual one, and consists of

  a Thiamine (or Vitamin B_1)
  b Riboflavine (or Vitamin B_2)
  c Nicotinic acid (or niacin)
  d Other less important substances (including B_6, Folic acid, Pantothenic acid, Biotin and B_{12}).

Thiamine is important because it helps the body to obtain energy from carbohydrate, and stimulates growth. Deficiency causes *a*. checked growth, *b*. depression and irritability, *c*. neuritis, *d*. the disease beri-beri, which is very uncommon in this country but was widespread among prisoners in occupied countries during the Second World War.

Thiamine is found in wholemeal bread, yeast, bacon, oatmeal, peas, nuts, meat and, to a lesser extent, in most other foods except sugar.

Riboflavine further aids the production of energy from food.

Deficiency causes *a*. checked growth, *b*. sores on the skin, particularly at the corners of the mouth, *c*. sore tongue, *d*. misted eyes.

Riboflavine is obtained from milk, cheese, eggs, liver and yeast.

Nicotinic acid further assists the conversion of food into energy.

Deficiency causes *a*. checked growth, *b*. roughened skin, *c*. sore tongue, *d*. diarrhoea, *e*. symptoms of mental confusion, *f*. the disease pellagra, the severe form of the previous symptoms.

Nicotinic acid is obtained mainly from meat, also from fish, flour, bread, vegetables, fruit, milk, yeast, liver.

Note As from 1974 food packages in the U.S.A. bear not only the vitamin value of their contents but also the recommended daily allowance of each vitamin.

Vitamins

Name	Function	Results of Deficiency	Source
A (fat-soluble)	a To promote growth b to maintain the perception of light c to keep mucous membranes healthy	generally impaired health and checked growth	fish liver oils, liver, butter, cheese, eggs, margarine, sardines, meat, carrots, spinach and green vegetables
D (fat-soluble)	To assist calcium in its work of forming strong bones and teeth	a rickets in children b osteomalacia in adults	animal products particularly fish liver oils and margarine
E (fat-soluble)	little evidence as yet		plants, seeds, milk, egg yolk, vegetable oils
K (fat-soluble)	Essential for normal clotting of blood	—	green vegetables, cereals, eggs
Thiamine (water-soluble)	a stimulates growth b keeps nerves healthy c assists in the digestion of carbohydrates	a checked growth b neuritis c depression and irritability d beri-beri	wholemeal bread, yeast, bacon, oatmeal, peas, nuts, meat, breakfast cereals; a little in most foods except sugar
Riboflavine (water-soluble)	a stimulates growth b assists in the digestion of carbohydrates	a checked growth b unhealthy tongue and eyes	milk, cheese, eggs, liver, yeast
Nicotinic Acid (water-soluble)	a stimulates growth b keeps skin and nerves healthy c assists digestion of carbohydrate	a checked growth b sores on skin and tongue c diarrhoea d mental confusion e pellagra	meat, fish, flour, bread, vegetables, fruit, milk, yeast, liver
C (water-soluble)	assists formation of connective cell tissue	a retarded growth b infection of mouth and gums c slow healing of wounds and fractures d scurvy	blackcurrants, green vegetables, oranges, lemons, tomatoes, rose-hip syrup, potatoes

VITAMIN C   (*Water-soluble*)

This vitamin is important because it prevents scurvy, a disease which was once the scourge of seamen and other travellers who were deprived of supplies of fresh fruit and vegetables for long periods. It was recognized that small doses of citrus fruit juice could offset the danger of scurvy long before the presence of vitamins as such was even thought of.

On a much less serious scale, deficiency of Vitamin C in the diet can cause *a.* retarded growth, *b.* infection of the mouth and gums, *c.* slow healing of wounds and fractures.

Vitamin C is apt to be deficient in the human system because

a it is easily destroyed by cooking

b it is easily destroyed by light

c it is contained in fruit and vegetables which are sometimes scarce and expensive. (The excellence of preserved fruit and vegetables nowadays, however, particularly when they are frozen, considerably reduces this possibility.)

Vitamin C is found in blackcurrants, green vegetables, oranges, lemons, tomatoes, rose-hip syrup and potatoes.

The Digestion of Vitamins

Fat-soluble vitamins are absorbed only in the small intestine. Water-soluble vitamins are absorbed in the stomach and in the small intestine.

MINERAL ELEMENTS

Mineral elements are used in the body

a to form bones and teeth—calcium, phosphorus, magnesium

b to help in the formation of body cells—iron, phosphorus, sulphur, potassium

c to give fluids their composition—sodium, potassium, chlorine

d to assist the various chemical reactions in the body—iron, phosphorus, magnesium.

Most foods contain small amounts of most mineral elements and it is unnecessary to pay special attention to the amounts being eaten, except in the cases of calcium and iron.

CALCIUM

This is a very important mineral element, as it is necessary to the body for

a the formation of sound bones and teeth (for which it combines with phosphorus)

b the normal clotting of blood—without which, of course, any minor scratch might have very serious results *c* the normal functioning of muscles.

It is, therefore, particularly important to

a children—in whom lack of calcium causes badly formed bones (the disease known as rickets, which used to be very common and is now almost unknown, except among the immigrant population) and teeth, and consequently less satisfactory growth than normal.

b expectant and nursing mothers—whose own supply of calcium will be heavily taxed to produce the child's bones and the milk with which to feed it. (Hence the now old-fashioned idea that 'each baby costs its mother a tooth'.)

c old people—whose bones may become brittle and easily broken without adequate supplies of calcium.

It is also important to all adults if their teeth are to remain sound and healthy.

Calcium is found in: cheese, milk, milk products, fish (particularly those of which the bones are eaten, e.g. sardines and salmon in tins), bread, green vegetables, and in 'hard' water.

IRON

This is important to the body because

a it gives blood its red colouring (haemoglobin)

b as a constituent of blood it carries oxygen round the tissues of the body.

Iron is used up very slowly by the body but it is essential that it should be constantly replaced because its loss is due to

a the general wear of the body and its normal functioning, particularly in excretion

b the loss of blood when any injury is caused.

Lack of iron causes *anaemia*—this is not due to insufficient quantities of *blood* in the *body* but to insufficient quantities of *iron* in the *blood*.

Iron is found in: liver, kidney, beef, eggs, peas, beans, lentils, apricots, wholemeal bread, oatmeal, cocoa, pulses.

Note Liver plays a large part in the diet of people being treated for anaemia.

SODIUM

It is better known to us in its combination with chlorine as salt. This is another very important mineral element as it is contained in all the fluids of the body and is essential to life. The amount of sodium in human blood *must* be maintained and, as it is continually being lost from the body, it must be just as consistently replaced.

It is lost in the urine excreted and in perspiration. It is, therefore, particularly important that this loss should be replaced in hot climates, after strenuous exercise and when working in high temperatures.

c

Mineral Elements

Name	Function	Source
Calcium	*a* formation of bones and teeth (combines with phosphorus and requires the help of Vitamin D) *b* assists the clotting of blood *c* assists the functioning of muscles	cheese, milk, milk products, fish, bread, green vegetables, 'hard' water
Iron	*a* gives blood its red colour *b* carries oxygen round the tissues of the body	Liver, kidney, beef, eggs, peas, beans, lentils, apricots, wholemeal bread, oatmeal, cocoa
Sodium	an essential constituent of all body fluids, particularly of blood	Bacon, kippers, cheese, cornflakes; a little in most foods; added in cooking
Potassium	an essential constituent of muscle and red blood cells	a little in most foods
Phosphorus	*a* combines with calcium to form bones and teeth *b* essential for the conversion of food into energy *c* maintains the fluidity of all body fluids *d* takes small part in the maintenance of body cells	liver, kidney, eggs, meat, fish, cheese, milk and oatmeal; a little in most other foods
Iodine	essential for proper functioning of thyroid gland	shellfish, fish, water, cod-liver oil, vegetables grown on an iodine-containing soil
Magnesium **Copper**	helps in production of $\begin{cases} \text{bones} \\ \text{teeth} \end{cases}$ helps iron in its work	normal diet

One of the most obvious results of insufficient sodium in the bloodstream is muscular cramp. Nowadays this is appreciated to the extent that manual workers, such as stokers, miners and others whose job entails great heat, are issued with salt tablets to take as compensators.

Sodium is found in: bacon, kippers, cheese, cornflakes, and to a lesser degree in most foods; it is also added (as salt) in cooking many foods.

POTASSIUM

This is an essential part of muscle cells and red blood cells. It is also lost in urine but not in sweat. Potassium is found in most of our foods.

PHOSPHORUS

This is important to the body because

    a it combines with calcium to form bones and teeth

    b it is essential in order that the body can obtain energy from food

    c to a lesser extent it assists in the maintenance of body cells.

Phosphorus is found in most foods, particularly liver, kidney, eggs, meat, fish, cheese, milk and oatmeal.

OTHER MINERAL ELEMENTS

Only very small quantities of these are required.

    a Copper helps iron in its work and is satisfactorily present in a normal diet.

    b Magnesium helps in production of bones and teeth and is essential for normal metabolism. It is also present in a normal diet.

    c Fluorine is an essential part of dental enamel and can reduce decay of children's teeth. It is found naturally in some drinking water and has been introduced deliberately in some other districts.

    d Iodine is essential for the proper functioning of the thyroid gland (the gland in the lower part of the neck which can cause goitre if it does not function adequately). Iodine is found in shellfish, fish, water, cod-liver oil.

The Digestion of Mineral Elements

Minerals are already nutrients in the form in which they are taken into the body—i.e. they are simple enough substances to be absorbed into the bloodstream without being broken down. Soluble mineral elements (potassium, sodium) are absorbed in the stomach and the small intestine. Calcium and iron are absorbed in the small intestine.

Amount of Foodstuffs Present in Food

(Amounts given are in 100 g of food)

Foodstuff	Best Sources	Amount	Poorest Sources	Amount
		g		g
Protein				
Complete	cheese	25·4	milk	
	beef (corned)	22·3	(owing to large	
	chicken (raw)	20·8	percentage of	
	sardines	20·4	water)	3·3
	kippers	19·0	onions	0·9
	kidney	16·9	turnip	0·8
	cod	16·0	butter	0·5
	beef (average)	14·8	apple, lemon, pear	0·3
	lamb	13·0		
	egg	11·9		
Incomplete	peanuts	28·1		
	lentils	23·8		
	peas (dried) ⎫ pulses	21·5		
	beans (haricot) ⎭	21·4		
	oatmeal	12·1		
Carbohydrate	sugar	105·0	potatoes (raw)	18·0
(as mono-	white flour	80·0	peas (fresh, boiled)	7·7
saccharide)	syrup	79·0	milk	4·8
	oatmeal	72·8		
	jam	69·2		
Fat	salad or cooking oil	99·9	milk	3·8
	lard, dripping	99·3		
	margarine	85·3		
	butter	82·5		
		μg		mg
Vitamin A	*Animal*			
(measured in	halibut liver oil	900,000	herring	45
μg retinol)	cod liver oil	22,740	milk	35
	ox liver	6,000	sardines	30
(measured in	*Vegetable*			
μg carotene	carrot	12,000	apple	30
—6 times	spinach	6,000	cauliflower	30
less valuable	apricots (dried)	3,600	pear	12
than retinol)	watercress	3,000		
Vitamin B complex				
Thiamine	yeast (dried brewers')	18·40	beef (average)	0·07
	pork	1·00	milk	0·04
	cornflakes	0·60	sugar	nil
	oatmeal	0·50		
Riboflavine	yeast (dried brewers')	3·68	beef	0·20
	liver	3·00	milk	0·15
	cheese	0·50	sugar	nil

Foodstuff	Best Sources	Amount	Poorest Sources	Amount
Nicotinic Acid	yeast (dried brewers')	*µg* 53·4	bread (white)	*mg* 1·4
	liver	13·0	potatoes (raw)	1·2
	beef	5·0	milk	0·1
Vitamin C	blackcurrants	200	tomatoes	20
	brussels sprouts (raw)	100	lettuce	15
	cauliflower (raw)	70	apple, plum, pear	3–5
	cabbage (raw)	60		
	lemons	50		
Vitamin D (measured in *µg*)	cod liver oil	*µg* 217·50	liver	*µg* 0·75
	herring, kipper	22·25	cheese	0·35
	salmon (canned)	12·50	milk (liquid)	0·05
Mineral Elements		*mg*		*mg*
Calcium	dried, skimmed milk	1277	meat (average)	10
	cheese (Cheddar)	810	potatoes (raw)	8
	sardines	409	rice	4
			margarine	4
Iron	cocoa	15·0	white fish	1·0
	liver (average)	13·9	cabbage (raw)	1·0
	kidney (average)	13·4	potatoes (raw)	0·7
	beef (raw)	4·0	milk	0·1
Sodium	bacon	1220	beef	69
	haddock (fillet)	1220	milk	50
	cornflakes	1050	peas (fresh)	1
	kippers	990		
	cheese (Cheddar)	612		
Potassium	prunes (dried)	864	cornflakes	114
	potatoes (raw)	568	bread	100
	brussels sprouts	515		
	liver	325		

Note The figures quoted above are based on those published by H.M.S.O. in *Manual of Nutrition* (1970).

   With the exception of sugar, which shows complete absence of the B complex of vitamins (all other foods containing *some*) 'poorest sources' refer only to the foods containing some of the nutrient concerned. It does *not* include all foods.

WATER

Although the body can live for a short time without food, it will very soon die for lack of water. Approximately 66 per cent of the body consists of water and as this is continually being lost through the normal functions of perspiration, respiration and excretion, it must be replaced.

The Functions of Water

1 It is the chief constituent of all body fluids, and these are distributed throughout all the tissues of the body.

2 It helps to dissolve food and aids digestion.

3 It helps to remove waste matter from the body and prevents the digestive system from becoming clogged.

4 It helps to regulate the body temperature—evaporation of perspiration reduces the heat of the body, and the rate of perspiration is increased as body temperature rises.

5 It regulates the degree of fluidity of all the body fluids in order that they may flow satisfactorily.

The Absorption of Water

Water plays an important part in the transport of food and nutrients through the digestive system and the greater part of it is re-absorbed into the body from the large intestine. It is excreted, holding in solution various waste products, from the kidneys, rather than from the rectum with the faeces. In this way, not only are the waste products of the kidneys excreted, but the loss of moisture from the body is more efficiently regulated.

Water in the Diet

All solid foods contain a certain amount of water, particularly fruits and vegetables. Many foods have their natural water content supplemented by that in which they are cooked. Even so, this does not provide replacement for the amount of water excreted from the body each day. At least one litre of liquid should be drunk as such in order to compensate the loss fully, but this may include any beverage, such as fruit drinks, tea, coffee, milk, and soup, as well as plain water.

BEVERAGES

All drinks are valuable in adding liquid to the diet, and even plain water, if 'hard', can contribute useful calcium as well. In some districts, too, fluorine has been added to the drinking water supply in an attempt to safeguard the enamel of children's teeth.

Generally all beverages can be classed as one of these

a stimulants: tea, coffee, cocoa

b foods: milk, egg/milk, beef tea

c refreshers: mineral waters, fruit drinks.

Mineral waters   true mineral waters are those which come from natural wells such as those at Bath and any of the spas.

Artificial mineral waters   ordinary water is saturated with carbon dioxide.

Soda water   usually this is produced in a similar way to artificial mineral waters; some can contain a very little sodium bicarbonate (which explains why some people find it easier to digest milk when mixed with soda water than when it is served alone).

Soft drinks (fruit)   These are usually 'still' and are flavoured with natural or synthetic fruit essences. Concentrated forms may have oil from the fruit peel added as well. Sugar content in non-synthetics is high, but synthetic forms are valueless as nutrients. Natural juice may also contain traces of Vitamin C.

Tea   produced by drying the leaves of an Indian or Chinese plant. It contains a nerve stimulant, caffeine, and traces of B complex.

Coffee   the beans of the coffee plant are dried, rolled, skinned and roasted before being ground. Coffee also contains caffeine. Most coffees as purchased are a blend of several different types of bean.

'Instant' coffee and tea is made by infusing the dried leaves or beans and roller-drying, spray-drying or freeze-drying the liquid, leaving a very soluble powder.

Cocoa   produced from the bean-containing pods of the cocoa (or cacao) plant. It contains a stimulant similar to caffeine, and also a little iron, carotene and Vitamin B.

Serving

All beverages should be served in clean vessels, as attractively as possible and at the correct temperature (very hot *or* chilled).

FURTHER STUDY

THINGS TO DO

1 Find out the standard scientific tests for the presence of protein, carbohydrate, fat and minerals in foodstuffs. Then

a bearing in mind that the chemical formula for sucrose is $C_{12}H_{22}O_{11}$, prove in the laboratory that all the elements shown are present.

b Repeat with protein, having ascertained the formula.

c Repeat with fat, having ascertained the formula.

2*a* Produce the ash of a sample of egg yolk and carry out an experiment to show the presence of *one* of the mineral elements you know it to contain.

b Repeat with the ash of a sample of meat.

c Repeat with the ash of a sample of cheese.

d Repeat with the ash of a sample of milk.

3 Find the names of as many digestive enzymes as you can, and which foodstuff each one affects during the breaking down of the food eaten. On a diagram of the human digestive system indicate where each enzyme does its work.

4 Using plain flour, demonstrate
a its insolubility in cold liquid
b its gelatinization in liquid when heated
c the necessity for blending with cold liquid before hot liquid is added
d the dextrinization of dry starch when heated
e the solubility of dextrinized starch in cold liquid.

5 Heat *a*. dry, and *b*. dissolved granulated sugar to demonstrate charring and caramelization. Repeat with brown sugar and with caster sugar to compare the effects.

6 Heat equal quantities of vegetable oil and melted lard to the same temperature. Note the time taken to bring both to a degree of heat which will brown equally-sized cubes of bread immediately.

7 Demonstrate a simple example of saponification, using a greasy frying pan:
a half-fill with hot water
b add a large knob (about the size of a walnut) of washing soda
c bring to the boil and note the cloudy, frothy (sudsy) effect produced.
(cf. equation on p. 51).

8 Demonstrate oxidation of foodstuffs (i.e. the release of energy) as follows:
a place a small amount of sugar in a test tube
b add a similar quantity of black copper oxide
c fit the test tube with a stopper and a dry delivery tube ⎫
d pass the free end of the delivery tube into limewater ⎬ see sketch on p. 174
e heat the test tube gently. ⎭

Results will show:
sugar+copper oxide → copper+water + carbon dioxide

Discover the chemical formulae and convert the equation into scientific terms.

9 Find out what you can about the production of synthetic 'meat'.

10 Find out the nutritive problems particularly applicable to
a immigrant children
b immigrant adults
c elderly people
d overweight adolescents
e overweight adults.

11 Find out the names of the essential amino acids.

12 Find out what an essential fatty acid is.

13 Using the tables provided, weigh out the amounts of the following foods supplying a day's supply of the nutrient indicated:

    a liver supplying riboflavine

    b liver supplying Vitamin A (retinol)

    c beef supplying protein

    d cheese supplying protein

    e potatoes supplying Vitamin C

    f cocoa supplying iron

    g sugar supplying MJ for an 18-year-old boy

    h cornflakes supplying nicotinic acid.

14 Weigh out portions of the following foods, each containing 100 mg of calcium: potato; cabbage; watercress; milk; cheese; flour.

15 Compare the bulk of 100 g of the following foods: meat; cheese; milk; bread; oranges; cabbage; sugar; butter.

QUESTIONS TO ANSWER

1 Write out the following statements, and complete them, using only the words in the right-hand column to fill in the blanks.

Section A

    a The foods we eat cannot nourish our bodies until they have been rendered into their simplest .... form.

    b When they have reached this stage they can be called ....

    c In order to be of value they must then be .... into the bloodstream.

    d The process of breaking down foods by chemical substances in the body is ....

    e The foodstuff required for growth and repair of human tissue is ....

    f The first digestive enzyme encountered by food being eaten is ....

    g Cellulose is of no nutritive value to the body because it is ....

    h Bodily processes are regulated by small quantities of ....

    i For the formation of bones and teeth we require calcium and ....

    j Proteins consist of carbon, hydrogen, oxygen and ....

phosphorus

protein

nitrogen

ptyalin

soluble

insoluble

nutrients

mineral elements

digestion

absorbed

Section B

    a The mineral elements which form bones and teeth cannot perform their functions without the presence of . . . .

    b If there is insufficient iron in the diet the condition known as . . . . may result.

    c The connective tissue between body cells cannot be formed without . . . .

    d Pellagra is caused by deficiency of . . . .

    e In the loss of perspiration and urine the mineral . . . . is also lost.

    f The production of energy is regulated by the thyroid gland which contains . . . .

    g Carbohydrates consist mainly of sugars and . . . .

    h Mono- and di-saccharides are types of . . . .

    i Fructose is the sugar found in . . . .

    j The carbohydrate which is used to assist in the setting of jam is . . . .

fruit

starches

iodine

pectin

Vitamin D

sodium chloride

anaemia

nicotinic acid

Vitamin C

sugars

Section C

    a When moistened and heated, starch . . . .

    b When dry starch is heated it . . . .

    c Fats consist of fatty acids and . . . .

    d The amount of energy provided by 1 g fat is more than twice that provided by 1 g of . . . .

    e When oil is broken up into tiny globules distributed throughout a liquid it is said to have been . . . .

    f When an alkali reacts upon fat, the process is known as . . . .

    g Thiamine and aneurin are two other names for . . . .

    h Another name given to nicotinic acid is . . . .

    i A yellow pigment found in plants and which can become Vitamin A is called . . . .

    j A complete protein contains all the essential . . . .

glycerol

niacin

saponification

amino acids

dextrinizes

gelatinizes

carotene

carbohydrate

emulsified

Vitamin B_1

    2 How does the body obtain its energy? How and why do the energy requirements of different types of people vary?

3 Explain, in detail, what happens to the following nutrients (found in buttered toast), from the time they enter the digestive tract until they are absorbed by the body:

    a gluten (protein in the flour)
    b starch (carbohydrate in the flour)
    c fat (as in the butter).

Why may cheese cause indigestion and how can this be prevented?   (A.E.B.)

4 What is the value of protein in the body? Explain the differences between complete and incomplete proteins.

    a Name *four* foods which are good sources of complete protein and *four* which are good sources of incomplete protein.

    b How would a knowledge of these facts help in the planning of well-balanced family meals?   (C.U.B.)

5 What is the nutritive importance of mineral elements in the maintenance of good health? Name *three* mineral elements which should always be included in the diet and give a detailed account of the value of each of them. Suggest meals for yourself for one day, showing how the three mineral elements have been used.

How can loss of mineral elements be prevented during the preparation of food?   (C.U.B.)

6 Why are vitamins essential for the health of the human body? Give as many examples as you can and state a good source of each.

7 What are the following? Describe their function in the diet.

a riboflavine	*c* lactose	*e* rennin
b albumen	*d* gluten	*f* ptyalin

Name one food which is a good source of each of *a*, *b*, *c* and *d*.
       (A.E.B.)

8 Explain what the following are and why they are important in the diet.

a fructose	*c* carotene	*e* water
b myosin	*d* calcium carbonate	*f* margarine

Name *two* foods which are a good source of *a*, *b*, *c*, *d* and *e*.
       (A.E.B.)

3

METHODS OF COOKING

Why do we cook food? What is cooking? From the very earliest days of history Man has found it necessary to cook his food. He knew even then that cooking made his meat more attractive to taste and easier to eat. We know now that it also makes food more easily dealt with by our digestive systems, and to a certain extent reduces the risk of our being infected by bacteria contained within it. So we can define cooking as the preparation of food for eating, usually involving the application of heat; the rendering of tissues palatable, digestible, attractive and safe for eating.

How is the food to be cooked? The choice of method depends on:

a the food to be cooked
b time available
c fuel available
d amount of cooking to be done
e personal taste
f type of person catered for.

BOILING

The cooking of food by immersing it in boiling liquid (i.e. 100°C) and keeping it at simmering point until tender. (A liquid is 'simmering' when the surface is just broken by an occasional bubble—*not* when it bubbles continuously.)

Suitable foods: vegetables, eggs, the more muscular parts of mutton and other meats (e.g. knuckle end of leg, middle neck, best end of neck, cow-heel), bacon, ham.

Aim

By boiling it is intended to keep in as many of the natural juices of the food as possible, while softening tissues right through. Therefore meat is kept in a large piece and plunged into boiling liquid. The heat coagulates the albumen present in the tissues of the meat and forms a coating which prevents the juices from escaping.

(The most easily recognized form of albumen is egg-white. To see how easily heat affects albumen, drop a small quantity of white of egg into rapidly boiling water. It will very quickly set and become opaque and, if the rapid boiling continues, soon becomes tough and leathery. This principle applies equally to the cooking of meat—once the outside is sealed the cooking should be continued with the liquid at simmering point only.)

Old potatoes and other old root vegetables are often placed in cold water and brought to the boil. This is because as the vegetables become older the cellulose (i.e. the cells of which the vegetable is composed) becomes tougher and needs gradual softening.

Prepared foods, such as fish, may be purchased with instructions to 'boil in the bag', i.e. in the plastic covering in which they are sealed. In fact, the boiling water does not reach the food, which is heated in its own steam. As the pressure of steam within the bag builds up, a simple 'pressure cooker' is evolved.

Advantages

    1 A simple method, needing little attention.

    2 Various types of food may be cooked in this way.

    3 The liquid may be used for making stocks, soups, sauces and gravies.

    4 Garnish may be cooked at the same time and in the same pan as the main dish, e.g. boiled beef and carrots.

Disadvantages

    1 Food may be broken down by over-boiling and flavour may be lost.

    2 A lengthy process.

STEWING

The long, slow cooking of food in liquid, using a covered pan.

Suitable foods: fruit, cheaper cuts of meat (flank, shin, neck, tail), fish, rabbit, liver, tripe.

Suitable liquids: stock, syrup, milk, water.

Aim

Stewing is intended to soften all tissues and to serve the liquid and its contents as a complete dish.

Because much of the juice from the food may be drawn out into the liquid without being wasted, the food may be cut into small pieces, thus exposing a larger area of food to heat, placed in cold liquid and brought very gradually to just below simmering point.

Note This is quite opposite to preparation for boiling.

Only sufficient liquid to cover the food is required. The natural juices of the food will be drawn out to increase the amount and a common fault of stews is that there is far too much liquid in proportion to solid matter. Juicy fruits such as rhubarb and gooseberries should be cooked in just sufficient liquid to cover the bottom of the pan and prevent sticking. The sugar necessary for sweetening these sour fruits dissolves, making more liquid; the natural juices added to this can easily make the total amount of liquid very excessive, and the flavour is diluted.

'A stew boiled is a stew spoiled.' You have seen what happens to the outside of meat when it is boiled and, in a stew, this results in tough, unappetizing portions. However, poor quality meat can easily become flavourless and insipid if stewed for too long. This may be avoided by frying the portions in fat before stewing them, which seals in some of the juices, thus helping to retain the natural flavour, improves the colour of the stew, and adds to the fat content of the dish, usually deficient when cheap cuts of meat are used.

As this is a long, slow method of cooking, with liquid to aid the softening process, cheap cuts of meat unsuitable for roasting or grilling may be used. This is therefore also an economical method.

Cheaper, coarser foods are often lacking in flavour and by this method flavourings may be added to supplement the natural ones, e.g. onions stewed with steak, cloves with apples.

Advantages

1 An economical method of cookery as far as fuel consumption (only a very low heat is required), cost of food and complete use of finished dish are concerned. There is no wastage with this method.

2 May be carried out on top of the stove or in the oven.

3 Needs very little attention, an occasional stir to prevent sticking being all that is necessary.

Disadvantage

A slow method which cannot be hurried.

CASSEROLE COOKERY

The slow cooking of food in a small quantity of liquid in a covered utensil in the oven. In fact the food is cooked by a combination of stewing and steaming. The utensil used is also known as a casserole.

This is a very popular method of cookery, perhaps more so since automatic ovens have become more widely used. The working housewife finds the oven-to-table process very convenient, economical, labour-saving and safe to leave while she is away.

Advantages

1 It is economical in the use of fuel, as several dishes can be cooked at the same time, and the temperature used is low.

2 There is little loss of food value in cooking since the meat/fish/vegetables are served in the liquor in which they are cooked. This is not a thickened liquid; it moistens the ingredients but does not mask them.

Oven Temperature Chart

Description		Gas Mark	Temperature	
	Suitable for		Celsius	Fahrenheit
Very Cool	Meringues	Below thermostat setting	100°	200°
Very Cool	Fruit bottling	$\frac{1}{4}$	110°	225°
Very Cool	Slow stewing	$\frac{1}{2}$	130°	250°
Very Cool	Milk puddings	1	140°	275°
Cool	Casseroles Rich fruit cakes	2	150°	300°
Warm	Slow roasting Shortbread	3	170°	325°
Moderate	Victoria sponges	4	180°	350°
Fairly Hot	Small rich cakes Sponges	5	190°	375°
Fairly Hot	Plain buns Short pastry	6	200°	400°
Hot	Quick roasting Scones	7	220°	425°
Very Hot	Bread	8	230°	450°
Very Hot	Puff pastry	9	240°	475°
Some electric ovens reach these higher temperatures			250° 270° 290°	500° 525° 550°

Note These figures are those presently quoted by the Gas Council and equivalent temperatures may vary a little from cooker to cooker. The Celsius and Fahrenheit temperatures shown are not necessarily direct conversions.

3 Inexpensive foods can be used since, as the cooking process is long, slow and in liquid, the ingredients are rendered tender and digestible.

4 One course of a meal can be cooked completely in one utensil. Root vegetables and the main ingredient can all be cooked and served in the same vessel, whereas several different pans and dishes would be needed for alternative methods of cooking.

The vessel used, the casserole, may be very decorative as well as functional, being made of plain or decorated ovenproof glass, glazed earthenware or cast iron or steel coated with vitreous enamel.

GRILLING

The cooking of food by direct heat over or in front of a smokeless fire or beneath the glowing reflector of a gas or electric grill.

Suitable foods: fish, bacon, tomatoes, mushrooms, sausages, thin pieces of good quality meat, e.g. fillet or rump steak, pork chops, lamb chops.

Preparation of Food
    1 Wipe and dry.
    2 Brush with cooking oil to prevent scorching.
    3 Grill until golden brown on one side, turn and grill other side.

Aim
Grilling is intended to make food tender and palatable without losing any of the natural juices, and therefore only thin slices or fine-grained foods should be used.

Advantages
    1 A quick and appetizing method.
    2 Grilled foods are more easily digested than fried foods.

Disadvantages
    1 Only good quality and therefore more expensive foods can be cooked by this method.
    2 Needs careful attention.

Note Grill burners must be red-hot before food is placed beneath them, otherwise outside is not sealed immediately and some juices may escape.

    (Test this with a piece of bread. If placed below red-hot grill toast is crisp and light; if placed under a cold grill it is leathery and heavy.)

    Do not prick the surface of the food. This also allows juices to escape.

ROASTING

The cooking of food with fat in an enclosed space (formerly on a roasting 'jack'). Over-cooking is a common mistake in roasting and one which can ruin the flavour and texture of rather expensive meat. Particular care should be taken when a small joint is being roasted, when the rule given for timing may have to be modified. (For roasting times see p. 109).

Suitable meats: better quality cuts such as best end of neck, chump end of loin, best end of loin, leg and shoulder; and poultry.

Aim
Roasting coagulates the surface albumen, seals in the juices and renders all the tissues tender.

This is a 'dry' method of cooking, the moisture coming from the food itself, apart from the fat added to the tin before it is put into the oven, which acts as a basting to prevent scorching. Therefore only good quality meats are suitable. Whenever possible, buy cuts with a small amount of bone, as it weighs heavy and adds to the price.

A good deal of evaporation takes place during this process, which is therefore more suitable for large than for small joints. However, by wrapping meat in cooking foil before placing it in the oven, moisture in the form of steam is retained in contact with the meat and shrinkage is reduced. The use of roasting bags (clear plastic) allows meat and poultry to brown while remaining moist. In either case far less oven-cleaning is involved than when no covering is used. Earthenware 'bricks' are also in vogue for use when roasting poultry. These are brushed over inside with oil before use and serve a similar purpose to roasting bags.

As the aim of this method of cooking is to retain as many of the juices as possible it is advisable to place the meat in a hot oven to seal the outside, then after about ten minutes to turn down the heat so that the inner tissues may be cooked fairly slowly without burning the outside. However, when making use of the new automatic ovens, it is possible to achieve satisfactory results by placing the meat in a cold oven and setting the switch for the required time.

Advantages
    1 An appetizing method of cookery.
    2 Needs little attention.
    3 Oven can be used for other dishes at the same time.

Disadvantages
    1 Only good quality meat is suitable.
    2 There is some shrinkage and loss of weight however good the quality.
    3 A great deal of fuel is required for heating the oven.

BAKING

The cooking of food in an enclosed space with no fat.

Suitable foods: starch mixtures, juicy fruits or vegetables, i.e. foods containing sufficient fat or moisture to assist cooking, whether it be necessary to burst starch grains (cake mixtures, etc.) or soften cellulose (apples, marrow).

Baking and roasting are closely allied and one method very often becomes a modification of the other. In both cases it is necessary for the heat to be lowered soon after the food is placed in the oven, i.e. after the outside has been sealed. Baked dishes only require fat for preventing the mixtures from sticking to the tins in which they are cooked.

FRYING

The cooking of food in heated oil or fat, either added or in the food itself. The best solid fat to use is clarified dripping or lard, which contains no water to cause spurting. Cooking oils are becoming increasingly popular and can be extracted from corn (e.g. 'Mazola'), cotton seed, groundnuts, olives and sunflower seeds; sometimes these or some of these are blended together to form a product such as 'Twirl'.

Advantages of frying
    1 A quick method.
    2 An attractive method.

Disadvantages of frying
    1 Expensive (food and fat must be of good quality, fuel consumption is high).
    2 Constant attention is necessary.
    3 Food is indigestible if not well cooked and drained.

Advantages of oil for frying
    1 Quick and easy to use.
    2 Remains liquid even in cold weather.
    3 Can be used several times if:
    a oil is not overheated
    b food is adequately coated
    c no flavour has been absorbed.
    4 Can be kept indefinitely.

Disadvantages of oil for frying
    1 Initial expense is quite high compared with solid fats (more economical if bought in large-size bottles or cans).
    2 Can be a fire hazard if not handled carefully. (Do not fill pans more than one-third of their depth and do not allow a kettle to boil close enough to the pan for it to spurt water into the oil.)

Types of Frying

    1 Dry frying: No additional fat is used, e.g. bacon, kippers.
    2 Shallow-fat frying: Pan contains sufficient fat to prevent food from sticking. Food must be turned, e.g. pancakes.
    3 Deep-fat frying: Food is completely immersed in hot fat, therefore does not need turning, e.g. fish and chips.

Test for readiness of fat
There should be no bubbles on the surface and it used to be said that a blue haze should be rising. This is not a sufficiently accurate test nowadays, however, when there are so many excellent cooking fats and oils with varying compositions on the market. A small cube of bread should be dropped into the fat; if it rises immediately and becomes light golden brown in 30 seconds, food may be fried successfully; if it sinks, the fat is not ready.

On removing food from fat it should be placed on crumpled kitchen paper (*not* greaseproof) to drain off excess fat.

Coatings used for Fried Foods
Seasoned flour: 1 tbsp. flour; ½ tsp. salt; pinch pepper. This may be used for shallow or deep-fat frying but must not be applied until immediately before cooking; otherwise flour becomes damp and lumpy.
Milk and seasoned flour: for shallow frying only, otherwise water content makes fat spurt.
Egg and breadcrumbs: for deep and shallow frying. Particularly suitable for deep-fat frying, as albumen sets immediately upon contact with hot fat and forms an attractive and effective coating. Egg must be beaten very well and breadcrumbs should be very fine and patted well against the food. (Fine oatmeal, raspings or crushed vermicelli can be substituted.)
Batter: used for fritters and very suitable for fish. Inclined to be indigestible to some people.
Reasons for coating foods
    1 To protect the food from the extreme heat of the fat and prevent it from becoming over-cooked.
    2 To prevent food from becoming soggy with fat.
    3 To prevent food juices from escaping.
    4 To prevent food from breaking up.
    5 To make food more attractive.
Preparation of food for frying
    1 Dry well before coating.
    2 Apply coating evenly.
    3 Do not allow pieces to overlap each other after coating.

STEAMING

The cooking of food in the steam from boiling water. Steamers are not now common pieces of kitchen equipment, probably because it is a long slow method of cooking which requires constant attention in order to replenish the boiling water. The most commonly used methods of steaming are:

Indirect steaming
The steam does not actually touch the food. This is a suitable method for warming-up cold cooked foods for late-comers and for cooking delicate pieces of meat or fish for invalids.

Pressure cooking
The food is cooked by direct contact with the steam but it is at such a high pressure that the cooking-time is accelerated considerably.
    The pan is a specially made, thick-walled vessel with a tightly-fitting lid which is clamped into position. The interior may be used as a

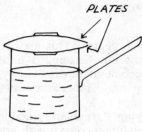

PLATES

Indirect steaming

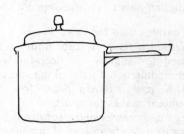

Cooking under pressure

single pan or for several different foods placed in the shaped containers provided.

It is very important that the manufacturer's instructions are followed in using these pans.

Suitable foods: fish, poultry, meat; root vegetables, pulses; fruits, pudding mixtures, jam, marmalade, (i.e. nearly all foods, green vegetables being exceptions. The cooking of these is quite acceptable but the colour sometimes deteriorates).

CONSERVATIVE COOKING

The cooking of vegetables to conserve the flavour and food value as much as possible.

The main vitamins found in vegetables, particularly green ones, are B and C, which are soluble in water. Vitamin C is also easily destroyed by light and heat. It is therefore not only necessary to buy fresh vegetables but to cook them in such a way as to retain as much of their vitamin and mineral element contents as possible.

Method

1 Cover the bottom of the vessel (saucepan if cooking is to be carried out on top of the stove; casserole if done in the oven) with half an inch of salted water (or melted fat) and heat it to boiling point.

2 Divide the vegetables into small sections for quick cooking and place in pan.

3 Place on a tightly-fitting lid.

4 Boil or heat rapidly for 10 minutes.

5 Strain off the small amount of liquid remaining and use it for stock.

It will be seen that this method combines those of boiling and steaming. The long, slow process of normal steaming destroys much of the food value and colour of green vegetables and makes the texture soggy and unappetizing.

THE EFFECT OF COOKING ON VARIOUS FOODSTUFFS

Starch
When dry, starch grains quickly become brown and charred. When the outer covering of starch grains is softened by liquid the grains swell and burst and the mixture becomes thick and transparent (this is what happens when making laundry starch).

Sugar
Sugar grains melt and become syrupy as the water content evaporates. The syrup turns brown (caramelizes) and finally chars, smelling strongly.

Cellulose
Stems, peel, etc., of vegetables and fruit become softened and palatable when cooked, particularly when liquid is used.

Fat
Melts very quickly and either becomes absorbed by other foodstuffs (particularly starch) or becomes browned and charred, when the flavour is most unpleasant.

Protein
Fibres become tender and easily divided, but if over-cooked the albumen in the fibres becomes hard and leathery (compare egg-white at various stages of cooking). Albumen begins to coagulate immediately upon contact with heat. Juices, if first sealed in by strong heat, are absorbed into the tissues of the muscle fibres.

Thiamine
25–50 per cent may be lost.

Vitamin C
Destroyed by heat. (See p. 56.)

Other Vitamins
Loss by cooking is not important.

FURTHER STUDY
THINGS TO DO

Section A
1 Prepare and cook a selection of root vegetables in as many different ways as possible.

2 Cook green vegetables by *a*. boiling, *b*. conservative method of cookery, and compare *a*. colour, *b*. bulk, *c*. flavour, *d*. liquid remaining. Make a note of the advantages and disadvantages of each method.

3 *Group work:* Prepare a midday dinner consisting of a roast joint, roast potatoes, rhubarb stewed in the oven; runner beans, and a simple custard sauce may be cooked on the top of the stove. Serve the dishes attractively and lay the dinner table for four people.

4 *Group work:* Prepare a midday dinner consisting of fish, potatoes, carrots and a simple steamed pudding cooked on one gas-ring. Lay the table and serve the meal attractively for four people.

5 Cook potatoes by the following methods: boiling; roasting; baking; frying. Serve each dish attractively, choosing from the following: creamed potatoes; duchesse potatoes; potato cheese; potato croquettes; chips; crisps; French fried; potato scallops.

6 Prepare and serve a fried breakfast for two people. Tea or coffee and toast must be included.

7 Prepare a mixed grill for one person. Cook vegetables to accompany it.

8 Plan and cook a simple midday meal using the oven only.

Section B

1 Separate the white from the yolk of an egg and drop equal quantities of each into luke-warm water. Continue to heat the water until each coagulates. Find the temperature at which this happens to *a*. the white, *b*. the yolk, *c*. a mixture of both.

2 Using equal-sized unpeeled potatoes, place one each at the top, the bottom and the middle of a moderate oven. Compare the speed of cooking at each position.

3*a* Using plain flour, blend 1 tablespoonful with (*i*) cold, (*ii*) hot water. Note the difference in the results.

b Blend 1 tablespoonful of flour with sufficient cold water to produce a smooth, thin paste and add boiling water until a thick paste is formed, stirring continuously. Notice the texture and colour. Compare this with similar mixtures of *a*. cornflour, *b*. laundry starch. What conclusions can you draw?

c Heat 1 teaspoonful of flour in a frying pan until evenly browned. Mix it into cold water and compare the result with that in *a*. What have you proved?

4 Use a fat thermometer to discover the temperatures at which *a*. lard, *b*. dripping, *c*. margarine, melt. Compare the temperatures at which *a*., *b*., and *c*. and cooking oil
    (*i*) fry a cube of bread as described on page 74
    (*ii*) smoke.

QUESTIONS TO ANSWER

1 Write out the following statements, and complete them, using only the words in the right-hand column to fill in the blanks.

a A method of cooking which can be carried out both in the oven and on top of the cooker is	soluble
	lard
b Foods cooked in an enclosed space with the addition of fat are cooked by	gelatinized
c When foods are completely immersed in hot fat they are being cooked by	grilling
d The best solid fat for frying is .... because it contains no	melts
e When starch grains are softened and burst by the action of liquid and heat they have been	dextrinized
f When starch has been heated without moisture it has been .... and made	water
g When protein is heated its solidification is properly called	coagulation
h When toast is made in front of a fire it is cooked by	stewing
i When sugar is warmed without any liquid it	dissolves
j When sugar is stirred into a cup of tea it	roasting
	deep-fat frying

2 Conduction, convection and radiation are means of transferring heat. Give a definition of each, showing its application to the cooking of food.   (C.U.B.)

3 What do you understand by frying as a method of cooking? What precautions would you take to obtain good results when frying *a*. pancakes, *b*. chips, *c*. fillets of plaice, *d*. eggs?

4 Describe briefly how you would cook the following foods, in each case stating any particular care which must be taken: *a*. liver; *b*. spinach; *c*. swedes; *d*. sponge pudding; *e*. herrings.

5 How do you account for the popularity of casserole cookery? Give examples of its use.

6 Giving reasons, suggest a suitable method of cooking for each of the following: beetroot; rice; fresh herrings. In each case indicate in note form how the food would be prepared, cooked and served.

(A.E.B.)

4
DAIRY PRODUCE

MILK

Milk must be the earliest known of all foods. Very ancient nomad tribes were always accompanied by their herds of goats, asses, ewes and sometimes camels, which were valued during their life-time largely as milk-producers. Even today the most simple-living and primitive peoples cherish their animals particularly for the milk they yield. All animals, including human animals, live solely upon milk for the first days of their lives—the length of time during which it remains their only food varies with the rate of development of the particular animal. Human babies live and thrive on it for several months.

MILK AS A FOOD

Milk is often called a 'perfect food' because:

1 It contains some of all the essential food values, particularly calcium.

2 It is usually easily obtainable.

3 It is reasonably priced—the actual cost varies according to the grade of the milk and the seasonal yield, etc.

4 It is usually easily digested, particularly if drunk slowly.

5 It can be used as it reaches the consumer, without any further preparation.

6 It can be drunk raw or it can be cooked, used as a basis of a large variety of dishes or as an accompaniment.

7 There need be no waste—even if allowed to go sour, it may still be used for cooking.

8 The flavour is very bland (i.e. not distinctive, plain), so that even if large quantities are drunk the palate does not easily tire of it.

It cannot, however, truthfully be claimed that milk has no faults as a food for adults, because:

1 It contains very little Vitamin B and not much iron.

2 What little Vitamin C is present is easily destroyed by light and there are extremely small quantities remaining after a bottle of milk has been left on a doorstep for any length of time, especially in sunshine.

80

3 A large percentage of the bulk of milk is water, which means that a good deal has to be drunk for its food value to be appreciated. Adults should drink at least half a litre a day and children at least a litre. This quantity can, of course, be spread over a day and need not be drunk all at once; nevertheless, drinking plain milk can often produce a very 'full' feeling without satisfying for long.

4 It will go sour unless kept at a very low temperature. If kept in a refrigerator milk will keep sweet for a fortnight or more, but if kept at room temperature the bacteria in the milk will begin to act upon the milk-sugar (lactose) and convert it into lactic acid. This acid coagulates the chief soluble protein in milk, known as *caseinogen*, and this brings about the condition we commonly call 'curdling'. Although these curds do no harm to the body and, indeed, are eaten in modified form as cheese, their flavour in raw milk is unpleasant and distasteful to most people. (See p. 85 for 'Safeguarding Milk in the Home'.)

5 Milk contains no roughage and an exclusively liquid diet will eventually dislocate the digestive system, particularly in the intestines where undigested bulk is required to help in the elimination of waste products.

6 Following on the previous point, a too soft or all-liquid diet very easily palls. Everyone feels the need at some time to eat foods which they can 'bite on' and variety of texture in the diet is one of the important points to be observed in planning meals.

The composition of milk

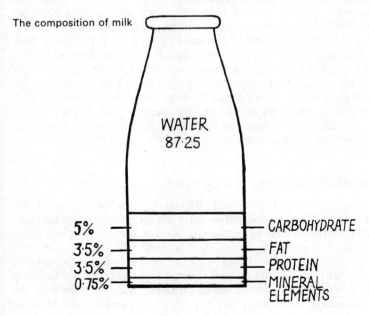

WATER
87·25

5% — CARBOHYDRATE
3·5% — FAT
3·5% — PROTEIN
0·75% — MINERAL ELEMENTS

THE DISTRIBUTION OF MILK

We have become so accustomed to the daily appearance of hygienically produced and safe milk on our doorsteps that we seldom think of the long story and drastic changes which lie behind its distribution.

For centuries milk taken from herds of cows, ewes, asses and goats was drunk in its rawest form. No kind of special precautions were taken in preparing the animal, the milker, or the utensils used, to avoid contamination. Indeed, the primitive method of milking the animal directly into the mouth of the consumer *may* have been a considerably safer way than the more usual process of using a collecting vessel.

In Tudor times, when the country farmers had begun to appreciate the financial gain in supplying town-dwellers, animals were taken from door to door and literally milked on the doorstep of the would-be consumer. This meant that an added source of pollution arose from at best the dust and at worst the sewage present in the Tudor roadways and streets. Many of the devastating epidemics which swept the country during these and earlier times must have owed a good deal of their strength to milk-carried bacteria.

Into the 1920s it was still a familiar sight to see the milkman carrying his can (filled from a storage churn on his cart) from house to house and ladling the customers' requirements into their own jugs and bowls. Although the milk had been purified before distribution, much of its purity must have been lost during sales.

Today it is fully realized that milk is as satisfactory a food for bacteria as it is for less dangerous creatures, and every effort is being made to produce and distribute entirely safe milk. Every stage of production is scrupulously inspected by officials and distribution is controlled by the Milk Marketing Board, which works out the shortest routes which can be taken between supply depots and consumers. So efficient has the purification of milk become that specially treated milk can be stored in waxed-paper cartons for weeks—even if not refrigerated. In aluminium foil packs it will keep 'fresh' for several months, although the flavour may deteriorate slightly.

THE PRODUCTION OF CLEAN MILK

'Clean' milk is *not* milk from which all bacteria have been removed—in fact it may contain up to 200,000 bacteria per cubic centimetre and still be perfectly safe for human consumption. There are, however, three diseases whose germs can thrive in milk and which can cause very serious illness in human beings. These diseases are tuberculosis, diphtheria and typhoid, and no milk is considered to be 'clean' unless it is officially free from germs of these diseases. The rate at which the number of cases of them (and every one must be reported to the Medical

Officer of Health) has dropped in recent years is an indication of the success of the measures taken to safeguard the public.

Steps are taken at every stage of milk production to reduce the risk of contamination, and many people are concerned in this chain of processes, from the dairy farmer to the consumer.

Safeguarding the Herd
The bacilli of tuberculosis can very easily be passed from a cow to a human being by way of cows' milk. Great care is taken to make sure that cows are free from the disease and all Britain's dairy herds are officially guaranteed to be so. At half-yearly intervals a veterinary surgeon injects tuberculin into a fold of skin at the back of the cow's neck. If, after a few days, this tissue has thickened, the cow is known to be suffering from the disease. It is then removed from the herd and destroyed. No milk is now sold as 'T.T.' as it is no longer necessary to state that milk comes from herds with a certificate of immunity.

Cleanliness in the Milking Parlour
Every detail of the process of milking is most carefully supervised. The structure and finish of the building is such that it can be kept as clean as possible as easily as possible: floors are concreted so that they can be thoroughly hosed after every use; walls are whitewashed as well as ceilings so that they can be cheaply and efficiently re-covered. Most milking is now carried out by mechanical means, instead of by hand. This means that the milk passes directly from the cow to covered buckets, along tubes which at no time are exposed to the air. All this equipment is sterilized by means of steam or of chemicals, after every use. When milking is carried out by hand the operators are prepared in much the same way as are doctors for their surgical work. Sterile white caps and aprons are worn and hands are scrubbed. The same precautions are taken by the men who fix and control the milking machines.

None of these precautions would be of any value if the cows were allowed to bring into the milking parlours the dust, dirt and other impurities which they cannot help collecting while grazing. They are therefore carefully and thoroughly examined, the udders and hind-quarters are washed, and any loose hairs which might fall into the milk are removed.

Safeguards in the Dairy
The milk leaves the cow at the cow's blood heat and the first step in retarding bacterial activity (i.e. of the bacteria which cause milk to go sour) is to pass it over a cooling frame, a series of cold water-filled pipes. It is then poured into churns and transported to depots, or carried to them in large glass-lined, steel, motorized tanks. Churns are clearly marked with the date and time of milking.

At the depot the churns are opened and experienced dairy workers can tell by the smell of the milk whether or not it is fresh. Any suspect milk is tested immediately in the laboratory and, if found to be below the required standard of freshness, is returned to the farm. Emptied churns are steam-sterilized before being returned to the farmer.

GRADES OF MILK

Pasteurized

Nearly 80 per cent of all the milk drunk in this country is pasteurized —i.e. subjected to heat and then cooled rapidly in order to destroy harmful disease germs and to prevent the rapid breeding of acid-producing bacteria. This method was originated by Louis Pasteur. Sometimes the milk is raised to a temperature of 63–66°C and held there for 30 minutes before being cooled rapidly to 10°C. Most dairies nowadays, however, prefer what is known as the H.T.S.T. method—i.e. high temperature, short time—in which the milk is heated quickly to 71°C, held at that temperature for 15 seconds, and cooled rapidly. These methods cause very little change in the flavour of the milk, which retains its characteristic blandness.

During this process the milk is neither in contact with air nor directly handled at any stage. All the machinery is enclosed and is sterilized after every use. After treatment the milk passes directly into sterilized bottles which are filled and capped by machine. Throughout the purifying processes, samples are removed for analysis, so that contamination is detected at once and any kind of deterioration of quality noted. Bottles are also 'spot checked', both before and after leaving the depot.

Sterilized

To sterilize milk it is necessary to pre-heat the milk and homogenize it (see below) before filling the bottles which are then hermetically sealed. The bottles are then heated to 104–110°C and kept at this temperature for 20 to 30 minutes. Because sterilized milk contains no bacteria and the bottles are vacuum sealed, it will keep for several weeks unopened. The obvious visible effect of this method of treatment is that there is no cream line and another result is an alteration in flavour which many people find distasteful. This is due to the caramelization of the lactose (milk sugar).

Homogenized

Milk is first pasteurized and then forced through a fine aperture, under pressure, while still warm. This breaks up the fat globules so completely that a cream line never forms and the fat remains evenly distributed throughout the milk. It is, therefore, easily digested and has a smooth, creamy flavour.

Ultra-heat Treated (U.H.T.)
This is the latest method of milk treatment, the result being known as 'Long-Life' milk. It is first homogenized and then heated to 132°C for one second before being allowed to cool (see p. 84).

Channel Islands and South Devon
This milk is produced by Jersey, Guernsey and South Devon herds, renowned for the richness of their yield (at least 4 per cent fat).

Untreated
In 1964 this designation replaced the former 'Tuberculin Tested' guarantee, as by then all herds were free from tuberculosis. This milk has had no heat treatment and is usually only available from the farms where it is bottled, providing that the farmer holds the necessary licence.

Safeguarding Milk in the Home
Once the milk has reached the customer the responsibility of keeping it clean ceases to be that of the dairyman and becomes that of the house-wife, who should observe the following rules:

1 Provide a sheltered spot for the milk if it is delivered—do not cause it to be left standing in sunlight. Exposure to light and heat will very soon destroy the water-soluble Vitamin C content. Take in the bottles and store them in a cool place as soon as possible.

2 Keep milk cold. Store in a refrigerator if possible, but when none is available stand the bottle on a stone floor or shelf out of direct light. In exceptionally hot weather stand it in a bowl or tall jug of cold water; or make use of the commercial milk coolers which are made of porous pottery and keep the contents cool by the evaporation of the water in which they are soaked. If milk has already been transferred to an open vessel cover it with a cloth or muslin with the ends dipping into water.

3 Cover all open containers of milk with weighted muslin covers or plastic covers to prevent pollution from the air and contamination by flies.

4 Do not store milk, especially in open vessels, near to strong-smelling foods (e.g. fish, especially kippers, onions, etc.) as the flavour is very easily absorbed by milk.

5 Always use very clean containers for storing or serving milk. Stale milk clinging to the curved sides of jugs or caught in rims of mugs will quickly bring about the souring of new milk.

6 Do not mix one day's delivery of milk with another. This will mean that the fresher milk will become sour at the same rate as the staler liquid and both may become unfit for drinking.

7 Rinse out vessels which have been used for milk with *cold* water first, to remove the milk film (solidified lactalbumen), and then in hot water.

How the Body Digests and Uses Milk

'Drinka Pinta' campaigns need little justification but young people often need encouragement in drinking the amounts they require. They do not appreciate the value of a food which can add so much to their general health, nor the beauty which good health offers. A clear skin, bright eyes, glossy hair and good teeth are qualities which no cosmetics can produce as satisfactorily as can perfect health, nor can the value of strong bones, efficient muscles and a well-developed body be under-estimated.

The protein in milk (casein and lactalbumen) is more completely absorbed than that of any other food, and can supply about $17\frac{1}{2}$ per cent of the daily needs of an adolescent. The carbohydrate in milk is present in the form of lactose, which is not sweet and can supply 12 per cent of a child's daily needs. It is very easily absorbed and also helps in the absorption of calcium.

The fat in milk exists as tiny globules of butter-fat which, when the milk is allowed to stand, rise to the top as cream. It is this fat which makes milk as satisfying a food as it is, because fats take longer than any other foodstuffs to digest.

The mineral elements in milk include some of all those required by the body, particularly calcium. Milk can supply over half of the child's daily requirements of calcium, and its absorption is increased by the lactose which accompanies it.

The digestion of milk does not begin until it reaches the stomach, where it is curdled by the enzyme *rennin*. This is a similar process to that artificially induced during the early stages of cheese-making and, by separating the solids and liquid constituents, prepares the milk for the further breaking-down of its foodstuffs into nutrients.

Milk Dishes

Many dishes include milk among their ingredients, but only those in which milk is the chief one can be called 'milk dishes', e.g. milk drinks (flavoured with fruit juices, chocolate, proprietary products, spices, etc.), cornflour moulds, milk puddings (rice, semolina, etc.), batters, junkets, milk jellies, custards.

BRITAIN'S DAIRY COWS

Ayrshires: 20 per cent of the country's dairy cattle are represented by this breed of large brown and white cows. They have a high milk yield which is third highest in richness.

Friesians: these cows give a good yield. They are easily recognizable by their characteristic black and white colouring.

Guernseys: milk from these cows is exceptionally high in fat content. The cows themselves are sleek and fawn to brown in colour, with white patches.

Jerseys: like Guernseys, these cows give very rich milk, in good quantities. The cattle are small and vary in colour from fawn to reddish-brown.

Lincoln Red Shorthorns: named after their own reddish-brown colouring, they produce good quality milk which is often used in cheese-making.

Red Polls: these cattle are used in the production of both meat and milk. They are deep red in colour, marked with white.

Dairy Shorthorns: also dual-purpose cattle. They yield satisfactory quantities of good quality milk.

South Devons: dual-purpose cattle whose milk is rich in butter-fat and is used in the production of Devonshire cream. They are the largest of Britain's dairy cows.

Welsh Black: a hardy mountain breed of cows used for beef and milk production.

CREAM

Cream will collect naturally on the top of milk when it is left to stand, as the light fat globules float to the top. All that cream-making used to entail was carefully skimming off the top of the open pans of milk by hand. Nowadays it is mechanically and considerably more quickly separated by centrifugal force (i.e. in a rapidly revolving container which spins the heavier part, the skimmed milk, to the outside, while the cream flows towards the middle). The skimmed milk left behind is particularly good food for pigs, and dairy farmers often keep pigs as a sideline. The separated cream is then pasteurized (heated to $79 \cdot 5°C$ and cooled to $4 \cdot 5°C$) ready for packaging.

There are several grades of cream, as of milk

a Thick or double cream: the 'cream of cream'—contains 48–53 per cent fat.

b Pouring or single cream: contains 18–24 per cent fat.

c Clotted cream (Devonshire): contains 50–60 per cent fat. This is produced by heating the milk to $82°C$ in shallow pans in which the cream has been allowed to rise. After cooling overnight the 'clots' are skimmed off.

d Long-keeping cream: the cream is pasteurized (heated to $82°C$ for 15 seconds) and cooled, before being heated in the jars or bottles in which it is sold, to $115°C$ for 12 minutes.

e U.H.T. cream: treated as milk of this grade.

f Sterilized cream: cream is filled into cans or bottles and sterilized to kill all the bacteria. It contains a minimum of 23 per cent fat.

EVAPORATED MILK

This is a concentrated form of milk, with only about 40 per cent of the original water content remaining. It is a very convenient form because it is tinned and sealed and will keep almost indefinitely until opened.

The water is removed from the fresh cows' milk by evaporation and the remaining thicker liquid is homogenized. That is, the fat globules are broken down and evenly distributed, giving a smooth, creamy liquid which is the same texture throughout. This treatment gives evaporated milk three advantages over ordinary milk for cooking purposes:

    a it is richer, being more highly concentrated

    b it blends more easily into mixtures

    c it will whip satisfactorily, as it is able to hold beaten-in air bubbles and give a light, fluffy result.

It is possible to use evaporated milk for any recipe in which ordinary milk is required. If diluted by $1\frac{1}{2}$ parts of water to 1 part of evaporated milk it produces a strength approximate to that of fresh milk, but the amount of water can be reduced as required for richer results.

Diluted evaporated milk may also be used as fresh milk for drinks, although the characteristic flavour is unpleasant to some people unless it is disguised by the addition of strong flavourings (e.g. coffee, chocolate). As the added water does not emulsify the fat globules it is not satisfactory as a substitute for fresh milk in tea. A film of tiny greasy droplets separates out and floats to the top of the liquid.

The food value of evaporated milk is undiminished by its treatment—actually, volume for volume, it is greatly increased.

Condensed milk is evaporated milk which has had a great deal of sugar added to it and this, of course, considerably enriches its food value and keeping properties. On the other hand its use is somewhat limited, as it can only be used for sweetened dishes.

DRIED MILK

Dried milk must not be confused with evaporated milk. 'Drying' is reducing the liquid to a solid, 100 per cent of the normal water content being removed by evaporation. The remaining solids are reduced to a fine or granular powder and packed in tins. The milk may be skimmed before it is dried and this obviously reduces its fat content. Only the kind labelled 'whole milk' can be reconstituted to a liquid resembling fresh milk, but the flavour cannot be said to be as bland and neutral as that of fresh milk.

It is a very convenient 'emergency ration' to store, because it will keep for very long periods in airtight tins and no more liquid need be made up than is required at the moment.

Again, this form of milk may be used in any recipe which includes milk in the ingredients and may also be used for drinking purposes. Indeed, there are many excellent brands of milk powders on the market for use in feeding babies. Many of these have certain reductions of their constituents (usually fat) to increase their digestibility, and these modifications are usually set out in detail on the labels of the tins.

In reconstituting the liquid it is essential that the solids are thoroughly beaten into the water to give a smooth mixture. Usually the powder is sprinkled on top of the liquid and gradually whisked into it. Mechanical beaters are very useful for this purpose but if these are not available satisfactory results can be achieved by the use of a fork.

Many people find it advisable to disguise the rather distinctive flavour and slight powderiness by the addition of flavourings (e.g. coffee, chocolate, malted powders).

CULTURED MILKS

These are produced by adding souring bacteria to milk, thus converting some of the lactose into lactic acid. Although they have only lately become popular in this country, they have been known for many years in eastern countries, including Eastern Europe. The differences in flavour and consistency depend upon the type of milk and the culture of bacteria used.

Cultured buttermilk   A slightly acid, refreshing drink made by adding a specific culture to buttermilk.

Soured cream   Single cream cultured to give a piquant flavour, and added to made-up dishes to enhance their flavour and creaminess.

Yoghurt

The most popular of all cultured milks, being easy to digest, pleasant to eat and good food value for all ages (protein, calcium, Vitamin B). It can be produced in a semi-solid state or as a liquid (drinking yoghurt).

Manufacture

The milk used may be whole, partially or entirely skimmed, evaporated or dried, or it may be a mixture of any of these. The milk is pasteurized for 5–60 minutes to remove harmful bacteria, homogenized to give a creamier texture and then cooled. The yoghurt culture is then added, *lactobacillus bulgaricus* (yoghurt is a traditional Bulgarian dish) and *streptococcus thermophilus*, and the blend is poured into cartons in which it is warmed for $2\frac{1}{2}$ to 3 hours at 42–45°C and then cooled. The culture is added and the mixture warmed in vats or churns if fruit yoghurt is required; the pieces of fruit are gently stirred in before filling it into cartons.

Home production

Yoghurt can be made from fresh milk at home by heating it to 43°C, adding a tablespoonful of fresh yoghurt and leaving it undisturbed in a wide-necked vacuum flask for 8 to 10 hours.

Besides being eaten as a dish on its own, yoghurt may be used as a dressing for salad, a sauce (mixed with the juice of cooked food), a

D

dip (seasoned and mixed with chopped bacon, cucumber and/or tomatoes), flan filling, or an ingredient for cheese-cake type mixtures.

BUTTER

When cream has been removed from milk its water content can be further reduced, to form a solid we know as butter. This result is brought about by churning—the beating of the liquid with paddles. In olden days this process was carried out by hand and was a very laborious business, although accepted as a normal part of the duties of the farmer's wife. Churns were then usually made of wood and operated by pushing and pulling the paddle handles or by rotating them. In modern creameries all this labour is carried out by machines, usually in great, steel vats which are kept scrupulously clean.

To assist the solidifying process the cream is 'soured' before churning, by adding a ferment and 'holding' the cream at 10–18°C for several hours, and then cooled to 7°C before churning. The liquid left behind as the fat is collected into lumps is known as buttermilk and this is separated from the solid matter by mechanical means. This, too, is a good food for pigs.

Before being divided into blocks the butter is sometimes mixed with salt to increase its keeping properties and to reduce the 'freshness' of the flavour. The use of salted or unsalted butter is mainly a matter of personal taste.

Butter is usually eaten in its natural state with carbohydrate foods, e.g. bread, scones, biscuits, etc. It is the best fat to use for such dishes as rich sauces, pastries and creamed cake mixtures but as this makes them rather expensive it is often partly or wholly substituted by margarine.

Butter should always be left wrapped or placed in a covered dish and kept as cool as possible. If a refrigerator is not available, a cold slab or a plate standing on a cold floor is a suitable place for storage. It is advisable to buy butter as it is needed, for if kept for too long a rancid flavour develops. The speed with which this will happen depends largely upon the temperature and humidity of the atmosphere. It is also important that butter should not be stored close to any strongly flavoured foods, as it very easily 'picks up' foreign tangs.

MARGARINE

Originally conceived as a substitute for butter during the Napoleonic wars, when an attempt was made to blend various animal fats, margarine is now a mixture of oils, mainly vegetable, including palm, palm kernel, sunflower, groundnuts, rapeseed, cottonseed, coconut and soya beans. Normally whale oil is added (which contributes Vitamins A and D) but in specially produced vegetarian margarine this is omitted.

The production of margarine is very effectively automated; 220 packets can be produced in a minute. The steps of production are

    a refining: oils are neutralized, bleached, filtered and deodorized
    b pasteurizing of fat-free milk
    c adding milk to blended oils
    d adding synthetic Vitamin A and D
    e votating: the churn, or votator, stirs, cools and texturizes the blend
    f wrapping.

The vegetable oils are unsaturated fats and, although some hydrogenation takes place, margarine is sometimes preferred to butter by people with heart disease because it does not increase the blood cholesterol.

CHEESE

It is difficult to say exactly how long cheese has been used as an important part of man's diet, but we do know that references are made to it in the very earliest records we possess. In ancient Greece cheese was an integral item of the severely regulated diet of the Spartans; wrestlers, who were highly esteemed as skilled exponents of a specialized craft, ate a great deal of cheese; cheese-moulds from the kitchens of wealthy citizens have been excavated in Macedonia; the Bible speaks of David carrying cheeses to his brothers in the army; the Romans, missing the cheese to which they were accustomed before they invaded Britain, taught the Britons the art of cheese-making.

In more recent days it is recorded that in the Middle Ages, when rents were paid to lords of the manor in kind, cheeses were legal tender. As there was little or no distribution of milk, cheese-making was the prerogative of farmers' wives, and legend has it that the marriageable value of country girls was based largely on their manual strength, essential for the heavy labour of pressing and turning cheeses. Cheese fairs became occasions of public holiday and at these a 'great' cheese would be sold for fourpence, a medium one for tuppence and a small one for a penny. During the reign of Charles II cheese-eating became a fashionable custom and this raised its price and made it inaccessible to any but rich people. Samuel Pepys writes in his diary of having eaten a quantity of cheese and it was at this time, too, that 'whey-houses' became the haunts of men and women-about-town in much the same way as our modern coffee bars are frequented today.

Later the first cheese-exporting trade began, and once the establishment of cheese-factories had begun (the first one was opened in America but the idea very soon caught on in England) this trade flourished.

METHOD OF PRODUCTION

Despite its long history, the principles of cheese-making have remained basically the same.

The discovery of the process of converting liquid milk into solid cheese has no definite history. It may be that the ancient Arabian nomads accidently produced cheese by carrying milk in bags consisting of the stomachs of animals from the herds which moved with them. These bags would undoubtedly have been very inadequately cleaned and any rennin remaining on the stomach lining would curdle the milk, while the swaying movement of the animal on which it was carried would assist in the separation of curds and whey. Cheese for these people may have been made from the milk of cows, goats, ewes, asses and even camels.

The legend surrounding the production of Cheddar cheese tells of a boy who left a pail of milk in a cave during a thunder storm. The pail had a hole in it, the heavy atmosphere 'turned' the milk and the whey ran out, leaving the first Cheddar cheese!

The actual stages of production are as follows:

1 Pure, fresh, pasteurized milk is cooled and placed in a cheese-making vat. It is ripened by adding a 'starter'—i.e. lactic acid-producing organisms (1 litre to 80 litres). After about an hour it is warmed to 30°C and rennet is added (100 g rennet to 400 litres of milk). This causes the milk to separate into curds and whey, and is equivalent to the process of curdling which may have taken place originally as has been described above.

2 In order to free the whey more quickly the curd is warmed to 36–40°C and cut into small cubes.

3 The whey is drained off and the curds are cut into blocks about 20 cm long, called 'leaves'. During this process the curds shrink owing to the loss of moisture, and gradually become more solid. The blocks are piled up, redrained, repiled and so on until there is no further apparent loss of moisture, and then subjected to pressure to ensure complete drainage.

4 The curds are cooled and placed in an electrically driven mill where they are cut into small pieces.

5 The curds are transferred to large vats where salt is spread over them and mixed in with large forks. (The proportion used is 500 g salt to 400 litres.) The addition of salt brings out the flavour and assists in the preservation of the cheese.

6 The salted curds are packed into moulds which have been lined with cloth strips or 'bandages', and which contain approx. 30 kg cheese.

7 Metal discs are placed on top of the moulds and pressed for a short time. The cheeses are then sprayed with hot water to produce a thin, hard rind and repressed for 24 hours.

8 The cheese is date-stamped and left to ripen for 4 months. During this ripening process the cheese changes its composition and flavour owing to the bacteria present; at the same time the protein becomes more digestible. The cheeses are turned every day and the humidity of the atmosphere is carefully regulated to prevent drying and shrinking. Cheese 'tasters', using special scooping implements, test the cheeses for quality of flavour and texture before they are marketed.

Variations in flavour and texture of cheeses are due to a 'house that Jack built' series of circumstances—that is,

the bacteria in the soil which
grew the grass which
fed the cows which
provided the milk which
produced the cheese.

Added to this are the variations in acidity, the fat content and the amount of pressure applied during production.

Today there is a very great appreciation of the differences between various types of cheese, and the production of traditional, regional cheeses is being encouraged.

Note Bacteria can be cultured so that a so-called 'regional' cheese can be produced anywhere.

TYPES OF ENGLISH CHEESE

Caerphilly: a cheese much favoured by the Welsh miners because of its moist, salty flavour. It is mild and creamy, with a smooth texture.

Cheddar: the most widely known of all our cheeses. The cheddaring process is used all over the world, although the only true Cheddar is, of course, the English one made in the Somerset village of the same name. It is a solid, firm, pale-yellow cheese with a succulent texture and nutty flavour.

Cheshire: a red or white cheese (the colour is due to a colouring pigment added during production and has no effect upon the flavour), with a crumbly texture and a keen, tangy flavour.

Derby: a white, smooth cheese with a soft, mild flavour. 'Sage Derby', a rare version of this cheese, has layers of finely-chopped sage leaves incorporated into it during production.

Dorset Blue: a straw-coloured, blue-veined cheese with a stiff, crumbly texture (as it is made from skimmed milk the fat content is low) and an unusual strong flavour.

Double Gloucester: this also may be straw-coloured or light red, and has a close, smooth texture and a mellow, somewhat pungent flavour.

Lancashire: a white, crumbly, easily spread cheese with a mild flavour, which is especially good for toasting.

Leicester: shaped like a millstone, this cheese is a rich red in colour and is mild, soft, crumbly and flaky.

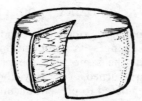

CHEDDAR PALE YELLOW

CHESHIRE RED OR WHITE

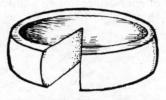

LANCASHIRE YELLOW-WHITE

WENSLEYDALE CREAMY-WHITE

DERBY WHITE

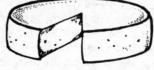

CAERPHILLY WHITE

DORSET BLUE
STRAW-COLOURED
WITH
BLUE VEINS

DOUBLE GLOUCESTER
STRAW-COLOURED or
LIGHT RED

LEICESTER
DARK ORANGE RED

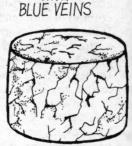

STILTON
CREAMY-WHITE
BLUE-VEINED

Stilton: originally collected from the surrounding farms and sold at the Bell Inn, Stilton, this cheese has always been known as the 'King of Cheeses'. It has a superb, rich flavour and is easily recognized by its wrinkled brown coat and creamy-white, blue-veined body.

Wensleydale: first made in the Middle Ages by the monks of Jervaulx Abbey, it is a creamy cheese with a sweet flavour.

These cheeses can be divided into classes for convenience:

a Hard-pressed cheeses: (i.e. those with a close, solid texture), e.g. Cheddar, Cheshire, Derbyshire, Leicester, Double Gloucester.

b Lightly-pressed cheeses: (i.e. those with a crumbly or friable texture), e.g. Caerphilly, White Wensleydale, Lancashire.

c Blue-veined cheeses: Stilton, Blue Wensleydale, Dorset Blue (Blue Vinny). (The blue/green veining is due to the deliberate exposure of the cheese to a harmless mould.)

d Cream cheeses: unripened, therefore of very mild flavour.

A modification of this simplest form of cheese is known to any economical housewife. Soured milk which is allowed to stand until it begins to separate is strained through a muslin bag and then beaten with salt and pepper to improve the flavour. This is known as 'cottage' cheese.

The Composition of Cheese

It takes 9 litres of full cream milk to make 1 kilogram of cheese, which, as a concentrated form of milk, consists of roughly $\frac{1}{3}$ fat, $\frac{1}{3}$ protein and $\frac{1}{3}$ water. There are also, of course, the vitamins and mineral elements present in milk: Vitamins A, D, B complex, calcium and sodium.

The Digestion of Cheese

Cheese has the reputation of being indigestible, particularly when cooked. This is due to the fact that each particle of protein is coated with fat which forms a waterproof covering and prevents the start of digestion of the protein in the stomach. The digestion of fat does not begin until it reaches the duodenum and until this is completed protein digestion cannot begin. This, of course, entails double work for the duodenum.

To aid digestion of uncooked cheese

1 Divide the cheese finely before serving by either grating or shredding. This helps to break down the structure of the cheese particles and makes the protein more easily accessible to the digestive enzymes.

2 Serve with a highly-flavoured seasoning, such as vinegar or mustard. This stimulates the flow of digestive juices and increases the rate of digestion.

To aid digestion of cooked cheese

1 Divide it finely before cooking—i.e. either grate or shred. This means that the cheese is cooked fairly quickly and quite evenly and there is no risk of over-cooking.

2 Avoid over-cooking—if cooked for too long or too fiercely the protein (cheese protein is called *casein*) hardens and the fat separates out.

3 Serve it with some starchy food or combine it with starchy ingredients. If cooked with starch the melted fat from the cheese is absorbed and the protein is more easily digested.

4 Serve it with some highly-flavoured seasoning such as mustard or vinegar. This stimulates the flow of digestive juices and speeds the digestion of the cheese.

5 Avoid serving cheese at late meals if it *is* found to be at all difficult to digest.

Suitable cheeses for cooking

Hard, strong-flavoured cheeses are best and most economical, e.g. Cheddar, Parmesan.

Methods of cooking

1 Grating and mixing into starchy substances, e.g. mashed potato, foundation white sauce.

2 Grilling: being a short, quick method the protein does not harden.

3 Frying: a teaspoonful of boiling water added to the grated cheese immediately it is put into the pan will prevent it from becoming stringy.

4 Baking: use a hot oven and take care not to cook the cheese for too long.

Some Cheese Dishes

Cheese sauce, Welsh rarebit, buck rarebit, cheese soufflé, cheese croquettes, cheese and tomato flan, cheese potatoes, cheese pudding.

The Value of Cheese in the Diet

1 It is a food rich in nutritive value—see p. 95.

2 It is an extremely concentrated food and is therefore an economical item of the diet.

3 There is very little waste—only the rind is not eaten.

4 It is easily transported and therefore valuable for those people who require packed meals.

5 It is suitable for children and old people, adding valuable calcium to their diets, as well as for sedentary and manual workers, vegetarians and invalids.

6 It can be eaten raw or cooked, as a main dish or as an accompaniment.

7 It is available in a large variety of textures and prices and is valuable for its distinctive flavours.

The Storage of Cheese

Buy and use cheese as fresh as possible (except for cooking) when its flavour and texture are at their best.

Keep wrapped in greaseproof paper or in a polythene bag in a cool place. It should not be wrapped too closely—some air should surround the cheese. If kept in a refrigerator, store in a plastic box to prevent drying out.

For short-time storing, use a cheese dish with air-holes in the lid.

FURTHER STUDY

THINGS TO DO

1 Visit a local milk bottling depot and find out:
a From where does the milk come?
b How is it transported to the depot?
c How old is the milk before it is bottled?
d How old is the milk before it is delivered to your home?
e What treatment has the milk received before it reaches the depot?
f If churns are used by the farmer, what happens to them before they are returned to the farm?
g What are the following tests: (*i*) resazurin test; (*ii*) gerber test; (*iii*) methylene blue test?
h What is the name of the instrument with which the water content of milk is tested?
i What is a heat exchanger?
j What other containers can be used for milk besides bottles?
k Why is any other method of packaging milk more expensive than bottling?
l What treatment do bottles receive before they are filled?

2 Using equal quantities of milk (150 ml), note and compare the effects of the following:
a storing at room temperature until 'soured' (note time)
b storing in a refrigerator for the same period of time
c boiling and repeating *a.* and *b.* for the same amount of time
d adding 1 teaspoonful of lemon juice
e adding 1 teaspoonful of rennet
f boiling and repeating *e.*
g repeat *b.* and bring to boil.
What conclusions can you draw from the results?

3 Make a sample of cheese from soured milk.

4 Make a sample of yoghurt using *a.* a commercial starter, *b.* a portion of existing yoghurt.

5 Draw a map of the British Isles and mark the chief dairy farming areas. List the chief dairy farming counties.

6 Find out what you can about *a*. French, *b*. Dutch cheeses, with particular reference to the district in which they are made, their characteristics and their current prices. Taste as many as you can and describe the appearance, flavour and texture of each.

7 Carry out experiments to show the effect of heating on cheese. What difference, if any, is made when cheese is treated *a*. in a mass, *b*. after grating?

8 Trace the history of cheese, using as a basis the brief account given in this chapter. In what respects has the manufacture of cheese changed since medieval times?

9 Having learnt the food value of cheese, carry out experiments to prove the presence of fat, protein and water.

10 Discover which animals are milked for human consumption in this country. How does the food value of these types compare with that of cows' milk? What differences are there between human milk and cows' milk? Why do you think these differences are necessary? What is 'humanized' milk?

11 Find out how a cow produces milk. Compare the yield of various breeds of cow.

12 Collect as many types of dried milk as you can and compare their composition.

Prepare liquid samples of each and compare with fresh milk, and with each other, *a*. their costs, *b*. their keeping properties, *c*. their flavours, *d*. their appearance, *e*. their usefulness.

13 Find out what you can about the experiments being made to produce *a*. lactose-free milk, *b*. imitation 'milk'. Why are these being made?

QUESTIONS TO ANSWER

1 Write out the following statements, and complete them, using only the words in the right-hand column to fill in the blanks.

a The most commonly used process of killing harmful bacteria in milk is	lactalbumen
b The process of heating milk sufficiently for it to keep for several days without refrigeration is	lactose
c The process of breaking up the fat globules in milk and distributing them evenly throughout the liquid is	pasteurization
d The chief proteins in milk are .... and	rennin
e The 'souring' of milk is due to the presence of .... produced by bacterial action on milk sugar.	casein
	Vitamin C

f The name given to the sugar in milk is	lactic acid
g Milk can be artificially coagulated by the addition of	iron
h The important mineral element found in milk is	sterilization
i An important mineral element which milk lacks is	homogenization
j Milk is not a 'perfect' food for children because it lacks not only an important mineral element but also	calcium

2 List as many forms as you can in which milk may be purchased. Give examples of the use of each and say why milk is an important item of the diet.

3 List the nutrients in milk and describe their functions in the diet. Why do bacteria multiply so rapidly in fresh farm milk? Outline *one* method of reducing the bacterial content of milk. Explain, with reasons, how fresh liquid milk should be stored in the home.   (A.E.B.)

4*a* List the nutrients found in milk and describe their function in the diet.

b In what nutrients is milk deficient and how can this be remedied in the diet of a one-year-old child?

c Describe the chemical action that takes place when milk goes sour.   (A.E.B.)

5 How would you ensure that your supply of milk stays fresh during hot weather when your refrigerator is out of order?

Describe one way in which you can make use of soured milk.

6 How can you explain the present-day popularity of yoghurt? Describe three dishes in which this product may be used.

7*a* List the nutrients present in cheese and give their functions in the diet.

b Explain why cheese is sometimes indigestible and suggest *four* different ways to remedy this. Give reasons.   (A.E.B.)

EGGS

The eggs most commonly eaten in this country are produced by hens and these are the ones referred to in any recipe including eggs. Duck and goose eggs may also be eaten but it is essential that they should be completely fresh.

The average weight of a hen's egg is 50 g and that of a duck or goose egg correspondingly more in relation to its size. If these larger eggs are used for cooking therefore, (e.g. in cake mixtures) the number should be reduced accordingly. (1 duck egg replaces $1\frac{1}{2}$ hen eggs; 1 goose egg replaces $2\frac{1}{2}$ hen eggs.)

THE COMPOSITION OF AN EGG

The Shell (*approx.* 12 *per cent of whole weight or* 6 *g*)
Consists of a chalky substance and becomes thinner as the egg develops and absorbs some of the calcium. It is porous and allows water to evaporate from inside the egg. The colour of the shell makes no difference to the food value of the egg within it and depends entirely upon the breed of the bird which laid it.

The Egg
If left to develop, a fertilized egg could produce a chicken with the help of no outside agency other than warmth. It must be, therefore, that the egg contains all the material necessary for the formation and growth of the chick, i.e. protein, fat, vitamins, minerals and water. As provision for bone and blood formation must be made, the mineral elements include calcium and iron. In fact the composition of the egg is approximately:

Protein: 12·0 per cent
Fat: 11·5 per cent
Water: 74·5 per cent
Minerals: 1·0 per cent
Carbohydrate: 1·0 per cent
Vitamins A, D, E and B complex.

The yolk (*approx.* 25 *per cent of weight or* $12\frac{1}{2}$ *g*)   The yolk is the more concentrated part of the egg, i.e. it contains less water than the white. It is suspended in the white by two gristly 'cords' called chalazae and is rich in fat, held in an emulsified form which is easily digested. The main protein in the yolk is vitellin and the yellow colouring (ranging from pale yellow to deep gold) is due to the pigment carotene (see p. 53) as well as to the sulphur contained in the protein. It is the sulphur which causes the characteristic odour of a boiled egg. In stale eggs the sulphur has combined with other substances to produce an obnoxious gas, and even in a fresh egg it combines with the iron and can form a greenish ring round the yolk when it is cooked. (To help to prevent this a hard-boiled egg should be plunged immediately into cold water.)

The white (*approx.* 60 *per cent of weight or* 30 *g*)   The white of an egg consists mainly of albumen, the chief of twelve proteins contained in viscous fluid, and the absence of fat allows it to hold a great deal of beaten-in air.

This albumen coagulates very quickly when it is heated, much more quickly than the protein in the yolk. It is, therefore, possible to cook an egg in such a way that the yolk remains fluid while the white sets. This is how most people prefer to eat an egg, whether boiled, poached or fried.

The Freshness of Eggs

An egg remains fresh for up to three weeks and can be boiled safely. If the housewife has any doubts as to its freshness she can carry out a simple test, based on the fact that the shell of the egg is porous. All eggs contain a small air pocket, which increases in size as the egg becomes older. This is due to the evaporation of water inside the egg and the passage of air through the shell to take its place. Consequently the egg becomes lighter and will float at different levels in a glass of water as it becomes less fresh.

VERY FRESH   LESS FRESH   STALE

When broken, a fresh egg comes out of the shell in a well-defined shape, with the yolk firm and domed and the white as a thick surrounding mass. A stale egg spreads as it leaves the shell, with the yolk flat and easily broken and the white watery and running away from the yolk.

A fresh egg has a clean, pleasant smell but a stale one develops an unmistakable obnoxious odour of sulphuretted hydrogen.

THE VALUE OF EGGS IN THE DIET

As a Very Compact Form of Important Food Values

One egg supplies as much complete protein as 25 g of corned beef in a more easily digested form and is therefore of particular value.

As a Food for Invalids

If lightly cooked so that the albumen is not toughened it is a valuable and easily digested form of the complete protein necessary to repair tissues broken down through illness. It may also be consumed in its raw state, but is more palatable if beaten well into milk than if eaten whole. Lime salts in the egg can sometimes cause constipation, but this can be overcome by eating the egg with brown bread and butter.

As a Main Dish

Owing to its complete protein content an egg can be used to replace meat occasionally as a main meal. In fact, it is a very common replacement for those vegetarians who allow themselves to eat eggs. Combined with carbohydrate and protective foods it can complete a well-balanced meal.

As an Ingredient of Other Dishes
Eggs may often be used in conjunction with other foods to increase their nutritive value and attractiveness: e.g. fish and egg pasty; cheese and egg flan; curried veal and eggs; ham and egg pie.

As a Garnish
If sliced or finely chopped, eggs make an attractive decoration for savoury flans, fish dishes, etc. If the white is separated from the yolk and the two parts chopped separately they may be used effectively in alternate rows, and combined with lines of paprika and finely chopped parsley. They may also be chopped into foundation white sauces for serving with white fish, etc.

As an Emulsifier
Beaten egg is capable of holding finely divided fat globules and prevents them from massing together to form oily patches in mixtures. This is particularly valuable in the preparation of salad cream and mayonnaise in which the oil is mixed to a smooth emulsion with the other ingredients.

As a Help in Raising Starch Mixtures
Eggs are not raising agents in themselves but are of great assistance in the use of air as a raising agent. When air is beaten into it an egg can hold a good volume until the air expands on heating, taking with it the surrounding starch mixtures, e.g. in batters, cakes. When the white is beaten alone it can form a thick white froth due to the presence of globulins (proteins) which enable it to hold large quantities of air, so for extra lightness the egg should be separated and the white and yolk beaten independently. For such dishes as meringues and soufflés the white is used alone, the separated yolks being used for other dishes.

As a Thickening Agent
Egg proteins coagulate when heated and will therefore thicken any liquid into which they are mixed, e.g. custards.

As a Binding Agent
Because it holds together finely-divided scraps of food, e.g. minced meat or flaked fish, egg is useful in making croquettes, rissoles, etc.

As a Coating
Delicate pieces of fish and other foods which are to be fried can be protected from the heat of the fat while cooking and prevented from being broken down by coating them in a layer of beaten egg (often made more attractive and easily handled by rolling them afterwards in fine breadcrumbs).

As a Glaze

Rich pastries, savoury pies, etc., can be made more attractive by brushing them with beaten egg which, when cooked, gives a rich, golden, shiny finish.

As an Enriching Ingredient

When egg is added to pastry, almond paste, milk puddings, etc., the colour and food value of the dish is improved, although little difference is made in the flavour.

METHODS OF COOKING EGGS

Egg white begins to set at a temperature of 58°C and becomes more and more tough as the heat is increased.

Egg yolk coagulates at 65°C and becomes more solid and crumbly as it is cooked beyond this temperature. If milk is added the temperature of coagulation is raised to 83°C.

This means that the egg is completely cooked at well below boiling point (100°C) and therefore custards and sauces into which eggs have been mixed should not be allowed to boil. If they do, the egg sets into uneven tough flakes which shrink and squeeze out some of the liquid with which they have been mixed, giving a curdled effect. This is why double saucepans and baking tins are recommended for cooking custards and why egg should not be added to a sauce until after it has been cooked and removed from the heat.

Boiling

a The egg should be gently lowered into boiling water and left to cook for

(*i*) $3\frac{1}{2}$ minutes—to give soft white and liquid yolk.

(*ii*) $4-4\frac{1}{2}$ minutes—to give moderately soft white and semi-set yolk.

(*iii*) 10 minutes—to give hard-boiled egg with very firm white and yolk suitable for slicing.

Very fresh eggs may require a little longer cooking to reach these stages, whereas those more than a week old may need a little less.

b The shell should be lightly cracked at one end as soon as the egg is removed from the water, to allow the steam to escape and prevent further cooking.

c Hard-boiled eggs should be placed immediately in cold water to prevent a dark ring from forming round the yolk.

Coddling

a This is a method particularly suitable for invalids' and young children's meals. The egg is set just sufficiently to make it non-liquid but not enough to make it in the least indigestible.

b It is lowered into sufficient boiling water to cover it and left in the pan with the lid on for 7 to 10 minutes. During this time the water should be kept hot but must *not* be allowed to boil.

Frying

a The egg should be broken into a cup or saucer and slid into hot fat. By doing this it keeps a good shape as the white begins to set immediately it touches the fat.

b The yolk should be basted with hot fat as the white is cooking *or* the whole egg may be turned over with a fish slice and cooked on both sides.

c The egg should be lifted out with a fish slice and the surplus fat drained off before serving.

Poaching

a Break the egg and slide it gently into a pan of boiling water (a half-filled frying pan or small, shallow saucepan is suitable) containing 1 tsp. salt and 1 dsp. vinegar in 500 ml.

b Simmer gently until the white is set.

c Lift out on a fish-slice and drain well before serving.

d A good shape may be obtained by dropping the egg into a greased metal pastry cutter.

or   *a* Grease the separate cups of an egg-poaching saucepan.

b Fill the pan with water and bring it to the boil.

c Break the eggs separately into cups and transfer them to the poaching pans.

d Keep the water simmering until the eggs are set.

Note   This method of poaching eggs involves the principle of steaming rather than of boiling.

Scrambling

a Break the egg into a basin and add a pinch of salt and pepper.

b Beat with a fork until the egg slips easily through the prongs.

c Add a tablespoonful of milk or water.

d Melt 12 g of butter in a small saucepan, without browning.

e Add the egg and cook it gently until the mixture is set but still very soft and creamy. It *must* be stirred continuously and removed from the heat while it is still soft as the heat of the pan will complete the cooking.

Baking

a Melt 12 g butter in each individual fire-proof glass or china container.

b Break the eggs and slip them into the containers.

c Bake in a moderate oven until set.

Egg Dishes

Omelettes (plain, sweet or savoury), soufflés (sweet, savoury), egg custards, Queen of Puddings, egg jelly, Scotch eggs, curried eggs, stuffed eggs, egg flip, egg and bacon flan.

Storing Eggs

Keep in a cool place. Place on end in a suitable tray, with the round end uppermost (i.e. with the air space at the top of the egg).

Keep away from strongly smelling foods as the flavour of these may be absorbed through the porous shells.

Refrigerators may be used to store eggs for short periods but if left for too long the liquid inside the egg freezes, expands and cracks the shells. Remove from refrigerator in time to allow eggs to return to room temperature before use.

Unbroken egg yolks which have been separated from the whites should be placed in a cup, covered with cold water and kept in a cool place, protected from dust. Broken yolks should be placed in a screw-top jar or polythene container and used as soon as possible.

Unused whites should be covered and stored in a cool place.

The Digestion of Eggs

The digestion of raw eggs begins in the stomach and is completed in the small intestine. The fresher the egg the more easily digested it is. The most easily digested cooked egg is that which is lightly boiled. The tougher the coagulated protein the more difficult it is to digest.

FURTHER STUDY

THINGS TO DO

1 Visit an egg-packing station and discover
a how eggs are graded
b what 'candling' is
c the faults which can be detected during testing.

2 Separate the white from the yolk of a new-laid egg and whisk it with an electric beater until the froth is stiff. Note the time this takes. Repeat, noting the time in each case, with
a a stale egg
b a chilled egg
c a pinch of salt added to the white
d a large bowl replacing the small one.

How do you account for the difference in facility of this operation?

3 Repeat the beating mechanically but use a whole egg. Compare the time taken to produce a 'froth' from the whole egg with that taken to whisk the white only. Compare also the volume of foam produced.

Repeat the beating and comparisons
      a adding a teaspoonful of caster sugar
      b beating over a bowl of warm water
      c combining *a.* and *b.*
What conclusions can you draw?

QUESTIONS TO ANSWER

1 Write out the following statements, and complete them, using only the words in the right-hand column to fill in the blanks.

a The correct name for the chalky substance of which the shell is composed is	carotene
b The main protein found in the white of egg is	coagulation
c The main protein found in egg yolk is	iron
d The yolk is suspended in the white by two	vitellin
e As the egg becomes staler the air space inside it becomes larger owing to .... of the liquid.	emulsification
f Beaten egg makes a good protective coating for food to be fried due to its .... on heating.	albumen evaporation
g Egg-white can be beaten into a froth because it can hold air due to its	viscosity
h The yellow colouring found in egg yolk is mainly	calcium carbonate
i The substance which causes the dark ring between the white and the yolk of a boiled egg is	chalazae
j The fat content of an egg yolk is easily digested owing to its degree of	

2*a* Give, with reasons, *six* ways in which eggs may be used in cookery. In each case name one dish as an example.

    b Give, with reasons, the practical cookery points which should be followed to ensure perfect results when making (*i*) a poached egg, (*ii*) a baked egg custard. (A.E.B.)

3 Why are eggs particularly valuable in the diet of children? Describe ways in which you could serve them attractively.

4 List the nutrients present in a poached egg on toast. Of what importance are these nutrients in the diet and in which main nutrient is this dish deficient? (A.E.B.)

5*a* Draw a diagram showing the structure of an egg and indicating the value of each part.

    b Describe the changes which take place when eggs are cooked.

5

OTHER MAIN FOODS

MEAT

The meat eaten in this country is the flesh of cattle, sheep, pigs and rabbits. It consists of bundles of long, tubular muscle fibres (which we refer to as 'lean meat') containing juices, in the same way as the segments of an orange are composed of 'sacs' filled with juice. Interspersed between these bundles are layers of fat, their thickness varying from part to part of the animal's body. The whole is held together with connective tissue, and this, when massed together, is called 'gristle'.

The more exercise the animal has had the tougher will be the tissues, although the flavour is often improved. Similarly, the parts of the animal which are most hard-worked are coarse in texture and have a certain amount of gristle, whereas the 'prime' or less energetic portions are finer in texture and fat is 'marbled' throughout the grain of the meat. This means that tender cuts may be cooked by dry heat in a relatively short time, while tougher cuts require moist heat and longer cooking.

The term 'meat' also includes edible birds such as chickens, ducks, geese, turkeys (poultry); pheasants, partridge, grouse (game). The flesh of these is generally more delicate than that of animals and consequently more easily digested. Exceptions, however, are water birds (ducks and geese) in which there is a high fat content; quite the opposite to game birds which are often 'dry' because they contain so little fat.

CHOOSING MEAT

1 Buy meat from clean, well-ventilated shops.

2 Choose the cut of meat suitable for the method of cooking which is to be used.

3 The flesh should be firm and elastic to the touch (although it is not suggested that customers should do their own prodding!).

4 The grain should appear fine and even.

5 The colour should be good for the type of meat:

a beef: dark red lean, and finely grained, yellow fat

b mutton/lamb: light red lean, and hard, white fat

c pork: pinkish lean, and soft, white fat

d veal: pale pink lean, and little fat.

6 There should be no unpleasant odour.

7 The amount of bone should not be excessive. (This is charged for at the same rate as lean meat.)

8 Young rabbits are much more tender than old ones and these can be identified by

a their pale flesh

b short claws

c brittle (easily cracked) jaw bones.

CHOOSING POULTRY

If a fresh bird is being purchased the breast should be plump and white, the bone and beak pliable and the legs smooth.

If frozen birds are being used they must be completely thawed before cooking. The package usually carries instructions and the process may take anything from four to seven hours. If time is short, the defrosting can be hurried a little by submerging the wrapped bird in cold water.

It is now common practice to buy chicken, at least, in packaged joints as well as a whole bird, and the comparatively reasonable price makes it an attractive main ingredient for a number of dishes. It may be stewed, fried, roasted, casseroled and even steamed if sliced thinly.

Remember to remove the giblets from inside the chicken before cooking; if the bird is to be stuffed, insert the stuffing (usually a mixture of sage, onion and breadcrumbs, or sausagemeat) at the neck end.

METHODS OF COOKING MEAT

Most methods of cooking can be used for one or other cut of meat, but general rules are as follows, bearing in mind that the object of cooking is to remove the raw appearance without over-coagulating the proteins or losing the minerals and extractives (see p. 68).

Roasting is suitable for good quality, tender, thick cuts, or for rolled and stuffed thin cuts (e.g. breast).

Boiling is suitable for salted meats.

Grilling should be used for thinly cut pieces of good quality.

Frying—as for grilling.

Stewing is suitable for inferior quality meats which require long, slow cooking to make them tender and need the added flavour of vegetables, etc., to improve the characteristic insipidity.

During cooking, the proteins in meat are coagulated and made pleasanter to eat but less easily digested. The ease with which they can be digested depends on

a the degree of toughness, often the cause of the success or failure of the cooking

b the amount of fat present

c the flavour.

When meat is boiled the outside albumen must be set to prevent the inner juices from being extracted. Therefore it should be placed initially in boiling water. If all the albumen is coagulated quickly, however, the resulting joint will be tough. Therefore, to soften the fibres slowly, the heat must then be reduced to simmering point. Some juices will still escape, so liquor in which meat is boiled should be used as stock for sauces and soups.

When meat is stewed the juices are allowed to escape and the resulting gravy is served as part of the dish. The long, slow cooking gradually softens tough fibres and these must on no account be hardened by boiling.

When meat is roasted the oven and the fat should traditionally be hot when meat is placed in it, in order to coagulate the surface albumen. After 10 minutes the heat should be lowered so that inner tissues are cooked slowly. The joint should be basted every half hour to prevent shrinkage and drying, unless cooked in foil or roasting bag.

However, automatic oven-roasting has shown that meat can be quite successfully cooked in what is initially a cold oven gradually raised to the prescribed heat.

When meat is grilled only thin pieces should be used (not more than 5 cm thick). If the meat has no fat of its own it should be brushed with oil before cooking. The slices should be turned frequently to prevent the outside from scorching before the inside is cooked, but care should be taken not to pierce the flesh with fork prongs because this would liberate juices.

General Rules for Cooking Meat

1 Wipe carefully.

2 Trim off fat, remove bones if necessary. Make use of all scraps: *a.* Render down fat by heating slowly at the bottom of the oven when other cooking is being carried out; strain off liquid fat. *b.* Use meat scraps and bones for making stock.

3 *a.* Cut meat which is to be stewed into cubes to expose as large an area as possible. *b.* Tie or skewer meat to be roasted into a good shape.

4 Calculate cooking time for roasting meat (see below).

5 Follow general rules for method of cooking being used.

6 Serve with suitable accompaniments and vegetables.

Cooking Time for Roasting

Lamb } Beef }	20 minutes per 500 g +20 minutes
Mutton	25 minutes per 500 g +25 minutes
Pork } Veal }	30 minutes per 500 g +30 minutes
Chicken	25 minutes per 500 g +15 minutes

Joints Suitable for Various Methods of Cooking

(See also pp. 68–75)

Meat	Boiling	Stewing	Roasting	Grilling	Frying	Pot Roasting
Beef	silverside flank brisket	buttock steak chuck flank shin	rib wing rib sirloin	rump steak fillet steak	rump steak	buttock steak top side top rump
Lamb/ Mutton	leg	breast middle neck best end neck scrag end	leg loin breast shoulder best end neck	chops cutlets chump chops	chops chump chops	leg
Veal		shoulder best end neck breast knuckle	shoulder best end neck loin breast fillet leg	chops	cutlets chops	
Pork	leg belly hand		leg loin spare rib	chops spare rib chops	chops spare rib chops	belly blade bone

THE FOOD VALUE OF MEAT

Complete Protein is the most valuable constituent of meat. The amino acids contained in the muscle of animals include all those essential to the human body. Their proportions are very closely related to those required by the body, which can, therefore, make use of them very easily. The chief protein in the living flesh is myosinogen and this is converted to *myosin* as the body cools after death. This causes coagulation and the carcass stiffens owing to the hardening of the muscles. Meat is therefore hung until the myosin liquifies and the muscles relax. Enzyme action causes this to happen and acids to form which improve the flavour of the meat and break down the connective tissue.

In the connective tissue of the meat there is present an insoluble, incomplete protein known as *collagen*. When exposed to moist heat (as in cooking) this is converted into soluble *gelatin*. It is completely deficient in the essential amino acid called *trytophan*, but it can be employed by the body to supplement other incomplete or partially complete proteins. The walls of the muscle fibres also contain a protein called *elastin* which is very tough and insoluble. The pounding of steak before cooking helps to break down the tough tissues and the enzymes can more easily reach the myosin.

Fat is distributed throughout the carcass of the animal, in layers between the muscle fibres and below the skin, and in masses around the delicate internal organs (e.g. the kidneys).

Vitamins C and D are almost entirely absent in meat, although liver may contain a small quantity of the fat-soluble Vitamin D.

The Vitamin B complex, however, is well represented in most meats, pork containing more than either beef or mutton.

The offal or internal organs of the animal (tripe, liver, sweetbreads, kidneys) are rich in vitamins, both the B complex and Vitamin A. Liver, especially, is a rich source of Vitamin A.

Mineral Elements in meat consist mainly of iron and potassium. Liver is particularly rich in iron, and tripe, because it is treated with lime during its preparation, contains more calcium than does any other meat.

Extractives have no actual food value but they give meat its characteristic flavour and stimulate the flow of digestive juices. Meat takes between three and four hours to be completely digested, and it is almost 100 per cent absorbed (i.e. there is extremely little excreted).

THE VALUE OF MEAT IN THE DIET

1 Its food value—the amount of meat required per day is less than that of carbohydrate-containing foods, as it is a more concentrated source of nourishment.

2 It is usually the most expensive item of the meal and forms the 'core' of it. Smaller quantities of meat than of its accompaniments are served, however, which balances costs somewhat.

3 It provides an important addition to the variety of flavours in the diet, and left-over gravies and meat stock can often be used to supplement the more insipid vegetable soups and sauces.

4 Left-over meat may be used to make attractive and satisfying réchauffé dishes.

5 It may be cooked in a variety of ways.

6 It is satisfying because it takes a fairly long time to digest, and hunger is not felt until three or four hours after eating a meal containing meat.

7 Offal (i.e. the internal organs of the animal—liver, kidneys, tripe, heart, etc.) has very concentrated food value and is comparatively cheap. It is usually easily digested, providing that it is not over-cooked. Whereas meat is composed of long, tubular fibres, liver, kidney, etc. are made up of round ones; over-cooking causes these to become hard and granular, and they do not fall apart as meat fibres do.

BACON

Bacon is the flesh of pigs specially bred to produce animals with long backs and less subcutaneous fat than is found in pigs used for pork.

Curing

Meat has been salted for hundreds of years to preserve it. The farmer's wife rubbed coarse salt well into the flesh and packed it under a thick layer of salt, so that it was eventually completely permeated by the solution formed by the dissolving of the salt in the meat's own juices. Today the same principle is carried out in bacon factories by injecting brine into the flesh at intervals and then steeping the sides of bacon-pork in brine-filled tanks.

Maturing

After being removed from the tanks the sides are stacked in cool rooms for 7 to 10 days to allow the flavour to develop.

In olden days this maturing was often carried out by hanging the carcass in the chimney to ensure a constant draught of fresh air on it. The flavour imparted to the matured meat by the smoke from wood fires no doubt gave rise to the now commonly practised method of smoking.

Smoking

Besides improving the flavour, this method increases the keeping properties of bacon and changes its appearance for the better.

The sides of bacon are hung from beams 6 metres above slowly smouldering oak or deal chippings for 30 to 60 hours.

Ham is cured by dry-salting (the process is secret to the famous ham-producers). Belfast hams are smoked but most hams are unsmoked. The 'ham' itself is the hind leg of a prime pig.

Gammon is the hind leg of a bacon pig but is cured while still on the carcass, with the rest of the side.

Green Bacon is cured but not smoked. (This is more popular in the north of England than elsewhere.) The flesh is pale and the rind almost white.

CHOOSING BACON

1 Rind: should be thin, smooth and not cracked.

2 Fat: should be white and firm, with no yellowish or greenish tinge.

3 Lean: should be of a good pink colour, with no trace of brown discolouration, moist and with no evidence of salt crystals.

4 Smell: should be fresh and pleasant.

COOKING BACON

1 Joints of bacon should be soaked before cooking to remove excess salt.

2 Allow boiled hams and gammons to cool in the water in which they have been cooked. (This improves the flavour and prevents the bacon from crumbling easily on the outside.)

3 When frying rashers of bacon:

a Remove rinds and fry them with the rashers. Dry and use for flavouring soups.

b Lay rashers in a cold frying pan and cook slowly or rapidly according to whether soft or crisp rashers are required.

c Let bacon cook in its own fat only—see 'dry frying', p. 74.

d Lay rashers with lean parts over fat ones when several are being cooked together.

4 When grilling rashers:

a Remove rind and snip the edges of the fat to prevent rashers from curling.

b Lay fat parts over lean ones when cooking several rashers.

STORING BACON

Bacon should be bought as fresh as possible and kept as cool as possible (3–4°C) in a larder. It should be wrapped in muslin or greaseproof paper to protect it from flies.

If kept in a refrigerator it should be wrapped in foil or film or placed in a plastic or glass container and stored away from the freezing unit. If bacon is left uncovered the moisture will evaporate, leaving the meat dry and unappetizing; moreover, refrigerator-coldness has no effect on the salt content, salt water having a lower freezing point than plain water.

THE FOOD VALUE OF BACON

1 The average cut of bacon is made up of: 45 per cent fat, 41 per cent water, 14 per cent protein.

2 Bacon is more easily digested than uncured meat.

3 It is an important source of Vitamin B.

Suitable Cuts (*See chart on p.* 122)

Boiling	Grilling/Frying as rashers
1 Hock	4, 5, 6 Streaky
7 Flank	7 Flank
8, 9, 10, 11 Gammons	12 Long Back
13 Oyster	13 Oyster (fat rashers)
16 Top Back	14 Short Back
17 Prime Collar	15 Back and Ribs
18 End Collar	16 Top Back

FURTHER STUDY

THINGS TO DO

1 Using small cubes of meat of exactly the same size, cook each until tender, using one of the following methods for each: grilling, roasting, frying, boiling, stewing.

Measure each very accurately before and after cooking to compare the amount of shrinkage caused.

2 Demonstrate the loss of juices from meat by:

a placing equal quantities of minced meat in each of two glasses

b pouring boiling water over one, sufficient to cover the meat and to form a deep layer above it

c pouring exactly the same volume of cold water over the meat in the other glass

d leaving both for half an hour.

Compare

a the colour of (*i*) the meat, (*ii*) the liquids

b the flavour of the two liquids.

What conclusions can you draw?

3 Observe the results of question 1 and list exactly the changes which have taken place during the processes. What has caused each of these changes?

4 Visit the butchery department of a supermarket and a small butcher's shop. Make lists of prices of as many joints as possible and compare the two sets.

Note the packaged cuts and prepared packs in the supermarket and compare these with the same quantity of unprepared amounts in both establishments.

5 Find as many facts as you can about the

a sources

b appearance

c preparation

d serving

e accompaniments

of poultry and game birds.

QUESTIONS TO ANSWER

1 Write out the following statements, and complete them, using only the words in the right-hand column to fill in the blanks.

a The red colouring matter of meat is due to the presence of	iron
b The main protein in the flesh of the living animal is	myosin
c The tissue connecting muscle fibres contain an insoluble protein called	offal

d The 'gravy' of a vegetable-free stew owes its flavour to .... from the meat.

e The main mineral element found in meat is ....

f The oldest method of preserving meat is by ....

g The edible internal organs of an animal or bird are known as ....

h Freshly-killed meat is unfit for eating immediately because enzymes have not been able to break down the coagulated proteins into ....

i When meat is cooked the insoluble connective tissue is converted into ....

j Edible birds which can only be killed at certain times of the year are called ....

haemoglobin

myosinogen

extractives

gelatin

game

collagen

salting

2 List the nutrients in meat and describe their functions in the diet. Explain the physical and chemical changes that take place in meat when it is stewed. (A.E.B.)

3 What do you understand by 'offal'? Give as many examples as you can and describe briefly how each would be cooked.

4 What cheaper foods would you use to replace or supplement meat now that it is so expensive an item? Give reasons for your choice and show how food values are maintained in spite of the omission of meat.

5 Name *four* examples of edible offal. What is its food value? Give directions for using *one* of these foods to provide an attractive main dish for a meal. (C.U.B.)

6*a* Upon what does the toughness and tenderness of raw meat depend?

b Name a method of cooking which renders tough meat tender and explain the changes that take place in the meat while it is cooking.

c Name *two* other methods of cooking meat. Explain briefly each method and give *two* cuts of meat which could be cooked by each method. (A.E.B.)

7*a* Name the cuts of bacon most suitable for
   (*i*)   roasting or baking
   (*ii*) grilling or frying
   (*iii*) boiling or braising.
Give cooking times and suitable accompaniments.

b Give hints for selecting the above cuts and their storage in the home. (C. & G.)

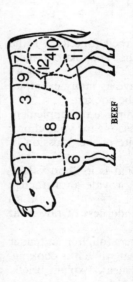

BEEF

No.	Joint	Appearance	Suitable Methods of Cooking	Accompaniments
1	Buttock steak (beef steak and stewing steak)		Steak puddings: steamed under suet crust Steak pies: oven-stewed Stews Beef olives Braising Pot-roasting (i.e. browned with a little dripping in a thick pan—add vegetables and herbs, cook very slowly)	Root vegetables, boiled or baked Creamed potatoes { Forcemeat balls (remainder of stuffing) Brown gravy
2	Chuck		Stewing Braising	Suet dumplings Diced carrot and turnips Brown gravy
3	Rib		Roasting May be boned, rolled and stuffed if preferred	Roast potatoes, brown gravy Cauliflower, carrots, parsnips Yorkshire pudding Horseradish sauce
4	Silverside		Boiling (salted or unsalted)—with whole onions and a bouquet garni	Boiled carrots, turnips, carrots, onions Suet dumplings Bread sauce

		Appearance	Suitable Methods of Cooking	Accompaniments
5	Flank		Stewing (used with other leaner cuts) Salting, boiling and pressing (eaten cold)	Creamed or boiled potatoes, root or green vegetables Salads
6	Brisket		(Similar to flank, but less fat) Salting, boiling and pressing	See above
7	Rump steak		Grilling Frying	Sauté, grilled or duchesse potatoes, peas, tomato sauce Fried onions
8	Wing Rib		Roasting (Boned, stuffed and rolled or left on the bone)	Horseradish sauce Tomato salad
9	Sirloin		Roasting	Rich brown gravy Horseradish sauce Yorkshire pudding Roast potatoes, green vegetables Cauliflower
10	Topside		Braising Pot-roasting	See 2 Cauliflower
11	Shin		Stewing Beef tea, soup, stock	
12	Top Rump		As for topside (similar joint but with more fat)	See 10

LAMB and MUTTON

No.	Joint	Appearance	Suitable Methods of Cooking	Accompaniments
1	Leg (shank end)		Roasting Boiling	Thick, brown gravy; onion sauce (m.); mint sauce (l.); redcurrant jelly; forcemeat stuffing (m.); new potatoes, peas, runner beans (l.); any baked or boiled vegetables (m.) Caper sauce, boiled vegetables
2	Leg (fillet end)		Braising Pot-roasting	
3	Leg (whole)		Roasting Braising Boiling	Young carrots, turnips Caper sauce and boiled root vegetables
4	Loin		Roasting, after boning, stuffing and rolling	
5	Chops		Grilling—included in mixed grill Frying	Serve with a pat of butter blended with lemon juice and chopped parsley

No.	Joint	Appearance	Suitable Methods of Cooking	Accompaniments
6	Breast		Stewing Boned, rolled, stuffed and roasted Stewed, boned, pressed, cut into small pieces, coated with egg and breadcrumbs, fried	Tomato sauce
7	Cutlets		Grilling	See chops Peas
8	Shoulder		Roasting—with or without bone (stuffed)	
9	Middle Neck		Stewing (hot-pot, Irish stew, Scotch broth)	
10	Best end of Neck		Stewing Roasting	
11	Scrag end		Stewing (haricot mutton, hot-pot) Oven stewing in mutton pies	
12	Chump chops		Grilling Frying	Tomatoes, onions

VEAL

No.	Joint	Appearance	Suitable Methods of Cooking	Accompaniments
1	Shoulder		This cut is often divided into two: *a* the 'oyster' lies towards the blade bone and is suitable for roasting or braising *b* the remainder is suitable for stewing	Lemon and parsley forcement stuffing Bacon rolls Thick, brown gravy Green vegetables, onions, tomatoes Baked or boiled potatoes Bread sauce
2	Best end of Neck		Whole: roasted Divided into cutlets: fry in butter or margarine Stewing	See above Fried, creamed or duchesse potatoes; tomatoes, green vegetables; brown sauce, young carrots Serve standing on end with cutlet frills on end of bone
3	Loin		Divided into chops; grilled or fried— coat with egg and breadcrumbs Boned, stuffed, rolled and roasted Roasting	Forcemeat balls
4	Breast		Stewing Used after cooking for galantines, aspics, etc. Bone, roll and stuff, roast	Boiled/creamed potatoes, root or green vegetables Salad Roast potatoes/boiled potatoes. Green vegetables
5	Fillet Leg		Veal escalopes Roasting	Bacon rolls, lemon butterflies Green peas Forcemeat balls
6	Knuckle		Braising Stewing	Diced/sliced root vegetables, onions

PORK

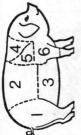

No.	Joint	Appearance	Suitable Methods of Cooking	Accompaniments
1	Leg		Roasting (score skin to make 'crackling') Salted, boiled	Apple sauce Pease pudding
2	Loin		As chops—grilled or fried Roasting	
3	Belly		Boiled, pressed Braising Pot-roasting	
4	Spare Rib		Roasting Cut into chops and grill or fry	
5	Blade Bone		Pot-roasting (boned and stuffed/on the bone) Braising	
6	Hand (or Shoulder)		Salted and boiled—served cold Braising	Pickled walnuts

BACON

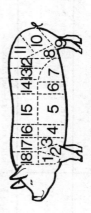

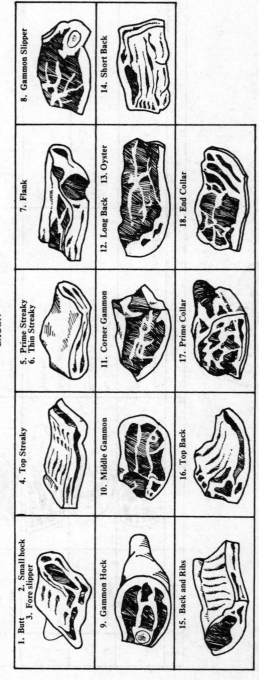

1. Butt 2. Small hock 3. Fore slipper

4. Top Streaky

5. Prime Streaky 6. Thin Streaky

7. Flank

8. Gammon Slipper

9. Gammon Hock

10. Middle Gammon

11. Corner Gammon

12. Long Back 13. Oyster

14. Short Back

15. Back and Ribs

16. Top Back

17. Prime Collar

18. End Collar

FISH

Fish is of great value in the diet because:

1 Its food value is similar to meat, although weight for weight its nutritive value is slightly less:

a it is a valuable source of complete protein

b it contains mineral matter in the form of calcium (especially that in which the bones are eaten), potassium, phosphorus, iron and iodine

c it contains Vitamin B (riboflavine, thiamine and nicotinic acid) and Vitamins A and D, particularly in oily fish

d some fish supply fat, either within their own structure or when cooked by frying.

2 It has a delicate, distinctive flavour which adds variety to the diet. The flesh of fish is similar to that of meat in structure, but contains a greater percentage of water, which accounts for the characteristic delicacy of its flavour.

3 It is more easily digested than meat. The connective tissue contains collagen but no elastin, and this is quickly converted into soluble gelatin as the fish is cooked. As the protein coagulates, therefore, the gelatin dissolves and the cooked fish flakes separate. Cooked fish protein, therefore, is less tough than cooked meat protein and can usually be satisfactorily digested by the most delicate systems. It is, therefore, an excellent dish for invalids.

4 It is sometimes less expensive than meat. Although prices vary a little according to the district and to the time of year, on the whole fish is cheaper than meat, weight for weight. There is often less waste in the form of shrinkage, but there could be up to 70 per cent wastage of the fish as purchased, when bone, skin and internal organs are removed. It must be admitted that fish is often found to be less satisfying than meat and greater quantities may be required.

5 It can be purchased already boned and prepared, and now that frozen goods are widely available, there is no 'season' for fresh fish.

6 It can be cooked by many different methods. Boiling, poaching, steaming, frying, baking and grilling are all suitable methods for cooking fish, and may be used according to personal taste.

7 It is suitable for any meal. Fish may form the main course of a midday lunch, supper, high tea or breakfast. It may be used as a filling for tartlets, pies, pasties, flans; or it may be one of many ingredients in an hors d'œuvre or salad. Expensive fish served in small quantities, e.g. smoked salmon, may be a preliminary to the main course of an evening dinner; or small portions may be served as a savoury at the end of a supper, e.g. roes or mashed sardines on toast.

8 Cheap fish may be served with stuffing or sauce to augment its food value and flavour. One of the cheaper white fish is cod, but the

texture and flavour are often slightly inferior to more expensive fish. If cooked slowly, however, the flesh can be rendered very palatable and to increase the flavour and food value good sauces may be served, e.g. chopped egg, shrimps, grated cheese, or anchovy essence may all be added to a foundation white sauce. Or forcemeat stuffing can be cooked with the fish, either inside boned cutlets or baked as small balls round the fish.

Round fish such as whiting or herrings should be opened, boned (if required), stuffed and sewn up again into their original shape. (*Note* sewing thread should be carefully removed before serving the dish.) Small herrings or mackerel may be boned and rolled after the stuffing has been spread on the inside flesh.

CLASSES OF FISH

White Fish
There is no fat distributed throughout the flesh, but some types store valuable supplies in their livers, e.g. cod, halibut, sole, plaice, hake, whiting, fresh haddock, etc.

Oily Fish
Fat is distributed throughout the flesh of the fish, giving a darker colour and making it a little more difficult to digest than white fish, but increasing the nutritive value, e.g. herrings, salmon, eels, mackerel.

Shellfish
The skeleton of the fish acts as its protective covering instead of as its support. They are usually cooked before being sold to the public and are served and eaten without further cooking. The flesh is considerably less digestible than that of the other two classes, the fibres being coarser than those of other types.

e.g. crustaceans: crabs, lobsters, prawns, shrimps, etc.

molluscs: oysters, mussels, winkles, cockles, etc.

Exceptions: Oysters are not usually cooked before eating; scallops are opened and cooked after purchase.

CHOOSING FISH

Much fish today is bought ready-prepared and frozen, requiring very little attention before cooking. Thin fillets, small steaks and cutlets do not even need complete defrosting before use, as the flesh is not dense and the danger of incomplete thawing and the multiplication of harmful bacteria while cooking is not present.

If fresh fish is available, however, the following points should be observed.

1 Purchase from clean shops where the goods are not exposed to dust and fumes from the streets.

2 Ensure that the fish is stiff (this is particularly important when choosing mackerel), that the gills, eyes and spots (as on plaice) are moist and bright in colour and that the smell is wholesome. Fish should smell of the sea!

3 Buy fish as close as possible to the time when it is to be eaten.

PREPARATION FOR COOKING

It is seldom necessary to bone or fillet fish at home. Even if it is purchased fresh and whole, the fishmonger will quickly and efficiently carry out these processes without charge.

All the preparation which is usually required is

a washing under a gently-running tap

b patting dry with absorbent paper or cloth.

Frozen portions need only be removed from the packing before cooking as required. Dark skin is more easily removed, if desired, after cooking, when it can be gently peeled away from the flesh.

COOKING

Boiling is a suitable method for cooking large fish with a good flavour. The flavour is slightly decreased during cooking and this method should not be used for delicate fish or for thin fillets. Use the liquor from cooking for making a well-flavoured sauce to serve with the fish.

Steaming is a very suitable way of cooking even the most delicate portions of fish. It is also a particularly good method of cooking fish for invalids, as it is very easily digested.

The result may, however, be a little insipid and colourless so steamed fish should be

a served with a good sauce

b garnished attractively.

During cooking the fish should be covered with greased paper to prevent it from becoming sodden with condensed liquid.

Stewing of fish is best carried out in the oven, using milk as the liquid. This can afterwards be used as the base of a sauce. This method is particularly suitable for fillets of white fish.

Smoked haddock may be similarly cooked on the top of the stove, either in milk or in water.

Baking is a method in which very little of the flavour of fish is lost. It should be placed in hot fat and cooked gently either as flat fillets or rolled fillets or stuffed whole.

Grilling is a quick and appetizing method of cooking small fish or fillets with no loss of flavour.

Round fish, e.g. herrings, are best boned and grilled flat.

White fish should be brushed with a little oil and laid on greased grill-pan bars.

If round fish is cooked whole, the body should be scored across several times to allow the heat to penetrate and cook the flesh without burning the outside.

Frying is an appetizing method of cooking fish, most of which should be coated first. This is particularly important if deep-fat frying is used, as the great heat and motion of the fat tends to break down the outside tissues.

Herrings can be coated very satisfactorily with oatmeal; white fish should be protected with seasoned flour, egg and breadcrumbs or batter.

Kippers, which contain a good deal of fat in their flesh, may be cooked by dry frying.

Sousing is a method of stewing fish in the oven, using vinegar as the liquid and adding seasoning and herbs (peppercorns, bay leaves, thyme, etc.) to give a highly flavoured, spicy dish. It is usually used as a method of cooking herrings or mackerel, which may be served hot or cold.

Note Herrings are one of our cheapest fish, rich in Vitamins A and D, and in protein, easy to prepare and to cook, and they provide a satisfying, economical addition to the diet.

FURTHER STUDY

THINGS TO DO

1 Compare the cooking time required for equal quantities of the same fish (e.g. fillet of haddock or cod) when steamed, boiled, grilled, baked and fried. Note the changes which take place in the appearance, bulk and texture in each case. How do you account for these?

2 To assess wastage of fish during preparation and cooking:

a weigh one fresh herring (whole) as purchased. Note price.

b clean and prepare fish for cooking. Re-weigh.

c grill until cooked and re-weigh.

d eat the cooked fish, weigh the unconsumed waste and calculate the weight of fish actually eaten.

Calculate the cost of the fish actually eaten, and percentage loss

a during preparation

b at table.

3 Select one type of oily fish, one white and one shellfish. Visit a fishmonger's and a supermarket and compare the prices of the following:

a the fish in its fresh state

b the same fish prepared for cooking

c the same type of fish from the deep-frozen fish counter

d equal quantities of the same type in a pack ready to be cooked

e if available, the same quantity of the same type in its tinned form.

QUESTIONS TO ANSWER

1 Write out the following statements, and complete them, using only the words in the right-hand column to fill in the blanks.

a The flavour of fish is more delicate than that of meat as it contains fewer ....   crayfish

b A commonly used example of white fish is ....   gelatin

c A popular oily fish is ....   roe

d One lesser-used shellfish is ....

e A fish which is usually eaten raw is ....   elastin

f When cooked, the flesh of fish flakes apart owing to the absence of .... in the connective tissue.   vinegar

g The .... quickly dissolves, and this increases the digestibility of fish.   oysters

h An important mineral present in fish and lacking in meat is ....   iodine

i The eggs of fish, which are often eaten, are known as ....   extractives

j In order to make shellfish fibres more easily digestible, it is often eaten with ....   pilchard

    hake

2*a* List the nutrients found in white fish and describe their functions in the diet.

b In which nutrients is white fish deficient and how can this deficiency be remedied?

c Give one method of cooking the following and in each case give reasons for your choice:

(*i*) a fillet of plaice for a convalescent

(*ii*) a fillet of cod for a manual worker

(*iii*) a fillet of fresh haddock for a weight-conscious housewife.

3*a* List the *three* classes of fish, giving *two* examples of each class.

b Name the main nutrients found in fish and give an account of the functions of these nutrients.

c Give *four* rules for the choice of fresh fish. (A.E.B.)

4 Compare the values of fresh, tinned and frozen fish to the housewife. Suggest four different ways of serving fish attractively.

5 What rules govern the choice of fish? When is pre-packed fish a suitable choice? Compare the nutritive value and digestibility of white and oily fish.   (C. & G.)

6 How can fish to be served to an invalid be made attractive?

FRUITS AND VEGETABLES

Fruits and vegetables not only add valuable nutrients to our diet but contribute a good deal of variety in texture, flavour and colour. Much aesthetic pleasure can be derived from their appearance and freshness, and altogether they form some of the most attractive types of food we eat.

THEIR FOOD VALUE

The most important nutrients to be found in fruits and vegetables are
    a vitamins
    b mineral elements.

Vitamins

a Oranges, lemons, grapefruit and blackcurrants are excellent sources of Vitamin C.

Watercress, parsley and brussels sprouts are also good sources and a syrup made from rose-hips (these cannot be eaten raw) is given to young children to make up for possible lack of fresh fruit and vegetables during the winter months. Potatoes and most other vegetables and fruits contain some of this vitamin. To obtain the fullest benefit from their Vitamin C content, these foods should be eaten as fresh as possible and preferably raw. (See p. 56 for the effect of light and heat on Vitamin C.)

b Green, yellow and red fruits and vegetables contain Vitamin A in the form of *carotene*, a yellow pigment. The liver is able to convert this carotene into Vitamin A.

Good sources are tomatoes, carrots, prunes, peas and green vegetables, the darker green leaves of which contain more carotene than the lighter ones. In carrots the richness of the vitamin content is indicated by the depth of the colour.

c Some of the Vitamin B complex are present in green vegetables and pulses.

Mineral Elements

Calcium is found in green vegetables.

Iron is present in raisins, watercress, green vegetables and peas. Although rich in iron, however, spinach is not a good nutritive source as the body cannot absorb that which is present.

Phosphorus is provided by cabbage, potatoes and oranges particularly, among most other fruits and vegetables.

Iodine is found in watercress and onions which are grown on iodine-containing soils.

Other Nutrients

Carbohydrates The most obvious carbohydrate provided by a vegetable is *starch*, found in potatoes and in pulses. *Sugars* are present (as fructose) in all fruits and are particularly evident in dried fruits such as raisins, currants, sultanas, dates and figs. *Cellulose*, which is not a nutrient but is most important to bodily health, forms the structure of all fruits and vegetables, and is important for the bulk which it provides as well as for its regulating properties and its stimulating effect on intestinal peristalsis.

Fats A little fat is obtained from nuts and from olives (olive oil is well known) but, in general, fruits and vegetables are almost completely lacking in the nutrient.

Proteins Vegetable proteins (incomplete) are present in minute quantities in many fruits and vegetables, but beans (particularly soya beans), lentils and peas are particularly good sources. Dried apricots and dried figs are the fruits which are richest in this nutrient but the amount is considerably less than in pulses.

Water

The value of water in the diet has already been mentioned and fruits in particular contribute a good deal.

Indeed, some fruits, such as grapes and cucumbers, are approximately 80 per cent water. The delicate flavours dissolved in this water, thus forming fruit and vegetable juices, are valuable for their freshness and appetizing properties. By stimulating the flow of digestive juices and so aiding the digestion of subsequent dishes, the practice of beginning a meal with a glass of fruit or tomato juice is a sensible one.

THEIR VALUE IN THE DIET

Accompaniments to Protein Dishes

In order to balance meals and to provide adequate supplies of all the essential nutrients regularly, it is necessary to accompany the staple protein foods by those containing good reserves of mineral elements and vitamins. Fruits and vegetables supply these needs and have become the customary accompaniments to main dishes: e.g. boiled beef and carrots; fish and chips; custard and stewed fruit. Starchy vegetables are particularly useful in adding bulk to meals and in providing energy and warmth economically.

Foods to be Eaten either Cooked or Raw

The food value of many fruits and vegetables is considerably greater when they are eaten in their uncooked state than when they have been cooked. This is because much of the Vitamin C content and many soluble mineral elements may be lost when the food is heated in water Although most ripe fruits are pleasant to eat raw, some of them (e.g. rhubarb, cooking apples, damsons and most vegetables) are quite unpalatable in this state. Several types of vegetable, however, may be rendered attractive and enjoyable to eat raw in salads by dividing them finely, e.g. cabbage shredded or chopped, and carrots and young turnips grated.

Foods which may be Cooked in Many Different Ways

Although the most satisfactory method of cooking vegetables is by the conservative method, in order to preserve as much food value as possible, many other methods of cooking may be used for various fruits and vegetables. The time of cooking and the method used depend a good deal upon the coarseness of the cellulose. (See p. 134 for details.)

It is sometimes possible to increase the food value of the vegetable by the way in which it is cooked and served, e.g.

a potatoes cooked as chips provide more calories than those which are boiled, due to their fat content

b creamed swedes (i.e. swedes mashed and blended with a foundation white sauce) provide additional carbohydrate and fat, which is lacking in plain, boiled swedes

c cabbage served with a knob of butter melted over it is of more value than when served plain.

An Important Part of a Vegetarian Diet

Because vegetarians are unable to eat several of the sources of animal protein, vegetable protein is of great importance to them.

(See p. 150 for the place of fruit and vegetables in vegetarian diets.)

Useful Garnishes and Decorations

Most sweet and vegetable dishes are improved in appearance (as well as in their nutritional value) by the way in which they are garnished or decorated. Indeed, the most plain and commonplace dish may be transformed into a tempting and attractive one by imaginative presentation. The use of parsley and watercress is well known and widely practised, but there are many other ways in which fruits and vegetables may be utilized:

thinly sliced lemon used as twists or 'butterflies',
thinly sliced cucumber used as above,
tomatoes cut into 'water-lilies',

sliced (cooked or raw) carrot with the centres of the rings cut out to hold small onions or bacon rolls, etc.,
radishes cut down towards the stalk end and left to open in water to form 'roses',
thin slices of red-skinned apples, one overlapping the other,
skinned orange sections arranged in 'wheel' pattern,
cherries and grapes used in halves or cut into petal shapes.

Aids to Digestion and Appetite

By adding colour and variety of texture and flavour to the diet, fruits and vegetables form a tempting item of most meals. The increased flow of digestive juices induced by their attractiveness aids the digestion of these foods themselves and of other dishes eaten at the same meal. This is of particular value to invalids whose appetites require stimulation and whose digestion is somewhat impaired.

HOUSEHOLD ECONOMY

Much expense can be saved and much satisfaction gained by growing one's own fruit and vegetables. It is then possible to preserve surplus supplies in readiness for out-of-season months.

If home-grown supplies are not available, large quantities of fresh vegetables and fruit can be purchased while they are at their most plentiful and therefore cheapest. They may then be preserved in one of the following ways:

bottling — suitable for most fruits, beans, peas, carrots
salting — suitable for runner beans
pickling — suitable for onions and mixed vegetables (other than green ones)
chutneys — suitable for vegetables and tomatoes
pulping — suitable for apples, apricots, tomatoes
jamming — suitable for most fruits and marrow
freezing — suitable for fruits and root vegetables if a domestic deep-freeze is available.

Frozen Fruits and Vegetables

Although they are not so cheap to buy as fresh fruits and vegetables, the ever-increasing range of deep-frozen ones has the following advantages:

1 They require no preparation and are therefore excellent for emergency meals when time is short.

2 They are simple to cook. Clear directions are always given on the wrapper, both for the methods suitable and as to whether or not it is necessary to defrost the contents before use.

3 There is no waste. As the foods are already prepared the entire weight which is purchased is suitable for eating.

4 The quality is always good. Packers of these foods know that only the best quality is suitable for preserving and they will not risk their reputation by offering inferior goods.

5 Out-of-season fruits and vegetables may be obtained throughout the year.

VEGETABLES

For convenience, vegetables are divided into two main classes: root vegetables, and green vegetables.

So-called 'root' vegetables include the following parts of the plants:

a true roots and tubers, e.g. carrots, turnips, swedes, potatoes, parsnips, beetroot, Jerusalem artichokes

b stems: e.g. celery, chicory, asparagus.

'Green' vegetables include:

a leaves: e.g. cabbage, sprouts, spinach, lettuce, watercress, kale

b pods: e.g. French beans, runner beans

c seeds: e.g. peas, broad beans, lentils

d flowers: e.g. cauliflower, broccoli, globe artichokes

e fruits: e.g. cucumber, marrow, egg-plant (aubergine).

Choosing Root Vegetables

1 Buy from clean, well-kept shops likely to receive regular fresh supplies.

2 Buy local-grown produce when possible. This will have been transported the minimum distance and is less likely to have had its food value impaired by exposure to light.

3 Choose medium-sized vegetables, as nearly as possible of comparable size. If they are too small the amount of wastage per kilo is increased, and if too large the texture may be coarse.

4 Do not buy vegetables which are covered in earth. This adds to the weight and is charged for at the same rate as the vegetables. The small extra charge for pre-packaged vegetables is often money well spent.

5 Choose root vegetables with skins as unblemished as possible, with no signs of seeding or shooting, and with crisp, firm texture.

6 Pick roots of which any attached leaves are crisp and a good colour.

Choosing Green Vegetables

1
2 } See above.

3 Choose vegetables of a good, fresh colour.

4 Avoid any which are limp, slimy or withered.

5 Choose vegetables which have firm hearts.

Storing Vegetables

1 Keep roots and tubers in a dark, cool, airy position, packed in a wire or plastic rack or in a basket ensuring good ventilation.

2 Place green vegetables in a pan with a tightly fitting lid or wrap in polythene bags and place at the bottom of the refrigerator.

3 When replenishing the vegetable supply, do not place new ones on top of the remaining old ones—these will thus probably not be used in order and will sprout and become flabby.

4 Remove any vegetables which show signs of decay immediately, in order that it may not spread.

PREPARATION OF VEGETABLES

This should take place just prior to cooking to minimize the exposure of cut surfaces to the air. Not only is Vitamin C oxidized by this but vitamin-destructive enzymes are liberated from the ruptured cells.

Roots

1 Cut off any green tops.

2 Scrub under running cold water to remove any earth.

3 Peel or scrape according to the vegetable and the season:

new potatoes: scrape with vegetable knife, or wash and cook in skins.

new carrots: washing is usually sufficient.

old potatoes ⎫ peel thinly with potato peeler or vegetable knife. (Old
parsnips ⎬ potatoes may be cooked in 'jackets' and peeled before eating as 15 per cent of the Vitamin C content lies just under the skin.)

old carrots: scrape downwards on to board.

turnips ⎱
swedes ⎰ peel thickly to the depth indicated by the colour of the skin.

beetroot: peel gently *after* cooking.

4 Remove any eyes and discoloured portions.

5 Cut into smaller pieces if necessary.

Green Vegetables

1 Remove all discoloured leaves and unwanted stems.

2 Wash thoroughly under running water but do not soak, as this will help to destroy Vitamin C and soften the fibres of the leaves.

3 Prepare the following with especial care:

watercress: pick over very carefully to remove small snails which may adhere to leaves even after washing.

mustard and cress: cut off seeds attached to ends of cress; wash and drain through a colander.

cauliflower: break into small branches to cook more quickly, unless a whole flower is required for a special dish.

spinach: strip leaves from coarse central veins.

Other Vegetables

onions: remove thin brown skin, cut off the root end and slice if necessary.

leeks: remove roots, leave on some of the green stem and split lengthwise.

marrow: peel thickly, cut in half lengthwise or into thick slices and scoop out the seeds.

celery, chicory: remove all but completely white stem, scrub and cut into even lengths.

asparagus: cut into even lengths and scrape any discolouration from the stems. Wash carefully.

METHODS OF COOKING

The cooking of vegetables is necessary to soften the cellulose structure which becomes increasingly coarse as the vegetables become older. At the same time the starch is gelatinized. Care must be taken to prevent as much loss as possible of the soluble vitamins and minerals.

Conservative Cooking   Suitable for all vegetables. See p. 76.

Boiling
Root vegetables

    1 Place in boiling, salted water and cook as quickly as possible without breaking them down. Potatoes should be boiled in their skins and peeled after cooking to minimize the loss of Vitamin C.

    2 Cook with the lid of the pan on.

    3 Drain thoroughly before serving.

    4 Toss in butter before serving and sprinkle with finely chopped parsley.

    5 Serve as soon as possible after cooking, as at least 30 per cent of the remaining Vitamin C may be lost by keeping vegetables hot.

Note   To cream boiled potatoes mash thoroughly and mix with *hot* milk and a little butter. Beat well with a wooden spoon until white and fluffy and replace heat lost during this process by stirring over very gentle heat.

Green vegetables

    1 Place vegetables in a small amount of boiling, salted water and boil rapidly to conserve the colour.

    2 Cook with the lid on.

Note   Bicarbonate of soda is sometimes recommended to preserve the colour but this completely destroys the Vitamin C content. If vegetables are well cooked this assistance should not be necessary.

Pulses (*Dried*)   Wash thoroughly and soak overnight before cooking.

Other vegetables suitable for boiling: cauliflower, broccoli, celery, onions.

Steaming is suitable for all root vegetables and bulbs, but impairs the colour of green ones. The loss of Vitamin C is somewhat increased owing to the length of time taken.

Baking is suitable for all root vegetables but not for green ones. Use a casserole containing 1 tbsp. water and 12 g butter per 500 g of vegetables, and 1 tsp. salt.

Roasting is suitable for all roots, tubers and onions.

Frying in shallow fat is suitable for onions, sliced potatoes. Deep fat is suitable for chipped or sliced potatoes, sliced artichokes, cauliflower.

Vegetable Dishes
Soups, hot-pots, curries, pasties, pies, flans.

SALADS

Choosing Ingredients
    1 Choose good quality vegetables, as young and fresh and of as good colour as possible.
    2 Choose a good variety of colours.
    3 Mix fruits with vegetables—suitable ones are pineapples, apples, pears, oranges, sultanas.
    4 Make sure that dishes and ingredients are perfectly clean.
    5 Prepare each vegetable as attractively as possible, keeping the best specimens for the final decoration.
    6 Handle ingredients as little as possible.
    7 Arrange attractively on a flat dish or in a deep bowl.
    8 Serve as soon as possible after preparation.
    9 Sprinkle with chopped chives if liked.
    10 Serve with a good dressing.

General Rules for Assembling
lettuce: shred, or leave small leaves whole. Wash thoroughly and shake dry in a towel or in salad basket. Toss in French dressing (i.e. a mixture of salad oil, vinegar and seasoning) immediately before serving in a separate bowl, using only a little in the arranged salad.
cabbage: wash thoroughly and shred finely.
tomatoes: slice, or cut into quarters or into water-lily shapes, making short diagonal cuts with the point of a sharp knife in alternate directions round the fullest part of the tomato.
    If required, peel by pouring boiling water over tomatoes and removing loosened skin gently, or turn gently in a gas flame, supported on a fork, until the skin 'pops', then peel.

cucumber: remove narrow strips of peel lengthwise all round the cucumber before slicing it thinly; a similar result may be obtained more quickly by scoring it lengthwise with a large fork.

radishes: cut lengthwise towards the stalk end and leave in water to open.

beetroot: dice and serve in heaps, or slice thinly.

carrots: grate fairly finely.

potatoes: cook and dice when cool; serve mixed with mayonnaise.

swedes: grate finely.

sultanas: soak for 1 to 2 hours previously until juicy and smooth; dry.

orange: peel, remove pith and slice thinly; remove pips.

apple: slice or grate; add a little lemon juice to prevent darkening.

pear: cut in half lengthwise, remove core; dice if required.

Suitable Additions: eggs, cheese, cold meats, galantines, croquettes, fish. All salads should be served with an accompaniment of French dressing (see above), salad cream or mayonnaise.

Winter salads are best made from cooked vegetables. Summer salads are made from fresh ones, except for potatoes (tiny new boiled potatoes are attractive for this purpose).

Coleslaw An attractive variation of the conventional salad can be served by mixing grated cabbage (savoy), celery, apple and carrot together with a salad dressing (oil and vinegar/lemon juice or salad cream).

Potato salad Use firm, boiled potatoes; slice them thickly and cut the slices into even-sized cubes. Mix with mayonnaise. Finely-cut chives or a little grated onion may be added if required. Serve in a small bowl or dish and sprinkle with chopped parsley.

FRUITS

There are two classes of fruit:

soft fruits, e.g. currants, raspberries, blackberries, gooseberries.

stone fruits, e.g. plums, greengages, cherries.

Choosing Fruits

1 Buy and use fruit as fresh as possible.

2 Buy under-ripe rather than over-ripe fruits and use as they reach their prime condition. (*Note* Pears need particularly careful watching to 'catch' them at the right moment.)

3 Serve as much fruit as possible raw.

Storing See 'Storing Vegetables', p. 133.

PREPARATION OF FRUIT FOR COOKING

The cooking of fruit is necessary in some cases to render the cellulose more palatable than it is in its raw state, and also to reduce the acidity.

Soft Fruits
> *a* remove stems
> *b* wash gently and drain well
> *c* cook gently to avoid breaking down of fruit flesh, using very little liquid (the sugar used in cooking and the natural juice are usually sufficient).

Stone Fruits
> *a* cut in half and remove stones
> *b* peel if necessary.

METHODS OF COOKING

Stewing is the most commonly used method of cooking fruit and is suitable for most fruits (except bananas).

Baking is suitable for apples and bananas.

Frying is used for cooking sliced fruits coated in batter—e.g. bananas.

As Fillings for pies, tarts, puddings, flans.

Fruit Dishes
Fruit in jelly, fools, flans, pies, pasties, tarts, steamed puddings, summer pudding, crumbles, charlottes, mousses, salads.

Pectin Fruits contain a non-nutritional cellulose called *pectinogen*. As they ripen the pectinogen is converted into pectin which forms a jelly when mixed with sugar and acid. It is this pectin on which the success of jam-making depends; the ease with which the jam sets depends on the amount of pectin which the fruit contains.

Gooseberries, currants, plums and citrus fruits are rich in pectin.

Strawberries, cherries and rhubarb are deficient in pectin and to produce a well-set jam they must be mixed with good pectin fruits or cooked with prepared commercial pectin.

FURTHER STUDY

THINGS TO DO

1 Collect equal weights of fresh (whole), dried and tinned apples. Compare the prices and uses of each of the three forms and work out which is the most economical buy.

2 Repeat with dried, frozen, tinned and fresh peas.

3 Repeat with dried, frozen, tinned and fresh potatoes.

4 Using equal weights of potato, compare the cooking time required, the texture and the flavour of those
> *a* boiled in their skins
> *b* peeled and boiled

   c steamed in their skins
   d peeled and steamed
   e baked in their skins
   f peeled and roasted
   g shallow-fat fried
   h deep-fat fried
   i parboiled and fried
   j parboiled and roasted.

5 Using the standard chemical tests, prove the existence/non-existence of starch, fat and protein in potatoes, peas, bananas and apples.

6 Discover as many unfamiliar (i.e. not traditionally used in this country) fruits and vegetables as you can. Classify them and learn how to cook and serve each. Find their countries of origin.

QUESTIONS TO ANSWER

1 Write out the following statements, and complete them, using only the words in the right-hand column to fill in the blanks.

a The best sources of vegetable protein are	Vitamin C
b The carbohydrate found in fruits which is responsible for the setting of jam is	gelatinization
c Vitamin A is present in green vegetables in the form of ...., a yellow pigment often masked by the presence of chlorophyl.	Vitamin D
d When starchy vegetables are cooked they lose their 'glassiness' and become opaque owing to the .... of the starch.	carotene
e Although of no nutritive value, the .... framework of fruit and vegetables is valuable for regulating intestinal activity.	pectin
f Most green leafy vegetables contain ...., one of the highest contents being found in spinach; it is unfortunately, however, not able to be absorbed by the body.	pulses
g Vegetarians require a large variety of vegetables in their diet in order that they may obtain as much ·....... as possible.	incomplete protein
h The vitamin which is almost completely deficient in fruits and vegetables is	cellulose
i The nutrient most easily destroyed during the preparation and cooking of vegetables is	dextrinization
j When peeled potatoes become brown on the outside during baking this is due to the .... of the starch.	iron

2 Why are fresh fruits and vegetables important items of the diet? How would you maintain their value when storing, preparing and cooking these foods?

3*a* List the nutrients found in (*i*) pulse vegetables, (*ii*) green vegetables, and state the functions of each of these nutrients in the diet.

b Give *six* ways, each with a reason, of preserving the vitamins and mineral elements in vegetables during their preparation and cooking.   (A.E.B.)

4*a* List the forms in which potatoes may now be purchased.

b Why are these popular?

c Why are potatoes valuable as items of the diet?

6

PLANNING MEALS

GENERAL RULES

When she has learnt the value of food to the body, the cook will understand that her work is to see that meals are

    a adequate—i.e. that they will satisfy the needs of the body

    b warming and conducive to good health

    c tempting, so that there is no difficulty in persuading the family to eat them.

    The choice of dishes included in each meal will depend upon several considerations. These are

Their Food Value

Some food from each class should be eaten at each meal. It is usually most convenient to decide what is to be the main dish, or 'core' (usually the protein dish) of the meal, and plan the accompaniments accordingly, so that all the foodstuffs are included. This is called *balancing* a meal. In other words, no one foodstuff or type of dish should far outweigh the others. For example, a midday dinner consisting of steak and kidney pudding, potatoes and beans, followed by jam roll and custard, would be badly balanced—the carbohydrate proportion would greatly outweigh that of protective and body-building foods. Using the same 'core,' a balanced meal could consist of steak and kidney pudding, potatoes, green vegetable; fruit fool.

Individual Requirements

Differing amounts of energy-giving foods (i.e. varying numbers of joules) are required by men, women, children, old people, invalids, sedentary and manual workers. Therefore the sex, age and occupation of those who are going to eat the meal must be considered.

Examples

A schoolboy would consider the following dinner adequate, whereas an old lady would find it far too heavy a meal.

    1st Course   Meat pie, creamed potatoes, cabbage, carrots.

    2nd Course Rice pudding.

Recommended Daily Intake of Nutrients and Energy

Age and Sex	Occupation	Body Weight kg	Energy MJ	Protein g	Thiamine mg	Riboflavine mg	Nicotinic Acid mg	Vitamin C mg	Vitamin A µg	Vitamin D µg	Calcium mg	Iron mg
Boys and Girls												
0–1 year		7·3	3·3	20	0·3	0·4	5	15	450	10	600	6
1–2 years		11·4	5·0	30	0·5	0·6	7	20	300	10	500	7
2–3 years		13·5	5·9	35	0·6	0·7	8	20	300	10	500	7
3–5 years		16·5	6·7	40	0·6	0·8	9	20	300	10	500	8
5–7 years		20·5	7·5	45	0·7	0·9	10	20	300	2·5	500	8
7–9 years		25·1	8·8	53	0·8	1·0	11	20	400	2·5	500	10
Boys												
9–12 years		31·9	10·5	63	1·0	1·2	14	25	575	2·5	700	13
12–15 years		45·5	11·7	70	1·1	1·4	16	25	725	2·5	700	14
15–18 years		61·0	12·6	75	1·2	1·7	19	30	750	2·5	600	15
Girls												
9–12 years		33·0	9·6	58	0·9	1·2	13	25	575	2·5	700	13
12–15 years		48·6	9·6	58	0·9	1·4	16	25	725	2·5	700	14
15–18 years		56·1	9·6	58	0·9	1·4	16	30	750	2·5	600	15
Men												
18–35 years	Sedentary	65·0	11·3	68	1·1	1·7	18	30	750	2·5	500	10
	Fairly active		12·6	75	1·2	1·7	18	30	750	2·5	500	10
	Very active		15·1	90	1·4	1·7	18	30	750	2·5	500	10
35–65 years	Sedentary	65·0	10·9	65	1·0	1·7	18	30	750	2·5	500	10
	Fairly active		12·1	73	1·2	1·7	18	30	750	2·5	500	10
	Very active		15·1	90	1·4	1·7	18	30	750	2·5	500	10
65–75 years	} Becoming sedentary	63·0	9·8	59	0·9	1·7	18	30	750	2·5	500	10
75 and over		63·0	8·8	53	0·8	1·7	18	30	750	2·5	500	10
Women												
18–55 years	Average activity	55·0	9·2	55	0·9	1·3	15	30	750	2·5	500	12
	Very active		10·5	63	1·0	1·3	15	30	750	2·5	500	12
55–75 years	} Becoming sedentary	53·0	8·6	51	0·8	1·3	15	30	750	2·5	500	10
75 and over		53·0	8·0	48	0·7	1·3	15	30	750	2·5	500	10
Pregnancy			10·0	60	1·0	1·6	18	60	750	10	1200	15
Nursing			11·3	68	1·1	1·8	21	60	1200	10	1200	15

MJ = megajoule: 1MJ = 1000 kJ; kJ = kilojoule: 1kJ = 1000 J (joules)

Recommended Daily Intakes of Energy and Nutrients for the U.K. (Department of Health and Social Security, 1969) from *Manual of Nutrition*; reproduced with the permission of the Controller of Her Majesty's Stationery Office.

On the other hand, the same old lady would be satisfied with this meal, which would not be adequate for the boy.

1st Course   Grilled fillet of plaice, duchesse potatoes, peas.
2nd Course   Stewed plums, egg custard.

A similar meal to that first mentioned could be eaten by both a factory worker and a housewife, but larger quantities would be required by the man than by the woman.

Time of Year

It is obvious that during cold weather more warming foods are required than during warm weather. The consumption of fatty and carbohydrate foods is therefore usually increased during the winter months, while that of protective foods (fruit and vegetables) is generally greater during the summer because of their fresh, cool appearance, texture and flavour.

Example

A winter breakfast might consist of
>Porridge
>Fried egg and bacon
>Toast and butter
>Marmalade
>Coffee or tea.

An equally well-balanced summer breakfast could be made of
>Grapefruit
>Boiled egg
>Bread and butter
>Tea.

Time of Day/Week

It is usual to plan one main meal in each day with other, lighter meals at approximately 4-hour intervals. This is roughly the period of time taken to digest any meal completely, after which the flow of gastric juices in the stomach causes increasing sensations of hunger. The time of day at which the main meal is eaten depends largely upon the working habits of the family, but is best not delayed until too near bed-time. The complete relaxation required for sound sleep cannot be attained while the digestive system is working hard to absorb a satisfying meal.

Menus should be planned, at least as far as the main dishes are concerned, over several days, so that the cost of the more expensive items of the diet can be evenly distributed. Moreover, provision can then be made for using 'left-overs' from the main meal of one day to form the main dish of a lesser meal on another.

Example

1st Day, Midday dinner   Beef stew, boiled potatoes, carrots.
2nd Day, Supper   Meat galantine (using remains of meat and sliced carrots set in aspic flavoured with gravy), served with green salad and potato salad (cold diced potatoes mixed with salad cream).

Variety

Monotony of any kind in the diet will lead to jading of the appetite, and consequent reduced flow of digestive juices. On the other hand, any attractive smell or pleasant appearance of food will increase this—the common experience of mouth-watering is due to the exaggerated output of saliva caused by an appetizing odour or sight.

Variety can be introduced, or lost, in colour, texture and flavour:

1 *Colour* A mental picture of the complete meal should be built up while planning it and the combination of colours mentally criticized.

Examples

  a Steamed fish, white sauce, cauliflower and creamed potatoes present a completely colourless meal which, particularly if served on a white plate, would look most unattractive. Parsley in the sauce, carrots and peas instead of the cauliflower, and duchesse potatoes made from the creamed ones would present a very different appearance, while maintaining the original balance of the meal.

  b Beetroot, tomatoes and carrots are excellent ingredients of a salad but, if arranged in close proximity to each other with no other vegetables, can give an over-coloured effect. Interspersed with cucumber, peas, white grapes, 'pearl' onions and lettuce leaves, however, they look most attractive.

2 *Texture* All meals should contain some food which is crisp enough to require chewing. Too soft a diet leads to lazy eating habits—the food is easily swallowed without being properly divided and mixed with saliva ready for the processes of digestion. Contrasts in texture are not only aids to digestion but are more exciting for the eater.

Examples

  a See example *a*. above. The original menu has no crispness in it whatever. Fresh watercress could be served as a garnish to improve the meal, or the potatoes could be fried or sautéd. Fresh fruit salad as a second course might also be used to advantage.

  b A midday meal consisting of stewed minced meat and accompaniments, followed by rice pudding, presents two soft, granular dishes, of very similar texture. A fruit or Bakewell tart would be a better sweet to follow the main course.

3 *Flavour* Nearly every food has its own distinctive flavour and it is not so likely that flavours will be repeated in one meal as in a sequence of meals.

Examples

  a If the main meal of the day is to consist of a fish dish and its accompaniments, it is unwise to begin the day with kippers for breakfast.

  b A large joint which is not exhausted for several days should be served in as many ways as possible after its first appearance. The enjoyment of sliced cold meat served at several subsequent meals will soon pall.

Individual Taste

Everyone has his or her favourite dishes and pet dislikes. Within reason, personal taste should be considered, as any pronounced dislike of a food can retard the flow of digestive juices and impair digestion. On the other hand, favourite meals should not be served too frequently—even these can become monotonous!

Economy

Money for buying food should be evenly distributed over the week's expenditure, and, except in special circumstances, not used up in large, expensive items covering only a few days. This applies particularly to protein foods.

Foods Available

Nowadays there are few problems concerned with foods being available or unavailable. When not in season they are nearly always obtainable in frozen or tinned forms of excellent quality. An economical housewife will, however, make full use of the seasonal glut of eggs, fruit, vegetables and milk, when these foods are at their cheapest, and avoid extravagant use of them when they are scarce and dear.

ARRANGEMENT OF MEALS

The time at which meals are eaten, the nature of these meals and the amount of cooking involved in preparing them depend largely upon the circumstances in which the family lives. Factors to be considered are

1 The times at which the members of the family are at home— it is obviously far more convenient to the cook if the whole family is able to eat at the same time. If meal-times have to be 'staggered', dishes and methods of cooking chosen must be those which will not be spoilt by waiting.

2 The amount of time available for preparation of meals. A housewife who goes out to work during the day will usually find it more convenient to prepare the main meal of the day for early evening, instead of for midday. Even so, this will probably involve some overnight preparation of a meal for those members of the family who cannot have one at work or at school.

3 Economy—the number of cooked meals on one day's menu will depend a good deal upon the housekeeping budget. When only one cooked meal is possible—or desired—during the day, care must be taken to see that other meals are satisfactorily balanced and do not consist entirely of carbohydrates.

The traditional sequence of meals consisted of
1 Breakfast
2 Luncheon
3 Afternoon Tea
4 Dinner
but in most working households this has now been replaced by one of
two more economical and less elaborate arrangements

a Breakfast	*b* Breakfast
Midday dinner/lunch	Midday dinner/lunch
High Tea	Afternoon tea
Hot drink at bedtime	Supper

There is, of course, a very extensive variety of dishes which can be
served at each meal, but the general structure should be as follows

Breakfast
English breakfast
     Cereal or fruit
     Cooked dish
     Toast and marmalade
     Tea or coffee
Continental breakfast
     Rolls/toast and marmalade
     Coffee

Midday Dinner or Lunch
     Soup or grapefruit (optional)
     Main course
     Sweet course
     Cheese and biscuits (optional)
     Coffee

Afternoon Tea
     Tea
     Variety of small sandwiches, cakes, biscuits.
(All foods served must be easily handed round and eaten without the
use of any other cutlery than a small knife and, occasionally, a pastry-
fork.)

High Tea
     Cooked main dish
     Sweet dish, fruit or jam and cake
     Tea

Supper
> Savoury course
> Sweet course
> Cheese and biscuits (optional)
> Coffee

Dinner
> Soup
> Main course
> Sweet course
> Cheese and biscuits
> Coffee

(This is the minimum number of courses. Several different fish, game and meat courses may be served at full-scale dinners.)

Sizes of Portions

Food	Amount	Frequency
Milk	Adults: ½ litre Children: 1 litre	per day
Meat	100 g ⎫ uncooked	2 of these
Fish	125 g ⎭	per day
Cheese	75 g	
Eggs	3–5	per week
Pulses/nuts	100 g	to replace meat, etc.
Margarine or butter	25–50 g	per day
Potatoes	100–150 g	per day
Green vegetables or salad	150 g	per day
Fruit	2 servings	per day
Carbohydrates	bread, cakes, etc.	as appetite requires
Water (or other liquids)	1–1½ litres	per day

SPECIAL MEALS

CHILDREN'S MEALS

Once a small child has reached the stage of being able to chew and digest solid foods, his meals consist generally of modified portions of those eaten by the rest of the family. To avoid any difficulties in persuading the child to eat, however, there are certain points which may be observed to make his meals particularly attractive.

Meals must be well balanced.
Although the child will not be worried by lack of any one foodstuff he will quickly tire of excess quantities of one kind. It is essential that his

diet should contain adequate quantities of body-building materials (see p. 42).

Foods should require plenty of chewing
For the formation of strong teeth and firm, well-shaped jaw-bones, it is necessary for the child to learn to chew as soon as possible. This can be encouraged by providing some crisp food with each meal—e.g. toasted bread or rusks instead of bread and butter, peeled raw apple instead of stewed fruit, fresh watercress or grated carrot instead of cooked vegetables.

Food should be served in small quantities
Small, individual dishes are always more attractive to a child than portions of a family-sized dish. It requires little more trouble to prepare a miniature version of the main dish at the same time and it is very satisfying to the child to be able to finish an entire dish.

Food should be presented as attractively as possible
The use of moulds for cornflour mixtures and jellies, colourings for milk puddings and drinks, and a variety of decorations all call for imagination on the part of the cook, but the results can be obtained quickly and are well worth the trouble. This is particularly true in the case of children's party dishes, where the simplest foods can be 'dressed up' gaily:
      'Candles' made of half bananas set upright in jelly.
      Small cakes iced as 'parcels' and 'addressed' to each child.
      'Traffic Light' biscuits—two plain biscuits, the upper one pierced with three thimble-sized holes, sandwiched together with red, yellow and green jam.
      Small sandwiches cut into animal shapes with biscuit cutters.

Utensils, cutlery, etc., should be suitable for a child's use
A set of melamine or special 'china', thick enough for energetic handling without breaking, but decorated with attractive pictures, and small-sized spoons and forks will all help to make meal-times pleasant. The table should be sensibly laid for a child—plastic covers over his section of the table-cloth will prevent any worry over slopped food and absence of admonition will encourage his experiments in feeding himself.

Meals should be served punctually and regularly
While forming good eating habits it is important that a child should be *ready* to eat at each meal-time. As his day is usually shorter than an adult's there may be less time between meals but set times for these meals should be established, and no tit-bits should be given in between. In this way digestion of one meal can be completed satisfactorily before another is eaten and the child feels sufficiently hungry to enjoy it.

INVALIDS' MEALS

During illness and convalescence it is particularly important that food should make good the damage which the body has suffered, and that it should be protected from further infection. The most important rule when planning invalids' meals, then, is

Meals must be well balanced, and must contain plenty of body-building and protective foods
This is one of the factors which generally increase the cost of meals to be served to invalids. The main protein foods suitable for invalids are dairy produce, white fish and poultry; the protective foods which are suitable are fruit and vegetables, and all these foods should be of as good quality as can be afforded. However, although these special dishes may be somewhat more expensive than a normal diet, their value is in proportion to their cost and it is usually only for a relatively short time that their purchase is necessary.

Further Considerations
Doctor's orders must be obeyed
This rule is almost, if not equally, as important as the previous one and should be very strictly observed. At the beginning of an illness which produces high temperatures, he will usually forbid all solid food altogether, and during this period the patient should be given plenty of fluids—fruit drinks, milk drinks, meat broths, etc. As soon as a 'light diet' is ordered, however, the following rules should be obeyed:

Meals should be served punctually
Meal-times become very important to the patient, because they often supply the main interest of the day and help to relieve the monotony of being in bed. It is important that food should be served at regular intervals and that the patient is not kept waiting—this may cause him to lose interest and to be unable to eat the meal when it does come. If for any reason, though, he does not want to eat at the appointed time, it is advisable to remove the meal altogether and re-serve it later rather than to leave it in the room until required or to insist on its being eaten.

Meals must be prepared and served with scrupulous cleanliness
Great care must be taken when preparing invalid food that neither the food itself nor the cook is adding to the risk of further infecting the patient. It is particularly important that any food which is to be eaten raw is washed or otherwise cleaned before serving, and any stored ingredients must be covered to prevent bacteria from the air coming into contact with them. The cook must be very particular about her personal cleanliness and no one suffering from colds, coughs or other infectious

ailments should be allowed to handle the patient's food in any way. Tray-cloths, cutlery and all utensils should be spotlessly clean, not only in the interest of hygiene but also because it adds to the attractiveness of the meal.

Meals should be served as attractively as possible
The importance of cleanliness has already been mentioned, and there are several other points to be observed in making the meal as tempting as possible to a rather unenthusiastic appetite

a Use pretty china and serving dishes, matching whenever possible. Those not in everyday use will help to make the patient feel that he is receiving special attention and therefore more willing to co-operate.

b Serve small helpings which can be repeated if required. Use individual dishes whenever possible, rather than remove portions from a family-sized dish. It is most important *not* to overload the patient's plate—if he feels immediately that he will not be able to finish it he will often make little effort to do so.

c Make sure that hot foods are served really hot and cold ones thoroughly cold. It must be remembered that hot foods will lose some heat while being carried from the kitchen to the bedroom and they should therefore be covered if possible.

d See that an attractive colour scheme is presented by the food and its serving dishes. Garnishes of tomato, watercress, etc., can make quite an insipid dish attractive. Add colouring fluids to otherwise white puddings and sauces, etc.

e Do not overload the tray, but see that the patient has all the accompaniments he may need—salt, pepper, butter, etc. Try to keep the size of the vessels containing these in proportion to the space available.

f Add flowers to the tray whenever possible. Tiny posies in small, low bases which cannot be knocked over easily are best, but single blooms, such as roses, may be tucked into the table napkin or laid beside the plate.

Foods should be cooked by the most easily digested methods
Steamed food is more easily digested than any other, but care must be taken that meals do not become too soft and insipid when the main part is cooked in this way. Greasy foods should be avoided at all costs and frying should not be considered as a method of cooking an invalid's food.

Avoid foods which have very strong flavours or smells
Much of the skill of preparing a patient's meals lies in the element of surprise. It is not advisable that he should be able to smell it while it is cooking and so be able to anticipate what he is to be offered. Moreover,

strong flavours which cling to the palate after the meal is eaten soon pall. On the other hand, lack of positive flavour is as unfortunate a mistake, and care must be taken in adding seasonings, essences, etc., during cooking.

Ensure that the patient is comfortable before serving meals
It is as important to see that an invalid's room and bed are comfortable before a meal as it is to ensure comfort at the family table. The patient should be able to sit in a position which is convenient for eating, with tray or bed-table within easy reach. There should be no draughts and the room should be warm but not stuffy or over-heated.

Remove the remains of the meal promptly
Never leave dirty plates or used trays in the sick-room. Not only does this look most unpleasant to patient and visitors, but smells may develop from cooling foods and in summer these scraps may attract flies. A drink may be left by the bed within reach of the patient, but it should be covered, and the dirty glass removed as soon as it is empty.

Convalescent Stage
During convalescence the principles of preparing invalids' meals should still be observed, but with the following modifications
    1 More substantial dishes should be introduced.
    2 Slightly larger portions may be served.
    3 More energy-giving foods will be required as activity is increased.
    4 A greater variety of methods of cooking may be used (e.g. occasional roasting, frying).
    5 Meals may be served at table.

Suitable Dishes for Invalids
Egg nog, beef tea, lemonade, barley water; junket, egg jelly, savoury custard; soufflés (cheese, sweet), fish pudding, baked fish, cheese pudding, steamed chop; honeycomb mould, apple snow, milk puddings, fruit fools.

VEGETARIAN MEALS

The term 'vegetarian' is used to describe a person who belongs to one of several groups; those who merely do not eat meat, those who will not eat anything which entails the taking of life, those who will eat only vegetable proteins (known as 'vegans') or those who obtain their complete proteins from dairy products only (known as 'lacto-vegetarians').

The reasons for becoming a vegetarian may be any of the following:

    a for moral reasons—as already described

    b for health reasons—there are a few people who cannot digest animal proteins and who are therefore medically advised to observe a vegetarian diet

    c for reasons of personal taste; to those people who dislike meat, a wholly vegetarian diet is the best one to ensure that they are adequately nourished.

Whatever the reason, the main concern of the cook should be that the vegetarian's diet is well balanced, and care must be taken in particular that the protein content is adequate.

Planning Vegetarian Meals

The absence of meat and fish means that the richest sources of complete protein are lacking. Therefore, to compensate for this deficiency, the best possible use must be made of eggs, milk and cheese. The value of vegetable protein must also be considered, bearing in mind that greater quantities of this incomplete protein is required than of complete protein.

Meat and fish have very distinctive flavours which stimulate the flow of digestive juices by increasing the appetite. In a vegetarian diet these flavours may be sadly missing and it is important to compensate for their loss as fully as possible. Foods with less pronounced flavours must be carefully blended with herbs, seasonings, essences and strong-flavoured vegetables to make them more attractive (e.g. onions cooked with cheese, vegetable soup flavoured with celery, lentil cutlets seasoned with parsley and mixed herbs, scrambled eggs cooked with cheese, boiled eggs served with curry sauce).

With two very interesting types of food missing from the diet, the remaining dishes must be cooked in as large a variety of ways as possible. Vegetables, for instance, should be cooked by as many different methods and served in as many combinations as possible, with the importance of colour-blending and texture-mixing always in mind. Plenty of salads made from raw and cooked vegetables and many different fruits and nuts should be included in the diet (e.g. raw shredded cabbage, raw grated carrots, diced cooked carrots, sliced or diced potatoes, etc.; sultanas, grapes, pineapple, apple, orange, chopped brazils, walnuts, or almonds, whole peanuts). These add greatly to the bulk of meals, supply mineral elements, water, vitamins, vegetable proteins, add freshness and colour to the general diet and, not least important, can look most attractive.

Larger portions of vegetables should be served to vegetarians than to those eating a normal diet, in order that vegetable protein may supplement the restricted animal proteins. Good use should be made of pulses, i.e. peas, beans, lentils.

Owing to the absence of meat in the diet, fat may be somewhat restricted. Vegetable fats and oils specially prepared for vegetarian cooking should be used in pastry and cake-making, for frying, etc. Butter and some margarine can also be eaten, of course, without violating any but the strictest vegetarian principles. Meat flavourings, too, may be replaced by savoury vegetable extracts in the preparation of sauces, gravies, sandwiches, etc.

Fruits and vegetables should be preserved when they are cheapest so that the extra supplies required do not affect the housekeeping bills too severely.

As far as possible the vegetarian's dishes should be modifications of those eaten by the rest of the family, to save extra preparation and expense for the housewife (e.g. pastry made for Cornish pasties for the family may also be used for cheese and onion pasties for the vegetarian, using some of the vegetables that have been prepared for the meat pasties).

Some Suitable Dishes for Vegetarians

Vegetable hot-pot, vegetable and cheese flan, lentil cutlets, cheese and onion pasties, cheese croquettes, cheese pudding, macaroni cheese, curried eggs, stuffed tomatoes, stuffed marrow, omelettes (cheese, mushroom, etc.), cauliflower cheese, savoury rice.

PACKED MEALS

Packed meals may be required a. by workers who are unable to obtain midday meals at their places of employment, b. by children who do not enjoy or cannot afford school meals, c. by travellers, d. for picnics.

The occasion for which it is required will make a considerable difference to the preparation of the meal. A fairly substantial but quite simple meal is usually provided for the worker who needs a daily packed lunch, as this will be supplemented by a cooked meal later in the day; schoolchildren need plenty of energy-giving foods and must eat well-balanced meals, but girls particularly very soon become slimming conscious; a packed meal to be eaten while travelling by train or coach must, of necessity, be such as can be very easily eaten; and both these meals must be light to carry. On the other hand, organized picnics, usually transported by car, may involve considerably more elaborate preparations and a greater variety of dishes.

General Rules for Preparation

Include the preparation of daily packed meals in that of the dishes made for the family meals, e.g. make several small pasties with different fillings while preparing the family pies; cook extra fruit to be set in jelly in tartlets; mash left-over fish with a little of the sauce served at the family meal to provide filling for hollowed-out rolls or pastry cases.

Balance the packed meal as carefully as the main meal. There is always a danger of including too great a proportion of carbohydrates. The day of the traditional sandwich is now almost over—to avoid using too much bread, 'open' or Danish 'sandwiches' are often used instead, with fillings laid on one slice of bread, but not covered. Any of the many crispbreads on the market are suitable for this purpose, and it should also be remembered that pastry cases can hold fillings quite as satisfactorily as slices of bread. Pastry adds crispness and flavour to the meal in a way that bread cannot.

Packed meals can very easily be too dry to be very palatable. Apart from sensible wrapping, the food itself should be moist— fillings should be soft and juicy (although care must be taken with foods like sliced tomato, which can quickly cause bread to become soggy) or combined with chopped lettuce, watercress or cucumber, to give crispness and freshness.

Remember the importance of small accompaniments to meals, such as seasonings and sugar. Portable cruets are easily obtainable and should be added to every picnic preparation.

Always supply some kind of drink, *adequately stoppered* if carried in a flask or bottle. Tea is best strained alone into a flask, with the sugar and milk carried separately.

Make the fullest possible use of the large variety of plastic equipment available for carrying food. It is light to carry, easy to clean, cheap and unbreakable, e.g. wide-necked flasks for soup, ice-cream or fruit; screw-top jars for fruit in jelly, butter and other soft mixtures; polythene bags for salads.

Pack all the parts of the meal in a container suitable for the occasion, be it work or play, e.g. small case, saddle-bag, picnic basket.

Suitable Dishes for Packed Meals
Soup, meat and vegetable pasties, cheese patties, sausage rolls, fish patties, stuffed eggs, fruit 'saucer' tarts, jam or fruit turnovers, fruit in jelly, ice-cream.

Sandwich or Pastry Fillings
Date and chopped nuts or apple, egg and tomato purée, sardine and chopped apple, cheese and watercress, grated cheese and salad cream.

FURTHER STUDY

THINGS TO DO

1 Choose a meal which you would enjoy if served as a school dinner and which is nutritionally sound. Prepare, cook and serve this meal for yourself and two friends.   (C.U.B.)

F

2 You are helping with a project on basic nutrition. Prepare, cook and serve a three-course balanced midday meal which will form part of the practical work. Include a dish rich in calcium and a cooked green vegetable. Serve a beverage. (C.U.B.)

3 Prepare, cook and serve a fork buffet supper suitable for a sixth-form party, to include both sweet and savoury dishes. Serve cold and hot drinks. (C.U.B.)

4 The kitchen is being redecorated and the cooker cannot be used until evening. Prepare a two-course midday meal which could be cooked the previous day and then served cold. In addition, make and cook a hot savoury dish for supper which would be served in the evening. (C.U.B.)

5 Your pen-friend from France is visiting you for the first time, and you are entertaining her and your school friend to an evening meal. Prepare, cook and serve three courses including at least two typically British dishes.

6 You and two friends have rented a seaside flatlet for a cheap holiday. You have to do all your own catering with the use of two boiling rings and a grill only. Prepare, cook and serve a main meal which is both economical and nutritious.

7 Prepare, cook and serve *four* dishes for an evening party in summer that you are giving for *three* friends. Include *one* pastry dish. Serve a cold beverage and coffee. (A.E.B.)

8 Prepare, cook and serve a three-course midday meal for *two* adults to include grapefruit and a main course using pastry. (A.E.B.)

9 You have invited a friend to spend the weekend with you and your parents.

a Prepare, cook and serve a light two-course lunch that could be served when your friend arrives. Cater for *two* persons.

b Prepare, cook and serve *two* different dishes that will help with the weekend catering. (A.E.B.)

10 Prepare, cook and serve:

a a well-balanced packed midday meal for two teenage boys to take to school. Display the packing materials and a list showing the cost of the meal.

b the main course and a cake for their high tea. (A.E.B.)

QUESTIONS TO ANSWER

1 What advice would you give to a friend who is going to be married about planning, preparing and serving meals? Assume that, as a career girl, she has had very little previous experience.

2 What points should be considered when preparing meals
a for a convalescent
b for a vegan

    c using 'left-over' foods
    d for an overweight teenager?
In each case give a suitable menu for an evening meal.   (A.E.B.)

    3 Plan the meals for a winter weekend for a family consisting of mother, father, teenage son, six-year-old daughter and completely healthy grandmother.

    4 What special adjustments to a normal diet have to be made when planning meals for
    a an overweight adolescent
    b an elderly widower?
Illustrate your answer by planning a day's menus for each person.

    5*a* Why is it important to have a good breakfast?
    b Plan a breakfast for each of the following:
        (*i*)   a family with two children under five years of age
        (*ii*) a family of three adults with a limited budget
        (*iii*) a family with two teenage sons.
    c How can a housewife ensure that breakfast can be quickly prepared and promptly served to all her family?   (A.E.B.)

    6 Why is protein an important part of the diet of old people and why is it often deficient? Suggest six simple dishes which would supply adequate protein for six consecutive days' main meals for two O.A.P.s. Explain why you have chosen each one.

    7 State the nutritional needs of teenagers. Plan midday meals for a week for a family including two schoolboys and a girl for whom these meals are the main ones of the day. Mention any other dish or drink to be taken during the rest of the day which is required to supplement the nutrients.

    8 As food prices rise, what steps could you suggest to be taken in order to prevent food bills from becoming unnecessarily high?

    9 What special care would you take in planning, cooking and serving meals for your mother when she is confined to bed after an operation?

    10 Explain what is meant by *a.* a strict vegetarian, *b.* a lacto-vegetarian. What are the problems associated with the provision of meals for vegetarians? How can an adequate diet be assured for lacto-vegetarians?   (C. & G.)

7
STOCK AND SOUPS

STOCK

Stock is the liquid in which bones, vegetables, scraps of meat, etc., have been simmered gently for a long time. It is used as a basis for savoury sauces and soups, improving the flavour and colour. When stock is used as a substitute for water the actual food value is not greatly increased but the small amount of soluble flavourings (known as *extractives*), mineral matter and protein which it does contain increases the flow of digestive juices and so assists the digestion of solid food eaten immediately afterwards.

Foods Suitable for Stock-making
Scraps of lean meat, raw or cooked.
Bones—meat or fish.
Giblets.
Root vegetables other than potatoes.
Bacon rinds.
The liquid in which vegetables, meat or fish have been cooked.

Foods Not Suitable for Stock-making
Green vegetables.
Fat meat or scraps of fat.
The liquid in which salted meat has been cooked.
Starchy foods or liquids thickened with starch.

Points to be Observed when Making Stock
1 The pan used should be strong and deep, with a well-fitting lid.

2 In order to extract as much flavour as possible from meat scraps, they should be cut into small pieces before cooking.

3 Vegetables should not be divided for cooking as they might then break down and cause the stock to become cloudy instead of clear.

4 There should be no fat floating in the stock when it is used and therefore care should be taken to remove all fatty layers from meat before putting it in the stock-pot. If there *is* any fat content the stock

should be allowed to cool so that the fat rises and solidifies on top of the rest of the liquid. It can then be easily removed as a solid layer.

5 Starchy foods should not be included because they cloud the liquid and, because of their poor keeping qualities, may cause the stock to become sour.

METHODS OF MAKING STOCK

Convenience Stock
Stock cubes of various flavours are available which only require the addition of hot water to produce 'instant' stock.

Brown Stock
1 Remove fat (or bones) and cut meat into small pieces.
2 Remove marrow from bones.
3 Fry the meat in a little hot dripping until quite brown.
4 Strain off all surplus fat.
5 Leave meat and bones soaking in cold liquid (1 litre water to each $\frac{1}{2}$ kilo of meat) to soften the fibres.
6 Bring the liquid slowly to the boil and skim off any scum which may form.
7 Add seasoning and bouquet garni; simmer for one hour.
8 Add vegetables and continue to simmer for 4 to 5 hours.
9 Strain off the liquid and leave to stand and cool.
10 Remove any solidified fat from the liquid.

White Stock
Use pale meats (veal, chicken scraps, etc.) and do not fry, but otherwise proceed as for other stocks.

Fish Stock
1 Use fish scraps, heads, bones and trimmings.
2 Prepare as for white stock but do not simmer for more than 45 minutes. Longer cooking time may cause the stock to taste bitter.

Vegetable Stock
Proceed as for white stock but omit meat.

The Care of the Stock-pot (*If a constant supply of stock is required*)
1 The pan must be kept perfectly clean and, if enamelled, must not be chipped.
2 Only suitable ingredients should be used.
3 Solid ingredients should be strained off as soon as the stock is prepared in order that the stock may remain clear.
4 The lid should be kept tightly in position to prevent evaporation and contamination from the air.

5 The stock should be inspected daily for signs of mould or souring. Daily boiling-up should prevent any kind of deterioration providing that the correct ingredients are used and scrupulous cleanliness observed.

SOUPS

The food value of a soup depends upon the value of its chief ingredient, i.e. protein in meat soups (e.g. kidney), vegetable protein in pulse soups (e.g. lentil), starch in thickened soups (e.g. potato). It must be remembered, however, that the proportion of solid ingredients to liquid is very low and that therefore the amount of actual nutrient in a portion of soup is very small.

The aim of soup-making is to draw out into the liquid the maximum amount of flavour and food value from the solid ingredients. Flavour is of great importance because it stimulates the flow of gastric juices and facilitates digestion. This is why soup is such an excellent food for people who are exceptionally tired or shocked—conditions in which normal digestion is impaired. It also accounts for the practice of serving soup as the first course of a meal—to encourage the flow of digestive juices to deal with subsequent courses.

Soups may be stored for 2 to 3 days providing that they are kept in a cool place or a refrigerator, and it is usually more economical to make a large quantity at one time and store the surplus than to prepare several small quantities. If stored in a deep-freeze cabinet they may be kept for up to four months.

For packed meals, soups may conveniently be carried in thermos flasks and so form a hot item in what would otherwise be a cold meal.

Really nourishing soups (i.e. those made with good-quality ingredients and with cream or beaten egg added at the last moment) are easily digested and attractive dishes for invalids or those suffering from loss of appetite.

A good glaze can be made from surplus stock by boiling it rapidly until it thickens to a treacle-like fluid. Impurities must be skimmed from the top of the liquid as it thickens and the hot liquid poured into a warmed glass jar, preferably with a screw-top. It can then be used as required to finish galantines, meat loaves, etc., or, in an emergency, re-diluted to form stock.

Soups are classified according to their ingredients and methods of preparation:

Broths
Small pieces of meat and vegetables served in seasoned liquid. For invalids' diets the meat and vegetables may be strained off before serving.

The liquid is thickened by the addition of a cereal ingredient such as rice or pearl barley.

Varieties of broths   Scotch, chicken, mutton, rabbit, sheep's head, veal.

Clear Soups or Consommés

This type of soup is quite distinctive and requires special treatment to clear the liquid completely before special garnishes (e.g. finely shredded carrot or celery, diced vegetables, etc.) are added. It consists of adding egg white and crushed egg shell to the other ingredients during preparation and straining the soup through a cloth before serving. The egg shell and coagulated egg white act as additional filters.

Varieties of consommés (named after their garnishes—the basic recipe is the same for all)   à la jardinière, à la royale, à la Julienne.

Thickened or Cream Soups

These soups have no thickening ingredient in their recipes but the liquid is thickened before serving by the addition of starchy mixtures such as flour, cornflour or sago, or by gently stirring in a beaten egg mixed with cream.

Varieties of thickened soups   cream of tomato, celery, kidney, potage à la bonne femme.

Purées

The basic ingredients of the soup are sufficient to thicken it and the texture is refined by passing the mixture through a sieve before serving. If necessary a small amount of flour or other starchy ingredient may be blended into the liquid after sieving for further thickening.

Varieties of purées   lentil, pea, potato, kidney, celery, tomato, ox-tail (these last require additional starchy thickening).

Common Faults and Remedies

1 Poor flavour is prevented by
   a using well flavoured stock
   b careful seasoning
   c cooking slowly
   d dividing the ingredients finely.
2 Poor consistency is prevented by
   a cooking slowly
   b using correct proportions of solids to liquid
   c thorough sieving of purées
   d the addition of some starchy thickening.
3 Greasy appearance is prevented by
   a making sure that stock has no fat layer on top
   b thorough sauté-ing of vegetables so that they absorb fat
   c thorough skimming.

4 Curdling is prevented by

a heating milk separately before adding to an acid soup, e.g. tomato

b cooling the soup before adding cream or egg

c re-heating soup very gently after the addition of cream or egg.

Serving Soups

1 Serve either *a*. iced or *b*. *very* hot.

2 *a*. Chill or *b*. heat plates or bowls before pouring in the liquid.

3 Serve finely-grated hard cheese for sprinkling over the surface of unthickened soups.

4 Serve croûtons (squares or cubes of toasted or deep-fried bread) as an accompaniment to cream soups rather than rolls or slices of bread.

FURTHER STUDY

THINGS TO DO

1 Find out what the Victorian stock-pot looked like. Find examples of and draw pictures of a soup tureen, a soup ladle, soup spoons, soup plates, individual soup cups and covered bowls.

2 Find as many names of soups as you can. Classify them and note the chief ingredients.

3 Soups may be home-made *or* purchased in tins *or* bought in packets ready for quick and easy preparation. Using tomato soup as an example, prepare:

a a portion of home-made soup equal in bulk to *b*.

b a tin of tomato soup

c the same quantity of 'packet' soup.

Compare

a the cost of each amount and calculate the cost of one helping

b the time involved in the preparation of each

c the fuel required for the preparation of each

d the flavour, colour and texture of each.

QUESTIONS TO ANSWER

1 Write out the following statements, and complete them, using only the words in the right-hand column to fill in the blanks.

a The liquid in which bones, vegetables and fish or meat scraps have been cooked is called	cream
	bones
b This is a better basis for soups than water because of the .... it contains.	croûtons

c When poultry is being roasted the
.... make a good basic liquid for gravy.

d Vegetables which are not suitable for
stock-making but are good ingredients for a thick
soup are ....

e One type of food not suitable for stock-
making is ....

f Soups which are thickened by the main
ingredient having been passed through a sieve are
called ....

g Clear soups which are called after their
garnish are ....

h The nutritive value of soups may be
improved by the addition of ....

i When .... are used for stock-making,
all fat and marrow should be removed first.

j Soups should be accompanied by ....
when served.

green
vegetables

stock

extractives

potatoes

giblets

purées

consommés

2a Describe in detail the preparation of stock from uncooked
bones, and give examples of its use.

b How would you keep stock fresh?

c What is the nutrive value of bone stock? (C.U.B.)

3a How may stock be prepared quickly and easily for immediate
use?

b Select two quite different types of soup and show how their
nutritive value depends on the ingredients used. Give instructions for
making either a purée or a broth. (C.U.B.)

4 Of what value is soup in the diet? Describe in detail how you
would make a. a white purée soup, b. a thickened brown soup.

5 What are the reasons for using stock instead of water in the
preparation of sauces and soups? Describe a. a traditional, b. an up-to-
date method of preparing a stock and give directions for its use in a
particular soup recipe.

6 Why is soup a useful item in the diet? Compare the food values
of clear soups, broths and thickened soups. How can the nutritive
value of a soup be increased?

8

THE PRESERVATION OF FOODS

Much of the variety we enjoy in our diet is due to the fact that foods can be preserved when they are available and used when they are actually out of season. So we may eat summer fruits and vegetables all through the year and reserves of all types of foods may be built up for emergencies.

Foods go bad because they contain micro-organisms which multiply to a dangerous extent, and because they are 'attacked from the air' by moulds and yeasts. The enzymes which cause normal ripening, moreover, will cause unpleasant deterioration in time.

Most 'bad' food can be detected by its unpleasant smell but this is not always so and it is wise never to take risks by eating stale food, however harmless it looks.

The principle of preserving food is the removal of conditions which allow the continued action of ripening enzymes and the growth of bacteria and moulds by

    a removing moisture—i.e. dehydrating
    b reducing temperature—i.e. freezing
    c excluding air ⎫
    d sterilizing   ⎬—e.g. bottling, canning
    e adding substances which prevent the action of organisms, such as vinegar, salt, sugar—e.g. pickling, jamming.

Dehydrating
From the earliest days the heat of the sun has been used to preserve such items as meat and fruit. Both of these, vegetables, milk, etc., can be successfully deprived of their water content by mechanical means, and this lack of moisture prevents the action of bacteria and the growth of moulds and yeasts.
Suitable foods: fruits, potatoes, pulses, milk, fish, meat.

Freezing
This is now one of the most widely used means of preservation and has been developed into a most successful process of retarding bacterial and

enzyme activity by lowering the temperature. In the early days of experimenting the texture of the foods was spoilt by the formation of large ice crystals within them. This disadvantage has been overcome by speeding up the process of freezing and, when defrosted, frozen goods are hardly distinguishable from fresh foods.

A domestic deep-freeze cabinet, one of the latest additions to a housewife's equipment, can be used for actually freezing large supplies of home-grown produce as well as for storing ready-frozen foods for long periods (see p. 165).

Suitable foods: large varieties of fruit, vegetables, fish, meat, prepared sweet and savoury dishes.

Accelerated Freeze-drying (*known as A.F.D.*)
This is a method of preserving such foods as peas and beans by a combination of quick-freezing and dehydration. It is not necessary to store these in a deep-freeze cabinet.

Canning
The food is cooked to destroy the bacteria and sealed to prevent contamination from the atmosphere.

So long as the tin remains airtight the contents will remain absolutely fresh. Any flaw in the tin will allow the entrance of air and pollution, and poisonous substances may develop, accompanied by the production of gas. *Never* use food from a tin which is rusty, badly dented or swollen.

Suitable foods: large varieties of fruit, vegetables, meat, fish, soups, etc.; milk, syrup, etc.

Bottling
The aim in bottling foods is to heat the food sufficiently to destroy the harmful micro-organisms and to seal it immediately to prevent contamination from the air.

Suitable foods: fruit, vegetables.

Pickles, Chutneys and Sauces
The fruits and vegetables are sterilized (in most cases) by boiling and then preserved from air pollution by increasing their acidity—i.e. by adding vinegar and spices.

JAM, JELLY AND MARMALADE MAKING

The fruit is sterilized by being heated to boiling-point for some time, and the growth of yeast is prevented by providing a high concentration of sugar.

General Rules for Jam Making

1 Carry out the preparation of preserves when supplies of the foods concerned are most plentiful and therefore at their cheapest.

2 Foods to be preserved should be in as nearly perfect condition as possible. No over-ripe fruit should be included.

3 All jars and bottles should be thoroughly cleansed and if possible sterilized before use. A quick and easy method of doing this is to place the open end of the jar over the spout of a steaming kettle.

4 Jars should be labelled with the name of their contents and the date on which they were prepared. This assists the housewife in deciding which preserves should be used first.

5 Preserves should be stored in a dry, cool place and inspected periodically for any signs of deterioration. If mould or 'working' is visible the jars should be used immediately. Usually a thin coating of mould can easily be removed from jams before the rest is affected. If the deterioration is at all extensive, however, the entire contents of the jar should be discarded rather than risks of food-poisoning taken.

Common Faults and Their Causes

Note   All recipe books give a good selection of methods of jam, jelly and pickle making.

Jam

Jam does not set: insufficient pectin in the fruit. Jam should be reboiled with the addition of 2 tbsps. lemon juice to every 2 kg fruit.

Fruit rises to the top: jam has been placed in jars while still too hot.

Jam crystallizes (i.e. becomes sugary): too little acid in the fruit. Lemon juice should be added when the next batch of similar fruit is used.

Mould appears on the surface:

    a moisture has formed between the outer cover and that immediately above the jam (usually because cover is not airtight)

    b jam has been covered while still warm

    c jam has been stored in a damp place.

Scum streaks are visible in the jam: inefficient skimming during cooking, and the stirring-in of the scum formed. A knob of butter stirred in after the jam is cooked will help to disperse the scum, but a thick layer should be skimmed off after boiling.

Jelly

Jelly is not clear:

    a jelly-bag not thoroughly clean

    b jelly squeezed through the bag instead of being allowed to drip through

    c jelly boiled too rapidly and so filled with air bubbles.

Jelly does not set: insufficient pectin—see Jam.

Jelly does not set in large jars but will do so in small ones: due to length of time taken to cool in jars. Jelly must be allowed to set quickly and should therefore be poured into small jars only (never larger than 500 g).

Marmalade
Marmalade does not set:
    a insufficient boiling
    b lack of pectin.
Peel rises, leaving clear jelly below: see Jam.
Flavour is bitter: pith was included when the peel was cut up.

HOME FREEZING

The domestic deep-freezing cabinet or chest is becoming a familiar item of household equipment, particularly in country districts because
    a it can reduce the need for shopping to a minimum
    b full advantage can be taken of the surplus produce of gardens or of seasonal gluts
    c meat may be bought as a portion of or as a whole carcass, making the cost proportionally cheaper
    d 'instant' meals may be stored for emergencies
    e dishes made in advance or in bulk may be safely stored.
There are certain disadvantages, namely
    a the substantial initial cost of the equipment
    b the cost of power used to run the machine
    c the cost of necessary packaging.
Micro-organisms are not killed by freezing, but below $-21°C$ growth is not possible. Enzyme activity is checked only at extremely low temperatures so vegetables and some fruits, e.g. apples, are scalded (or blanched) before freezing in order to render the enzymes inactive.

CHOICE OF FREEZER

    1 The chest type has a lid opening from the top and, because cold air falls, this type holds it more effectively than the cupboard type.
    2 The cupboard type takes less floor space and it is easier to pack and unpack than the chest. Cold air can be lost, however, each time the door is opened.
    3 Small free-standing models can be obtained for use in flats or for small families, which fit well on top of a refrigerator or a normal working surface.

Choice of Foods for Freezing
These should be
    a as fresh as possible
    b of as good quality as possible.

Preparation for Freezing

Vegetables   Scald (blanch) to

    a inactivate the enzymes

    b reduce by 80–90 per cent micro-organisms present

    c improve the flavour of green vegetables

    d remove trapped air.

Blanching time varies from 1 to 6 minutes according to the type (the more solid the vegetable, the longer the time). They should be cooled immediately in ice-cold water.

Fruits   Blanch apples. Remove skins and stems, and slice or halve. Remove any pulpy items of soft fruits. Wash, if necessary, and drain thoroughly. Pack in syrup or with/without sugar.

Meat   Trim and pack in conveniently sized portions. Chops/steak: place two thicknesses of paper or plastic between every two chops or steaks for easy separation.

Fish   Clean, dip in brine and wrap in polythene.

Unsuitable foods for freezing: boiled whole potatoes; bottled cream (unless whipped with sugar); salad vegetables normally eaten raw; mayonnaise; hard-boiled egg; desserts containing custard/cream; pears; bananas; whole onions; marrows; whole eggs (these can be separated for freezing).

Packaging Materials

Efficient packaging is necessary

    a to prevent food drying out

    b to keep food in conveniently sized portions.

Containers should be

    a grease and oil resistant

    b waterproof

    c strong

    d easy to handle

    e odourless, tasteless and harmless.

Types of containers

    a for foods which hold their shape: aluminium foil; polythene; special films; waxed paper and cellophane (for short-term use).

    b for foods which do not hold their shape: flat-topped, rigid, rectangular containers are better than round ones because they stack well, do not waste storage space and do not bulge like non-rigid containers, e.g. plastic 'boxes' with screw or push-on lids; bottling jars (which can be broken and are wasteful in space); tins with tight-fitting lids (which, unless the lid is sunken, should be sealed with sticky tape); ice-cube trays (for initial freezing of soups and sauces which, when solid, can be transferred to normal wrappings); wax cartons (which can be unhygienic); ovenproof glass (attractive, but wasteful in storage space).

Seals are necessary to prevent the entrance of water and water-vapour, e.g. Polytape, Scotch tape, pliable plastic strips or fibre-covered wire for small polythene bags.

Labels are necessary to show
    a the type of food inside
    b the quantity of food
    c the date when it was frozen.

They may be
    a stuck to the outside of opaque containers
    b placed inside transparent containers
    c written on rigid containers with a wax (chinagraph) pencil
    d fixed with Polytape.

Packing the Freezing Chamber

    a Do not overload the chamber.
    b Make sure that there is good air circulation.
    c Try not to place new packages too close to those already frozen.
    d Do not freeze too much at the one time. It is quicker and more efficient to freeze about 10 per cent of the capacity at one time.

Use
    a Use items in rotation according to date of freezing.
    b Arrange a six-monthly 'turnover'.
    c Do not refreeze any items unless some ice-crystals are still present. Re-date the label before returning the package to the freezer.
    d Vegetables: cook while still frozen.
    Fruit: thaw gradually, up to six hours at refrigerator temperature, and two at room temperature if necessary to thaw completely. Thaw fruits till they separate for tarts and pies. Do not thaw for sauces, jams and preserves. Serve with a few ice-crystals remaining for cold desserts (e.g. raspberries).
    Meat and Poultry: thaw thoroughly (up to 8 hours) before use.
    e Do not leave the door of a cabinet open for any longer than necessary. Cold air is heavier than that at room temperature and will 'fall out' if the door is open for long.
    f Defrost freezers regularly, cupboards two or three times a year and chests once or twice yearly.

Note It is rarely necessary to discard food due to a breakdown of power. Providing the door is not opened, the contents will remain in perfect condition for at least six hours. If an added safeguard is required, it is possible to take out an insurance against loss.

FURTHER STUDY

THINGS TO DO

1 Prepare a quantity of broth ($\frac{1}{2}$ litre) and divide it into eight equal portions:
  a deep-freeze one portion
  b place one on a refrigerator shelf, covered, and one uncovered
  c leave one in open air at room temperature
  d boil one rapidly for five minutes and leave at room temperature, uncovered
  e repeat *c*. and *d*., but cover the samples
  f leave one uncovered in a warm, damp atmosphere.
Compare the appearance and smell of *b*., *c*., *d*., *e*. and *f*. daily. (Do not taste after second day.)
  Notice the length of time required in each case for mould to form. After one week thaw *a*. and compare it with *b*., *c*., *d*., *e*. and *f*. Explain the results you observe.

2 Find recipes for three different kinds of chutney, three kinds of pickles, two jams made from soft fruit and two from stone fruit, two jellies and two marmalades.
  List in detail
  a the steps taken to prepare each type of preserve
  b how you would test the pectin quality in each fruit
  c how you would test the setting quality of each jam and jelly as it was being prepared
  d the scientific principles involved in each.

3 Find out what you can about the following: Appert; Birdseye; commercial gas storage; clostridium welchii; salmonella; botulism; staphylococci; streptococci; fermentation.

4 Look into the history of the preservation of foods and find as many interesting facts as you can about conserves, spices, herbs, wines and beers.

5 Cost the preparation of one kilogram of jam and compare it with that of three different proprietary brands of the same variety.

QUESTIONS TO ANSWER

1 Write out the following statements, and complete them, using only the words in the right-hand column to fill in the blanks.

  a Preservation is the prevention or retarding of the natural .... of foods.   curing

  b Foods contain living .... which bring about changes (e.g. ripening) within the food, which can continue, causing it to become unpleasant and dangerous.   dehydration

                                                                                              decomposition

c From outside the food can be attacked by .... which feed upon it and multiply.

d If the food temperature is raised sufficiently to destroy harmful micro-organisms it has been ......

e The oldest form of preservation is ...., whereby the moisture necessary for organic growth is removed.

f The use of salt as a preservative is most well known in the production of bacon; the .... produced prevents the growth of a number of harmful organisms.

g The process described in *f.* is known as ....

h .... will inhibit the growth of bacteria and the activity of enzymes but will not destroy either.

i Jam is able to set when fruit and sugar are boiled together due to the presence of ....

j The success of bottling as a method of preservation is due partly to sterilization and partly to the exclusion of ....

refrigeration

enzymes

pectin

bacteria

air

acidity

sterilized

2 What steps would you take to deal with a glut of the following produce from your garden:

a cooking apples
b gooseberries
c tomatoes?

Describe briefly the scientific principles underlying the methods of preservation you choose.

3 What are the most common faults to be found in home-made blackcurrant jam, strawberry jam, red-currant jelly? How would you prepare *one* of these preserves to achieve good results?

4 A country housewife may find shopping very difficult during hard winters. Suggest ways in which she could prepare in advance to feed her family adequately.

5 How are the principles of preservation applied to the production of cheese, wines and yoghurt?

6 What do you understand by 'convenience foods'? Give as many examples as possible and indicate when these are better 'buys' than their fresh equivalents.

9

RAISING AGENTS

A raising agent is a substance introduced into flour mixtures by mechanical or chemical means, providing a gas which expands on heating. The flour contains gluten which stretches and holds the mixture round the rising gas bubbles as it sets.

Air Introduced by Mechanical Means
Air is a mixture of gases and, like all gases, expands on heating. Its raising action is sufficient to make mixtures such as batters, soufflés, meringues, sponges and pastries light and porous.

It can be incorporated into mixtures by
1 Mixing it in with the ingredients:
a Passing dry ingredients through a sieve, thus collecting air among the particles as they fall from the sieve into the bowl.
b Creaming fat and sugar, and so beating in air during the process and making the mixture light and fluffy.
c Whisking together eggs and sugar, making a frothy mixture.
2 Trapping it in a liquid:
Eggs, particularly the whites, have the power to hold large quantities of air, and can be beaten from a viscous liquid into a stiff, frothy foam. Water has no power of holding air bubbles (unless these are introduced under pressure, as in soda water), and milk can only do so for a short time. However, both these liquids will give off steam when heated and this is how batters become risen and light upon cooking.
3 Rolling and folding dough:
In the preparation of rough puff and flaky pastries air is sandwiched between layers of paste.
Note Care must be taken *not* to overbeat or over-roll mixtures. Air bubbles carefully incorporated can then be burst and their value lost.

Gas Introduced by the Chemical Action of Baking Powder
Baking powder is a fine white powder composed of
    a bicarbonate of soda ⎫
    b food acid   ⎬ the important chemicals

c a starchy 'filler' mixed with the other two substances in order to keep them dry and finely distributed (this is often rice flour).

a Bicarbonate of soda A fine white powder which, when heated, breaks down into a simpler soda (which is what we know as 'washing soda'), giving off a gas called *carbon dioxide*. Carbon dioxide is a colourless, flavourless gas, therefore suitable for raising mixtures.

Unfortunately, when bicarbonate of soda (or sodium bicarbonate) is heated alone, only 50 per cent of the carbon dioxide it can produce is liberated, and the washing soda which is left has an unpleasant taste. It may also cause yellow stains in the mixture.

For a satisfactory, efficient raising agent, therefore, another chemical (an acid) is required. This should combine with the sodium bicarbonate (an alkali) to liberate all the available carbon dioxide and form a salt which is tasteless, non-poisonous and produces no discoloration. The action should be moderately slow and as even as possible, but the whole substance must be cheap.

The substance which will fulfil all these requirements most satisfactorily for domestic use is:

b Cream of tartar This is the food acid used in home-made baking powder mixture and is another fine white powder, slightly soluble in cold water but very soluble in hot. Because of this its reaction in baking powder takes place only slowly when cold but quickly when heated.

When mixed with sodium bicarbonate the following action takes place:

$$\text{Bicarbonate of soda} + \text{Cream of tartar} \rightarrow \text{Carbon dioxide} + \text{Rochelle salt} \left(\begin{array}{l} \text{colourless and} \\ \text{flavourless salt} \end{array} \right)$$

Proportions of acid to alkali

An acid can only combine with a certain stated amount of alkali, and vice versa. Therefore care must be taken that the correct amounts of cream of tartar and bicarbonate of soda are combined.

a If too much cream of tartar is used in proportion to bicarbonate of soda the excess remains unchanged in the mixture and imparts a sour, unpleasant flavour.

b If too much bicarbonate of soda is used in proportion to cream of tartar the excess decomposes into washing soda, causing an unpleasant taste and yellowish stains in the mixture.

It has been scientifically calculated that the proportions required are two parts of cream of tartar to one of bicarbonate of soda, and these are the proportions used in commercially-produced baking powders.

The Use of Baking Powder and its Components

1 Keep in dry place.
2 Store in tightly closed tin.

(The action of baking powder begins, however slowly, as soon as it becomes damp. When this happens carbon dioxide is liberated and the baking powder loses its 'strength'.)

3 It is advisable not to add liquids to mixtures containing baking powder until it is convenient to complete the mixing and cooking. However, present-day baking powders have a 'delayed action' and this is not so vital a matter as it used to be.

4 When the constituents are used separately make sure that they are used in the correct proportions.

5 Use bicarbonate of soda alone in mixtures in which the flavour and discoloration of washing soda is disguised, i.e. in strongly-flavoured dark mixtures such as gingerbreads, parkins and spiced bread.

Self-raising Flour
This contains ingredients similar to those of baking powder but it is obvious that the proportion of these to that of the flour is fixed and cannot be calculated. (The amount may be too much for rich cakes and too little for scones, for instance.) For really successful cooking it is always advisable to use plain flour with the correct proportions of raising agent added during the mixing.

Other Suitable Acids
Sodium bicarbonate will give off carbon dioxide when mixed with acids other than cream of tartar. Those most suitable for cookery are *Tartaric acid* (of which cream of tartar is the salt). This is often used in large-scale or advanced cookery when a quicker-than-normal action is required.

Lemon juice ⎫
Vinegar ⎬ Although results can be quite satisfactory when these acids are used, their acidity cannot really be guaranteed and the
Sour milk ⎭ amounts required cannot be accurately calculated.

Gas Introduced by the Growth of Yeast
Yeast is a living plant which has the appearance of a fawn-coloured, rather crumbly paste with a very characteristic smell. In favourable circumstances the yeast cells grow and multiply, producing carbon dioxide as they do so.

For cooking purposes special 'strains' of yeast are bred which are 'first cousins' to brewers' and distillers' yeast. It may be purchased as a compressed block or in small tins or packets after drying.

The essential conditions for growth are

a warmth: provided by warm working conditions, warm hands for kneading, warm liquid for mixing.

b food: provided by the sugar produced by the action of yeast enzymes on flour (starch). (A little sugar is added to the flour in order to start this action.)

c liquid: provided by the warm water or milk used in preparing the dough.
(For proof of the effects of the provision of each of these essentials see 'Things to Do' on p. 174.

These experiments will also show that although cold retards the growth of yeast it will not prevent it from growing when the correct conditions are substituted; and that great heat will stop its growth altogether.)

Because of these characteristics the following rules should be observed when using yeast

1 Keep yeast cool during storing.

2 Keep liquid used for mixing at lukewarm temperature.

3 Avoid draughts while preparing yeast mixtures.

4 Place yeast mixtures in a warm place to prove, i.e. for gas bubbles to form.

5 Place prepared yeast mixtures in a hot oven at first to prevent further expansion.
(For the use of yeast in bread and similar mixtures, the methods of creaming and of kneading, and the use of proving, see pp. 199–201.)

FURTHER STUDY

THINGS TO DO

1 To show the expansion of air on heating:
Blow up a rubber balloon as full as possible and tie it to prevent the air from escaping. Put it in a warm place (in front of the fire or over a stove). The balloon will shortly burst owing to the expansion of the air causing too great a strain on the balloon fabric.

2 To show that some liquids can 'hold' air bubbles, while others cannot:
Using a rotary whisk, beat air into *a*. a basin of water, *b*. a basin of milk, *c*. a whole egg, *d*. an egg white.

Notice that

a The bubbles on the surface of the water will very quickly break, leaving the water quite 'flat'.

b The milk will remain frothy for a short time but the bubbles will gradually burst and the milk return to its former consistency. The bubbles are smaller than in the water, however, and are closer together.

c The egg will remain full of small bubbles for a considerable time.

d The egg-white will quickly become stiff and frothy and will remain so unless over-beaten, when it will revert to a liquid state. Once this has happened it is almost impossible to re-aerate the liquid.

3 To show the effect of the addition of an acid to sodium bicarbonate:

a Add 2 tbsps. cold water to ½ level tsp. of sodium bicarbonate in a test-tube.

b Add 2 tbsps. hot water to the same amount of sodium bicarbonate in a second tube.

c Add ½ level tsp. of bicarbonate of soda to 1 level tsp. cream of tartar and mix with 2 tbsps. cold water in a third tube.

d As above, but add hot water.

Compare the amount of effervescence in each tube after 5 minutes—this is the effect of the gas escaping from the mixtures. Which is the most satisfactory mixture for providing a raising gas?

4 To demonstrate that the gas given off is carbon dioxide:

a Set up the following apparatus and observe the change in the limewater when the water is allowed to come into contact with the sodium bicarbonate and cream of tartar mixture.

HOT WATER

LIMEWATER

SODIUM BICARB. + CREAM OF TARTAR

b Repeat the above experiment, replacing the sodium bicarbonate and cream of tartar mixture with sodium bicarbonate alone, and the hot water with sour milk. Heat the mixture gently after the liquid and soda have been mixed.

c Repeat *b*., substituting lemon juice for sour milk.

5 To demonstrate the conditions necessary for the effective growth of yeast:

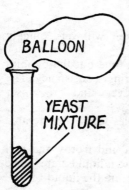

BALLOON

YEAST MIXTURE

Prepare a series of test tubes of equal size, each fitted with a small rubber balloon as shown, and containing mixtures as described below:

a Yeast creamed with sugar. (*Note* Sugar is used instead of flour so that the action is quicker.)

b Yeast creamed without sugar and with cold water added.

c As *a*. but with cold water added.

d As *a*. but with warm water added.

e As *c*. and stood in a beaker of ice.

f As *a*. with boiling water added. Keep mixture boiling for 5 minutes.

Leave each mixture for 1 hour and compare the size of the balloons.

Remove *e*. from the ice and warm gently. Observe the size of the balloon after 1 hour.

Note Equal quantities of each substance (yeast, sugar, water) must be used in each case.

6 To demonstrate that the gas given off by the growth of yeast is carbon dioxide:

Repeat experiment 4, substituting a mixture of creamed yeast and sugar and warm water for the sodium bicarbonate mixture.

7 Make a paste of flour and water, sufficiently thick to form a coherent mass. Tie it into a piece of muslin and wash it thoroughly under a running tap. Continue rubbing it out until the water is clear of suspended starch. Undo the muslin and examine the sticky, elastic substance which remains. What is it?

8 Find the names of the yeast enzymes which break down the flour starch and produce carbon dioxide and alcohol.

QUESTIONS TO ANSWER

1 Write out the following statements, and complete them, using only the words in the right-hand column to fill in the blanks.

a Starch mixtures become light and spongy in texture owing to the .... of steam and gas introduced into the mixtures by the ingredients.	yeast
b As the gases rise, the starchy mixtures thicken and set owing to the .... of the starch.	sodium bicarbonate
c They remain risen and firm because the .... of the flour sets around the gas bubbles.	warmth
d The liquids in mixtures produce .... when heated and this expands thus assisting the raising of the mixture.	carbon dioxide
e The gas produced by both chemical and natural raising agents is	gelatinization
f In chemical raising agents this gas comes from the combination of .... and an acid.	enzymes
g It is also produced when the action of the raising agent, ..., breaks down starch.	expansion
h This breaking-down is brought about by the activity of ...... in favourable conditions.	gluten
i These conditions are the presence of food, of liquid and of	steam
j The beery smell of newly baked bread comes from the production of .... as starch is broken down into glucose.	alcohol

10

STARCH MIXTURES
(*Basic recipes will be found on p. 206*)

Most people are familiar with the process of thickening a liquid by adding it to a starchy substance and heating it. It used to be a common item of routine to make laundry starch with which to stiffen cotton and linen goods; the stiffer the result required the higher the proportion of starch to water became. The fabric was immersed in the gelatinized mixture and this was 'set' by the heat of the iron. Nowadays the same basic method is used to make quickly produced white sauce (using cornflour) and custard sauce (using coloured, flavoured cornflour). Again, the higher the proportion of starch to liquid (cornflour to milk) used, the stiffer the mixture will be and the more firmly it will set on cooling (e.g. blancmange).

This principle can be applied to all starch mixtures made in cookery, starch being used in the form of flour, e.g.

a flour and liquid give us coating batters and, with the addition of flavourings, sauces. Richer batters are produced by replacing some of the liquid with eggs, and smoother sauces by adding fat.

b flour, less liquid and some 'shortening' (i.e. fat which gives the mixture a granular instead of a dense texture; see p. 178) produce crisp, solid masses, e.g. short crust pastry, biscuits.

c flour, shortening, some liquid and a raising agent give light, porous, spongy mixtures such as are required for cakes, puddings, etc.

THE CHOICE OF INGREDIENTS

FLOUR

In this country, flour is made by 'milling' the grains of wheat. Each grain consists of endosperm (84 per cent), germ (2 per cent) and bran (14 per cent). Milling is the breaking down of these grains into a fine powder suitable for cooking.

A wheat grain can be compared to a tiny grooved egg, wrapped in several layers of brown paper, glued together—these represent the husk. The grains pass between iron rollers to shear them open and expose the floury contents. The broken grains are then sifted to remove the bran particles and this process is repeated again and again until the final sifting passes the flour through a silk or nylon mesh.

Whole wheat or *wheat meal* flour contains up to 100 per cent of the grain and is easily recognizable by its coarse texture and brownish colour.

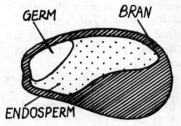

White flour, which is in much more common use, contains about 72 per cent of the wheat grain, mainly the endosperm. The bran and wheat germ as well as impurities are separated from the grain by passing it through rollers, and only the endosperm is ground. This means that there is some loss of iron and part of the Vitamin B complex (thiamine and nicotinic acid). Government Regulations insist that white flours are 'fortified' by addition of these nutrients. Calcium carbonate must also be added to all except wholemeal and self-raising flour (see p. 172). These regulations are reviewed from time to time and may well be changed.

Cornflour is made from maize and can only be used for mixtures which are not required to rise.

Flours vary in composition. As far as its use in cooking is concerned its most important constituent is a protein known as *gluten*. It is an elastic substance which, when mixed with liquid, will stretch and hold expanding gas bubbles. (See p. 175 for experiment to show presence of gluten in flour.) So the whole success of a 'raised' flour mixture depends upon the efficiency of the gluten in the flour. Flours are graded according to the quality of the gluten they contain:

Strong flours, such as Canadian spring wheat flour, contain good-quality gluten in slightly higher than average proportions. These flours are excellent for bread-making.

Medium flours are usually blends of strong and weak ones and are satisfactory for general purposes.

Weak flours, such as English winter wheat, contain gluten of a poorer quality and lower proportion and are suitable for very light spongy mixtures and pastries.

'Soft' flours are those with weak gluten.

'Hard' flours are those with strong gluten.

The finer the flour the lighter its appearance and the softer is its gluten. Cornflour, which is particularly smooth and fine, has no gluten at all and is sometimes used in shortbreads to reduce the proportion of gluten in the rest of the flour and so give a 'shorter' result. The degree of elasticity of gluten is improved by acidity. Where it is very important that the gluten should be able to hold gas bubbles in 'blown up' mixtures, e.g. puff and flaky pastries, lemon juice is added to the mixing liquid.

Although commercial bakers recognize and appreciate the differences between strong and weak flours and their suitability for various mixtures, the ordinary housewife often has no idea of the quality of the flour which she is buying. From among the many branded flours on the market it is usually by a process of trial and error that she is able to sort out the one which is 'good for sponges' or 'makes nice pastry'. However, some firms now produce 'strong' flours which are clearly labelled as such and it is likely that this practice will develop. As a general guide it should be remembered that:

1 Bread requires 'strong' flour, which is also suitable for rolls and plain buns, and for puff pastry.

2 Richer yeast mixtures (i.e. with fat or eggs) will become tough if flour is too strong, and a medium, general-purpose flour is better.

3 Scones, plain cakes and fruit cakes, short crust pastry and pudding mixtures are best made from medium flour—the usual 'plain' flour on the market.

4 Light sponges, biscuits and extra-short short crust pastry require a weak flour for best results.

Storing Flour   Keep flour in a dry place, preferably in bins or jars, and label it according to its type.

SHORTENINGS

To change the texture and structure of a jelly-like, glutinous flour and liquid mixture into that of the granular, crumbly but cohesive mass characteristic of cake and pastry mixtures, it is necessary to add fat. In the bakery trade, fats (whether in the form of solids or liquids) are always referred to as 'shortenings' and can include butter, lard, margarine and all the branded cooking fats and oils now on the market.

When mixed with flour the fat coats each grain of flour with a greasy layer which keeps the particles apart. When the flour grains are softened and burst by moisture and heat the freed starch absorbs the fat and is set (again by heat) as separate granules, giving the characteristic 'shortness' or crispness of biscuits and pastry.

If a raising agent is present the gas bubbles it produces 'blow up' the mixture while this process is taking place and the mixture sets around the bubbles, giving a porous, spongy texture.

If the amount of heat provided is only sufficient to melt the fat before the starch grains are ruptured and ready to absorb it, the mixture will be tough and disappointing. It is, therefore, necessary to place such mixtures in a hot oven, the richer (i.e. the higher the proportion of fat) the mixture, the hotter the oven.

The efficiency of shortening depends on
  a the ease with which it can be dispersed throughout the mixture to coat the flour particles

b its creaming property—i.e. its ability to trap and hold air when beaten. Although this air is not often sufficient to raise a mixture on its own it does help the action of the additional raising agent.

Lard is very easily dispersed throughout a flour mixture and is therefore very satisfactory for pastry-making. But it gives very soft results and is usually more successfully used in combination with a more stable fat such as margarine.

It cannot hold air when creamed and is therefore not suitable for cake-making by the creaming method.

Margarine and butter contain more water than does lard and make a more cohesive mixture which may be a little tough when margarine is used alone. Used in conjunction with lard, however, it gives good results and its colour improves the appearance of the mixture. Butter also adds a rich, characteristic flavour.

Cooking oils are becoming popular with those people who prefer not to use animal fats and these can be used satisfactorily as substitutes for solid fats in most short crust pastries and cake mixtures. It is easy to blend oil with flour and the hands do not need to be used in pastry-making, so the mixture can be kept cool. Generally speaking, it is advisable to use the recipes recommended by the makers of branded oils, usually involving a 25 per cent reduction in the normal proportion of fat.

Dripping is suitable for savoury pastries, as it is usually readily dispersed throughout the flour, but care must be taken that it is not 'oiled' during incorporation. This saturates the starch granules with fat before they are ready to absorb it and gives a heavy, tough result. Flavour, too, must not be disregarded—even when clarified, many drippings have a very pronounced flavour.

Suet is a hard fat which must be finely divided before use—grated or shredded. It is not readily dispersed and suet mixtures have a much coarser texture than those made with finer fats.

Cooking fats commercially produced under proprietory names are specially prepared for ready dispersibility and creaming.

SAUCES

Sauces are classified according to their consistency:

Pouring sauce, as its name implies, should be sufficiently fluid to be poured from a container and is used as an accompaniment, e.g. custard sauce with stewed fruit, parsley sauce with steamed fish, etc.

Coating sauce is thicker than a pouring sauce. It should be sufficiently fluid to be ladled over the food it is to coat, and to flow evenly over it before it begins to set, but thick enough to form a covering which does not slide off, e.g. cauliflower au gratin, coating for fish which has been steamed or baked.

Binding sauces or panadas are too thick to flow and are used to bind together finely-divided ingredients, e.g. croquettes, rissoles.

These are two methods of preparing these sauces:

a by blending, usually using cornflour

b by the roux method, when ordinary plain flour is used.

Blending Method

This method is very similar to that used in laundry starch-making, but a little fat may be added to improve flavour, colour and glossiness.

1 Blend the cornflour to a smooth cream with a little of the cold liquid.

2 Bring the remainder of the liquid to the boil and add seasoning, flavouring and fat.

3 Pour the boiling liquid on the blended mixture, stirring continuously.

4 Return all liquid to the pan and bring back to the boil. Stir continuously over a low heat for two minutes.

A similar method is used for preparing cornflour moulds, but these are poured into wetted containers while hot and allowed to cool before serving.

A good blended sauce should be

a perfectly smooth and free from lumps—this can only be achieved by thorough stirring throughout.

b a good colour—essences and colourings used should be added very carefully and gradually: chopped parsley should be added immediately before serving to prevent discoloration.

c of good flavour—seasonings and flavourings should be added gradually and the sauce tasted critically until the required flavour is obtained. Stocks used as part of the liquid should be perfectly fresh.

d glossy—the fat content will impart a certain sheen to the sauce and beating well will increase it. It must be remembered, however, that heat can be lost during beating and sauce should be re-heated before serving.

e quite free from 'powderiness'—the powdery taste and texture of some sauces is due to the fact that the starch grains have not completely gelatinized. This can only be surely avoided by continuing to cook the mixture for a minute or two after it has thickened.

f of the correct consistency for its purpose. The texture of a completed sauce depends upon the correct proportions of ingredients.

The Roux Method

This gives a more glossy and better flavoured sauce than does the blending method. It is always made with plain flour and fat. The liquid used usually includes some milk but this may be combined with meat or fish stock.

1 Melt the fat in the pan but do not allow it to brown.

2 Stir the flour into the melted fat and cook together until smooth but do not allow the mixture to brown.

3 Remove pan from heat and add one third of the liquid, stirring continuously. Continue to heat and stir until mixture is thick and smooth. Repeat this process with each of the other two thirds of the liquid.

4 Boil gently for three or four minutes to cook the starch completely, stirring continuously.

A good sauce should be

a smooth and free from lumps

b a good flavour

c glossy

d of the correct consistency

e free from 'powderiness'

f a good colour: fat and stock must be free from any food particles which could discolour the sauce; the roux must not be allowed to scorch.

Variations of Basic Sauce Mixtures
Cheese sauce: 50–100 g grated cheese to each 250 ml sauce.
Egg sauce: 1 hard-boiled, chopped egg to each 250 ml sauce.
Mustard sauce: 2 tsps. dry mustard and 2 tsps. vinegar to each 250 ml sauce.
Parsley sauce: 1 tbsp. chopped dry parsley to each 250 ml sauce.
Onion sauce: 250 g cooked chopped onions to each 250 ml sauce.
Anchovy sauce: 2 tsps. anchovy essence to each 250 ml sauce.

BATTERS

A batter is a mixture of flour and milk beaten together (hence its name) to form a smooth liquid, usually with the addition of egg. During the beating process air is incorporated into the mixture, is trapped and held by the egg and rises when cooked, giving a light texture.

Batters may be used

a as coatings for fish and other deep-fat-fried foods

b as puddings and pancakes.

Coating batters are not usually made with egg, for economy's sake.

Pudding or pancake batters contain eggs which hold beaten-in air which, together with the steam produced by the heated liquid, is sufficient to raise the mixture and no baking powder is required.

Method
1 Sieve the flour and salt into a deep bowl.
2 Make a well in the centre and drop in the egg.

3 Add sufficient of the milk to be able to mix in all the flour.

4 Stir until a smooth mixture is formed.

5 Add the rest of the liquid gradually and beat well until the surface is covered with bubbles. Tip the bowl sideways to do this and, using a wooden spoon, lift the mixture and let it fall back into the bowl. Do *not* beat the bowl! A rotary whisk may be used instead if preferred.

Cooking

a For Yorkshire Pudding: Pour into baking tin containing *hot* fat and bake for 15 to 20 minutes in the middle of a fairly hot oven (190°C or Gas Mark 5).

Continue cooking at top of oven (35 minutes in all).

b For pancakes:

(*i*) 'Season' the frying pan—i.e. heat lard in the pan until smoking hot, pour off excess.

Pour in sufficient batter to cover the bottom of the pan and cook till browned. Toss or turn to the other side and repeat. Roll pancake up and serve with lemon and sugar.

Re-season pan for cooking next portion of batter.

(*ii*) Drop spoonfuls of the batter on to the greased and heated hot plate of electric stove or griddle.

c For steamed batters: Grease small basins or moulds, pour in the batter ($\frac{2}{3}$ full), cover with greaseproof paper and steam.

Some Uses of Batters

Yorkshire pudding, toad-in-the-hole, pancakes, fruit in batter, fritters, black-cap pudding.

PASTRY

SHORT CRUST PASTRY

As the name implies, this pastry should be crisp, light and crumbly. Its success depends upon:

a the incorporation of fat into flour without 'oiling' the fat by the warmth of the hands. If oil is used it must be quickly and evenly distributed throughout the flour.

b the small amount of liquid used to hold the mixture together.

c the amount of air incorporated during the mixing.

d the heat of the oven being sufficient to burst the starch grains quickly so that they can absorb the melted fat.

Method

1 Sieve the flour and salt into the mixing bowl in order to remove any lumps and to entrap as much air as possible.

2 Cut the fat into pieces in the flour, using a round-bladed knife *or* add oil to flour, mixing well with a fork.

3 Rub the fat into the flour until the mixture resembles fine breadcrumbs. Use only the tips of the fingers to do this, as these are the coolest parts of the hands. Lift the mixture as it is made, and allow it to fall back into the bowl from a height, in order to aerate it.

4 Add cold water evenly throughout the mixture, until it forms a stiff dough. The last stages of mixing should be done with the fingers and the dough should be sufficiently stiff and dry to leave the sides of the bowl easily and cleanly.

5 Flour the rolling board or table-top lightly and roll out the dough with short light strokes. Turn the pastry, not the rolling pin, to roll it in the opposite direction.

6 Use the pastry as required and cook in a hot oven. Gas mark and temperature depend upon the dish which is being made and recipes should be followed accordingly. As the top of the oven is the hottest part, deep pies should be cooked near the top for the first few minutes to cook the pastry and then moved nearer the bottom where the contents can cook gradually while the pastry is browned. Small tartlets and shallow pies should be cooked as quickly as possible, i.e. near the top of the oven.)

Faults and Their Causes
Hard or tough pastry:

  a insufficient fat
  b inefficient rubbing-in
  c too much water
  d bad rolling.

Blisters on the surface: uneven addition of liquid (where there is more liquid in one portion than in another the steam from it blows out a bubble of gluten which hardens in the heat of the oven to form a blister).
Pastry sinking into fruit tarts:

  a insufficient fruit to support the pastry after it has softened with cooking
  b too cool an oven—melted fat not absorbed will run out of the pastry and the dough will collapse
  c slit made in the top of the pastry too large to allow the dough to support itself
  d pastry being stretched over the contents. As it shrinks with the evaporation of moisture it will come away from the sides of the dish.

Soggy layer of pastry just above the filling: the absorption of steam from cooking fruit/meat. After pastry has set a small slit should be made in the crust to allow the steam to escape.
Note The problem of allowing steam to escape without causing the pastry to collapse can often be overcome by using a pie-funnel. This

acts as a 'chimney' for the escape of steam and supports the crust at the same time. This is particularly valuable when using extra-wide pie dishes.

General Rule for Short Crust Pastry

Keep dough as cool as possible until ready for cooking. (In very hot weather it should be allowed to 'rest' in a cool larder or refrigerator after handling in order to allow the softened fat to harden before cooking.) Cook in a hot oven.

Uses of Short Crust Pastry

Jam tartlets and cases for other sweet or savoury fillings.
Pasties—sweet and savoury.
Fruit and savoury pies.
Rissoles—when pastry is wrapped around meat filling and fried in deep fat.

ROUGH PUFF PASTRY

Puff pastry has well-defined layers divided by air spaces and should be very light.

Its success depends on

a the successful distribution of fat through the flour

b the inclusion of as much air as possible to expand on heating and 'blow up' the mixture

c the elasticity of the gluten in the flour to hold the bubbles of gas

d the oven heat being sufficient to bring about complete absorption of the fat.

Method

1 Sieve the flour and salt together.

2 Mix the fats well together until they are evenly blended, divide it into pieces about the size of walnuts and allow it to cool and become firm.

3 Add the fat to the flour, still in lumps.

4 Add the water and lemon juice.

5 Using a round-bladed knife, mix into a stiff dough.

6 Draw the dough together with the fingertips.

7 Turn on to a floured board and form into a rectangle.

8 Roll lightly into a long strip, keeping a good rectangular shape.

9 Divide into three and fold bottom third over middle third, top third over other two, enclosing air between the layers. See diagram opposite.

10 Seal the ends with the rolling pin.

11 Turn so that folded ends are at the side.

12 Repeat 8, 9, 10, 11 four times more.

13 Leave in cold place to 'rest' for 20 minutes: this allows softened fat to harden and the stretched gluten to 'relax' (and thus be ready for re-stretching when required).

14 Use as required.

15 Cook in very hot oven (230°C or Gas Mark 8, reduced to 190°C or Gas Mark 5 when pastry has set).

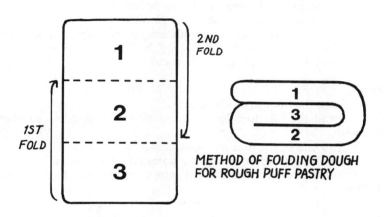

METHOD OF FOLDING DOUGH FOR ROUGH PUFF PASTRY

Faults and Their Causes

Pastry hard and showing no spaces between layers:
- *a* the addition of too much water during mixing
- *b* too cool an oven; fat has melted before starch is cooked
- *c* too much flour on board while rolling out
- *d* too heavy rolling and folding
- *e* omitting to cool pastry before use.

Pastry hard on the outside and soggy inside:
- *a* too hot an oven, causing outside layer to be cooked quickly and sealing in the steam from under it
- *b* insufficient cooking.

Pastry risen unevenly:
- *a* uneven rolling
- *b* fat unevenly distributed
- *c* poor shaping for folding
- *d* pastry not being allowed to 'rest' after rolling, for the gluten to relax.

Pastry shrinking during cooking:
- *a* stretching it during rolling and folding
- *b* not allowing it to 'relax' before cooking
- *c* placing pastry dish to one side of the oven for cooking.

Uses of Rough Puff Pastry
Savoury pies, sausage rolls, savoury pasties, mince pies, Eccles cakes.

FLAKY PASTRY

Its name describes the texture of this pastry. It is much less dense than short crust and the flakes of the cooked mixture should be easily discernible.

Its success depends upon:
a the method of incorporating the fat into the flour
b the inclusion of as much air as possible
c the heat of the oven being sufficient to bring about quick and complete absorption of fat
d the elasticity of the gluten in the flour.

Method
1 Sieve the flour and salt together.
2 Blend the fats together, divide into four and allow to cool and harden.
3 Rub one of the four portions of fat into the flour.
4 Mix to a stiff dough with the water and lemon juice.
5 Roll out on a floured board into a rectangular shape. Mark into three.

METHOD OF
DISTRIBUTING FAT
AND FOLDING
DOUGH IN
FLAKY PASTRY

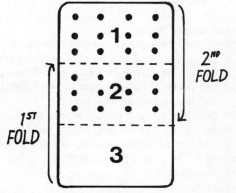

6 Divide another portion of the fat into small knobs and spread them evenly over the top two thirds of the pastry.
7 Fold the bottom third up over the middle one and the top third over both of them. See diagram above.
8 Seal the side edges with the rolling pin and turn dough sideways.
9 Re-roll into rectangle. Mark into three.
10 Repeat 6, 7, 8, and then 5–8 (all fat is now used up)
11 Allow pastry to 'rest' for 10 minutes.

12 Roll and fold twice more.

13 Allow to 'rest' as long as possible. If left overnight it must be wrapped in greaseproof paper to prevent moisture from evaporating.

14 Use as required and cook in a very hot oven.

Faults and Their Causes: See Rough Puff Pastry, p. 185.

Uses of Flaky Pastry

Savoury pies, savoury pasties, sausage rolls, Eccles cakes, vanilla slices, sweet and savoury patties.

Summary of the Differences in Methods of Pastry-making caused by Differences in Proportions of Ingredients

Distribution of fat through flour

1 Up to half the amount of fat to flour can be rubbed into it, ∴ fat is rubbed into flour for short crust pastry.

2 More than half the proportion of fat to flour and up to two thirds cannot be rubbed in without making the dough too soft, ∴ fat is mixed into flour in small lumps and rolled into the mixture for rough puff pastry.

3 More fat, i.e. two-thirds to three-quarters fat to flour, cannot be satisfactorily incorporated in such large pieces and is too great a quantity to be rubbed in, ∴ fat is incorporated into flour partly by rubbing in (to form a cohesive dough) and then by being spread on to the dough and rolled into it to make flaky pastry.

Amount of air included

The richer the dough the more air is required to make it light.

1 In short crust pastry air is included by sieving flour and by lifting mixture as fat is rubbed in.

2 In rough puff and flaky pastries additional air is included by the method of rolling and folding.

The inclusion of lemon juice

The more a paste is required to rise the more the gluten in the flour has to stretch, ∴ in rough puff and flaky pastry, which both have air folded into their layers, the gluten is made more elastic by the addition of lemon juice. In a short pastry this is unnecessary.

The heat of the oven

It is essential that the starch in the pastry mixture should be ready to absorb the fat as soon as it has melted, ∴ the greater the proportion of fat the more quickly the starch grains must be burst, and the hotter the oven should be.

SUET PASTRY

Like the three types of pastry already mentioned, suet pastry is a mixture of flour, fat and water. Its texture, however, is quite different from that of these other types and it may be cooked by different methods. The cooked pastry is of a coarser, more open texture and the colour is paler, usually quite white.

This is due to the fat used, whether finely-chopped butcher's suet (which is rarely used nowadays) or commercially prepared packet suet. Suet melts more slowly than the other fats used in pastry-making and there is the danger that the starch grains will be cooked before the fat has melted sufficiently for the starch to absorb it, with a resultant hard, close texture. To safeguard against this a small amount of raising agent is added to the flour.

Choice of Suet

Butcher's suet (i.e. that removed from round the internal organs of animals) Kidney suet is the finest; all fresh suets should be bought as required, but can be kept for a few days if buried in flour. All skin and connective tissue must be removed before finely chopping or grating the fat. (Mutton suet, being hard, is easily grated; beef suet, being softer, should be chopped, with a little flour to dry it if necessary.)

Packet suet (i.e. commercially shredded and mixed with a small amount of starchy substance to keep it dry and granular) This suet can be stored for some time providing that it is kept cool; if allowed to get warm it will soon go rancid. It is a slightly more expensive form of suet than that bought fresh from the butcher, but its convenience and storing properties make this a negligible disadvantage.

Method

1 Sieve the flour, salt and baking powder together.
2 Chop or shred suet finely if necessary.
3 Add the suet to the flour.
4 Add the water quickly, distributing it evenly over the surface of the dry mixture.
5 Mix with a round-bladed knife to a stiff lumpy dough.
6 Knead lightly with the fingertips until the dough sticks together in one elastic mass.
7 Use as required.

Cooking

Steaming is the most satisfactory method of cooking suet pastry because it gives the gluten in the flour opportunity to stretch as the raising agent blows up the mixture. The result is a light, spongy but substantial, cooked dough.

Boiling is a satisfactory method of cooking this pastry but the pressure of the boiling water, which restricts the expansion of the dough, gives a closer cooked texture. Any leakage through the pudding cloth can also result in a sticky outer layer on the dough.

Baking can be carried out in the same way as for other pastries but the hardness of the fat gives a less crisp and crumbly texture.

Faults and Their Causes
Heavy solid texture:
  a liquid added too slowly
  b too little raising agent
  c water for boiled pudding not at boiling point when pudding is immersed
  d mixture insufficiently protected from boiling water or condensed steam.
Hard, tough baked pastry:
  a insufficient raising agent
  b cooking too quickly *or* too slowly
  c too much handling and/or rolling.
Small lumps of uncooked suet in the cooked dough:
  a insufficient chopping or shredding of suet
  b cooking too quickly for the suet to melt.
Note Suet pastries should always be eaten hot; they become very solid with congealed fat on cooling.

Uses of Suet Pastry
Meat puddings, steamed fruit puddings, syrup layer puddings, spotted dick, dumplings (in savoury stews or enclosing whole apples), baked jam roly-poly.

SCONES

Scone-making can conveniently be placed midway between pastry-making and plain cake-making. The recipe is similar to that for rubbed-in mixtures, i.e. it contains flour, fat and a raising agent (the inclusion of some sweetening ingredient is optional), but as the proportion of fat is lower and eggs are not usually included, the proportion of raising agent must necessarily be higher. After mixing, the dough is treated as pastry, i.e. rolled out and cut into shape.

Sour milk is often used to provide some of the acid necessary to act on the bicarbonate of soda (see 'Raising Agents', p. 170).

Method
  1 Sieve flour, baking powder and salt together. (If bicarbonate of soda and cream of tartar are used separately, this sieving should be repeated three times in order to make sure that no lumps of baking soda are left. These can impart an unpleasant flavour and a certain amount of discolouration to the scones.)
  2 Rub in the fat.

3 Add all the liquid.

4 Mix with a round-bladed knife to an elastic dough.

5 Knead with the fingertips on a floured board to a smooth dough.

6 Roll out into a round 2 cm thick.

7 Divide into four with the back of the knife *or* form into four separate small rounds *or* cut into small rounds with a pastry cutter.

8 Brush with milk.

9 Cook in hot oven (220°C or Gas Mark 7).

Faults and Their Causes

Heavy texture:

    a insufficient raising agent

    b insufficient liquid

    c too cool an oven

    d too long a period of time between mixing and cooking

    e heavy handling.

Burnt underside, under-cooked top:

    a wrong placing in oven—i.e. with tray directly over the flame

    b baking tray too large for the oven, preventing satisfactory circulation of heat round it.

Uneven rising:

    a bad kneading

    b uneven rolling.

Strong flavour of soda and brown specks in mixture:

    a insufficient sifting of flour and raising agent

    b incorrect proportion of bicarbonate of soda to cream of tartar.

Spreading of scones and loss of shape:

    a too much liquid

    b too much fat used in preparing baking tray

    c too much raising agent

    d bad kneading.

Types of Scones

Wholemeal, cheese, fruit, potato, treacle.

CAKES

Cakes are classified according to the methods by which the fat is incorporated; this in turn is dependent upon the proportion of fat in the mixture. Therefore, the classes may be labelled as

    a rubbed-in, or plain, mixtures

    b creamed, or rich, mixtures

    c melted fat mixtures

    d whisked, or sponge, mixtures which contain no fat.

Note 'Plainness' or 'richness' of cake mixtures refers to the proportion of fat in the mixture and has nothing to do with the addition of fruit. (see pp. 206–209 for basic recipes.)

Choice of Ingredients

   1 *Flour* (see pp. 176–178)
   2 *Fat*

Butter always adds good flavour to starch mixtures and may be used alone or as part of a blend of fats. It is especially recommended for creamed mixtures, where fineness of flavour should be allied to delicacy of texture.
Margarine is the fat most commonly used for any mixture and is satisfactory used alone or with other fats, although the flavour is not so good as that of butter. In creamed mixtures which have fruit or other strong flavourings added it may well be used alone.
Lard is suitable for use in rubbed-in or melted mixtures.
Clarified dripping may be used in rubbed-in or melted mixtures, especially when strong flavourings are added.

   Neither lard nor good dripping contains water and this helps to produce a fine, close-textured mixture when cooked.

   Cooking oils may, obviously, be used in melted mixtures.
   3 *Sugar*
Granulated sugar is suitable for rubbed-in mixtures.
Caster sugar, the finer crystals of which more readily blend with fat, is best for creamed mixtures. Its finer texture also makes it more suitable for sponges.
Brown or demerara sugar is very suitable for melted mixtures and for any others in which a light-coloured result is not required. Demerara crystals, however, are too large for satisfactory blending with fat in creamed mixtures, and moist brown sugar should be used in preference.
   4 *Raising agents* (see p. 170)
   5 *Flavourings*
Dry powders, e.g. cocoa, spices, should always be sieved with the flour.
Dried fruit, if large, should be chopped before adding it to the mixture *after* the fat has been incorporated. Small fruits should be cleaned and dried thoroughly before adding.
Nuts with tough skins (e.g. almonds) should be blanched and skinned before chopping and added like fruit.
Essences should be added to the first half of the liquid to ensure even blending throughout the mixture. Careful tasting should ensure good flavour. Most mixtures, particularly those containing cocoa, are improved by the addition of a few drops of vanilla essence.
   6 *Eggs*
Most recipes refer only to hen eggs, but duck or goose eggs may be used provided they are quite fresh. Owing to their size, the number of goose or duck eggs required is smaller.

RUBBED-IN MIXTURES

As the proportion of fat to flour is not more than half, it can conveniently be rubbed in.

Method

    1 Sieve flour, salt and baking powder together.

    2 Rub the fat into the flour until the mixture resembles fine breadcrumbs *or* stir oil into flour with a fork, mixing well.

    3 Add sugar.

    4 Beat the egg and make up to the required amount of liquid with milk.

    5 Add the liquid to the flour all together.

A
    6 Mix with a fork to a soft, rather sticky dough. (The fork should be able to stand upright in it.)

    7 Divide into equal portions and place on a greased baking tray.

    8 Bake in a fairly hot oven (200°C or Gas Mark 6).

OR

B
    6 Mix with a wooden spoon to a soft dough which will just drop off the spoon without its being shaken, adding more liquid if necessary.

    7 Put into a greased cake-tin and level off the top.

    8 Bake in a fairly hot oven (190°C or Gas Mark 5).

Faults and Their Causes

Coarse, open texture:

    a too much raising agent

    b too hot an oven

    c insufficient mixing-in of liquid.

Heavy texture:

    a insufficient raising agent

    b too cool an oven

    c incorrect proportion of fat to flour

    d too much liquid

    e fat becoming oily while being rubbed-in.

Dry texture:

    a too little liquid

    b too much raising agent

    c insufficient quantity of eggs

    d over-cooking.

Large holes throughout the cake, giving very uneven texture:

    a fat insufficiently rubbed in

    b mixture transferred to the tin in small portions, trapping air between them.

Small buns burnt underneath and pale on top:

   a buns placed too low in the oven

   b tray placed over the flame, thus becoming very hot and preventing proper circulation of heat in oven.

Small buns spreading on tin:

   a too much grease used when preparing the tin

   b too slack a mixture

   c too cool an oven.

Large cake rising to a peak in the middle:

   a cake being placed too high in the oven

   b oven too hot at first but turned down before too much harm was done

   c mixture not levelled before cooking.

Large cake rising unevenly:

   a cake placed at one side of the oven instead of in the middle

   b too much raising agent

   c oven not heated to the correct temperature *before* cake was cooked.

Large cake sinking in the middle:

   a too slack a mixture

   b too much raising agent

   c opening oven door before cake had 'set', or perhaps slamming door shut

   d too cool an oven

   e insufficient cooking

   f draught through the kitchen.

Fruit in large cake sinking to the bottom:

   a too slack a mixture

   b fruit wet when added to the mixture

   c cake cooked in too cool an oven so that the mixture is not set quickly enough to support the fruit.

Uses of Rubbed-in Mixtures

Rock cakes, raspberry buns, fruit buns (currant, sultana, date, cherry), coconut buns; chocolate or coffee cakes; almond, lemon, orange cakes; seed, spice, ginger cakes.

CREAMED MIXTURES

The amount of fat is from half to equal that of flour and therefore it cannot conveniently be rubbed in. That of the sugar is equal to that of fat and the number of eggs used is from 4 to 12 to each 500 g of flour. As the number of eggs is increased the amount of raising agent is correspondingly decreased, as eggs can hold whipped-in air. Fat also can hold beaten-in air when creamed.

Method

1 Cream the fat and sugar together with a wooden spoon until the mixture is white and fluffy. If oil is used, add with the egg.

2 Beat up the eggs (break them separately into a cup before mixing together) and stand them for a few minutes in a bowl of warm water. By raising the temperature of the eggs there is less risk of curdling the creamed fat and sugar as they are added. (Curdling is caused when the coldness of the egg separates the fat from the sugar by solidifying it.)

3 Add the eggs gradually to the creamed mixture, beating well between each addition. (If mixture curdles, beat it well over a bowl of warm water to re-blend the fat.) Add any other liquid required.

4 Sieve the flour, salt and raising agent and fold gradually into the creamed mixture, using a metal spoon and only mixing the ingredients sufficiently to ensure even distribution. Consistency should be such that the mixture can be gently shaken from the spoon.

5 Place mixture in greased and lined cake-tin and make a hollow in the middle. If sandwich-tins are used dust with flour and sugar after greasing to give a thin crust to the cake. Care must be taken to tap out all excess flour mixture before tin is used.

6 Bake in a fairly hot oven (190°C or Gas Mark 5) until firm. For large cakes without fruit reduce the heat to Gas Mark 4 or 180°C until cooked. For large cakes with fruit, start cooking at 180°C or Gas Mark 4 and reduce to 170°C or Gas Mark 3 after half an hour.

Faults and Their Causes

Heavy, close texture:

a insufficient creaming of the fat and sugar and consequently little air being beaten into the mixture

b insufficient beating during the addition of the eggs, again decreasing the possible inclusion of air

c insufficient cooking

d too much liquid

e oven too cool, so that the air did not expand to its fullest extent before the mixture set

f oven too hot, setting the mixture on the outside before full expansion of the air has taken place

g too little raising agent.

Coarse, open texture:

a too much raising agent

b insufficient creaming

c incorrect proportion of fat to flour

d too hot an oven.

Dry texture:

a too much raising agent

b cooking too slowly.

Uneven rising:

    a cake badly placed in the oven, i.e. to one side instead of in the middle.

    b oven not heated adequately before cake was placed inside

    c oven shelf sloping.

Cake sinking in the middle:

    a too much liquid

    b opening the oven door before the mixture has set

    c too cool an oven

    d removing cake from oven before it is completely cooked

    e too much raising agent—mixture rises too quickly and collapses because the gluten has not set.

Cake rising to a point and cracking:

    a too hot an oven

    b placing cake too high in the oven.

Uses of Creamed Mixtures

Chocolate, coffee, ginger cakes; coconut, almond, walnut cakes; fruit cakes, Queen cakes, Eve's pudding, Victoria sandwich, simnel and Christmas cakes.

MELTED FAT MIXTURES

Adding fat by melting it together with the sweetening agent (sugar, syrup, treacle) is the method used for such mixtures as gingerbreads, parkins and malt bread. Alternatively the warmed sugar or syrup can be easily mixed with cooking oil (according to brand instructions). It gives a fairly soft, open but somewhat sticky texture, the amount of air included being decreased by the omission of creaming or even of rubbing-in.

    As most of these mixtures are dark in colour, dark syrups and sugars may be used. Black treacle alone, however, may impart a bitter flavour and is better combined with golden syrup. Bicarbonate of soda, which may also impair the colour and flavour of lighter mixtures, is satisfactorily disguised by the addition of ginger and other spices. Although bicarbonate of soda alone gives off its gas very slowly this is an advantage in a mixture already made heavy by the addition of the syrup.

Method

    1 Sieve the flour, salt, bicarbonate of soda and spices together.

    2 Warm the fat, sugar and treacle/syrup together in a pan.

    3 Add the melted mixture to the dry ingredients.

    4 Add the rest of the liquid and beaten egg.

    5 Mix all ingredients well together without beating.

6 Pour into a lined and greased tin.

7 Bake in moderate oven (180°C or Gas Mark 4).

Faults and Their Causes

Cake sunk in the middle:

    a too much raising agent

    b too much syrup or treacle

    c oven door opened too soon

    d too hot an oven.

Cake cracked when it has risen:

    a too much flour in proportion to other ingredients

    b insufficient liquid

    c too much raising agent.

Cake hard on the outside and doughy inside:

    a too much liquid

    b too much syrup

    c too hot an oven.

Uses of Melted-fat Mixtures

Gingerbread (plain, fruit, nut), parkin, malt loaf, Coburg cake.

SPONGE MIXTURES

A true sponge mixture is made by whisking together eggs and sugar to incorporate as much air as possible and folding in sufficient flour to form a light, open, cellular structure.

As the success of the cooked sponge depends upon the amount of air included while mixing, the proportion of eggs to flour is higher than in mixtures containing fat. When more than three eggs are used a little hot water may be added to the whisked mixture. This helps to set the albumen round the air bubbles and gives a light cooked sponge.

Method

1 Sieve the flour and place in a warm position.

2 Whisk together the eggs and sugar over a basin of hot water until thick and creamy. The bowl containing the mixture should not touch the water as the heat will coagulate the egg albumen and prevent it from holding air. If preferred, the eggs may be separated. In this case the yolks are beaten with the sugar and the whisked whites added afterwards.

3 Continue whisking away from warmth until the mixture cools.

4 Fold in the flour very lightly, using a metal spoon.

5 Pour into prepared tins.

6 Bake in fairly hot oven (190°C or Gas Mark 5) and reduce heat immediately (to 180°C or Gas Mark 4).

Faults and Their Causes

Heavy, close texture:
- *a* insufficient beating of eggs and sugar
- *b* fat and sugar over-heated during beating
- *c* flour added too quickly, squashing out the whisked-in air
- *d* flour stirred in instead of being folded in gradually
- *e* too much flour
- *f* too hot an oven—mixture sets before air expands.

Moist, 'sad' texture:
- *a* too much sugar
- *b* too hot or too cool an oven
- *c* insufficient cooking
- *d* oven door opened before cake has set.

Sinking in the middle:
- *a* too hot an oven
- *b* moving the cake before it has set
- *c* insufficient cooking.

Cracking of Swiss roll:
- *a* over-cooking
- *b* too close a texture
- *c* tin not lined with greaseproof paper
- *d* mixture not rolled over a damp cloth
- *e* rolling too slowly.

Use of Sponge Mixtures

Sponge sandwiches, sponge fingers, layer cakes, Swiss roll, Genoese sponge (using fat).

BISCUITS

Fat may be incorporated into biscuit mixtures in the same ways as into cake mixtures, i.e. by creaming, rubbing-in or melting, and the mixtures are made in similar ways, *but*
- *a* less liquid is added, to give a dough which can be rolled out
- *b* they are slowly dried rather than baked
- *c* when cool the texture should be such that the biscuit breaks

cleanly and does not merely crumble.

Choice of Ingredients

Flour As the mixture is not required to rise, flour with a low gluten content is most useful. Rice flour or cornflour may be mixed with the wheat flour to give added 'shortness'.

Fat Butter should be used whenever possible on account of its delicate flavour. Margarine may be wholly or partly substituted. For melting methods lard or cooking oil is suitable.

Sugar Caster sugar is preferable to granulated, as it gives a finer texture, and moist brown sugar is preferable to demerara.

Varieties of Biscuits
Rubbing-in method
Cheese straws, cheese, oatmeal, shortbread, spice, chocolate, coconut, almond biscuits.
Creaming method
Shrewsbury, shortbread, coffee cream, orange biscuits.
Melting method
Brandy snaps, ginger nuts, flapjacks.

PREPARATION OF BAKING TINS

Pastries
Brush tins with melted fat; the more fat there is in the mixture the less is required on the tin.

Scones
Grease tins lightly. If desired, dust with flour and shake well to remove surplus.

Rubbed-in Mixtures
Rock cakes: grease; dust with flour if required.
Large rubbed-in cakes: grease.

Creamed Mixtures
Queen cakes: grease lightly.
Large cakes: grease well and line sides and bottom with greaseproof paper. Use two layers for very large cakes.
Christmas fruit cakes: as above. For additional protection against the formation of a hard crust, fix a layer of brown paper or corrugated cardboard round the outside of the tin.
Sandwich cakes: grease and line *or* grease and dust with a flour and sugar mixture.

Melted Fat Mixtures
Grease and line with greaseproof paper.

Sponges
See creamed mixtures. Use flour and caster sugar dusting of a greased tin for sandwiches. Grease and line Swiss-roll tins.

Biscuits
Lightly grease baking tins for rubbed-in mixtures. Line tins for creamed mixtures.

Yeast Mixtures
Grease. Flour if required.

Lining Round Cake Tins
    1 Place tin on single or double greaseproof paper and draw round it.
    2 Cut out drawn circle, just *inside* pencil line.
    3 Lay tin sideways on single or double paper, with the seam of the tin to the side edge of the paper.
    4 Roll the tin along the paper until the seam is reached.
    5 Cut paper 3 cm outside measured length.
    6 Fold down 3 cm of the open edges of the paper, lengthwise.
    7 Snip at 3 cm intervals from edge of paper to fold.
    8 Stand length of paper upright round the inside of the tin (previously greased) with the snipped edges overlapping round the bottom, smoothing it evenly against the sides.
    9 Fit the cut-out circles of paper over the snipped edges.

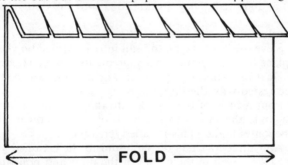

← ——————— **FOLD** ——————→

NON-STICK BAKEWARE

It is not necessary to grease any of these specially treated tins, but, if very special care is being taken, large cake tins may be lined with paper to guarantee a perfect result.

     BREAD

Bread is a mixture of flour and liquid which is raised or 'leavened' by the addition of a growing plant called yeast, giving it its characteristic texture and flavour.
    The success of bread-making depends upon the satisfactory action of the yeast and when its action is understood (see p. 174) it is clear that this requires
     a moisture
     b food
     c warmth.

Moisture is provided in the form of water or milk.

Food is given in the form of sugar added to the flour, and later produced by the action of enzymes on the flour.

Warmth is ensured throughout the process of bread-making by
a placing flour in a warm place before using
b eliminating draughts in the room
c using the hands for mixing
d warming the liquid to be incorporated
e covering the dough with a cloth while it is proving.

Choice of Ingredients

1 Flour should be 'strong' and may be white or wholemeal.

2 Yeast should be fresh and moist. If stale it is difficult to cream and imparts an unpleasant flavour to the bread.

3 Milk or water or a mixture of both may be used as required.

4 Salt should be included to improve the flavour.

5 Other ingredients, such as fruit, peel and chopped nuts, may be added as required. They are kneaded into the dough after mixing.

General Rules

1 Sieve the flour, sugar and salt into a warmed bowl and put into a warm place to stand while other ingredients are prepared.

2 Heat the liquid to tepid point, i.e. until it feels neither hot nor cold when tested with the little finger.

3 Pour a little of the liquid onto the yeast in a small basin and press it against the side with the back of a teaspoon until the whole mixture becomes liquid. This is called 'creaming'.

4 Add three-quarters of the liquid to the creamed yeast.

5 Make a well in the centre of the flour and pour in the liquid.

6 Sprinkle a little of the flour over the liquid and leave to stand in a warm place for half an hour, i.e. until the liquid becomes frothy. This is called 'sponging'. (This process may be omitted if time cannot be allowed for it.)

7 Mix the yeast mixture into the flour by hand to form a soft dough, adding the rest of the liquid as required.

8´ Knead the dough by hand until it becomes smooth and leaves the fingers and sides of the bowl quite cleanly. Knead by pulling up the outer edges of the dough with the fingers and pushing it into the middle of the lump with the knuckles.

9 Cover the bowl with a cloth and place it in a warm position for 30–45 minutes. During this time the gas bubbles from the yeast will blow up the mixture to double its size. This is called *proving*.

10 Turn the dough on to a lightly-floured board and knead again until the large holes (gas bubbles) are broken up into small ones and the texture is even throughout the mixture.

(Steps 9 and 10 may be omitted if small rolls are being made.)

11 Shape as required. Place in a greased tin if necessary, half-filling it.

12 Leave dough to re-prove until it has doubled its size.

13 Place in a very hot oven (230°C or Gas Mark 8) for 10 minutes, then lower the heat to 190°C or Gas Mark 5 and bake for 45 to 60 minutes.

14 Remove from oven and test by tapping the underside of the loaf with the knuckles. If a hollow sound is produced the loaf is cooked. Cool on a wire tray.

Note As cold retards enzyme activity, the unproved dough may be wrapped and stored in a refrigerator for several days if not required at once. It should be thoroughly and slowly thawed before re-use.

Faults and Their Causes

Close, heavy texture with little increase of size during cooking:

 a yeast enzymes were destroyed before loaf was placed in the oven, because added liquid was too hot

 b there was too much heat surrounding the dough during its first proving.

Large holes throughout the loaf when cut:

 a insufficient kneading after the first rising, leaving large gas bubbles which were not broken up

 b too cool an oven—yeast went on producing gas after the loaf was placed in the oven, instead of enzymes being quickly destroyed.

A heavy loaf with a close texture:

 a too dry a dough

 b too little time allowed for proving

 c too much salt was added, so inhibiting the action of the enzymes.

Bread tastes slightly sour:

 a stale yeast

 b too much yeast in proportion to the flour

 c too much time taken over proving, allowing acids to develop.

Uses of Basic Yeast Mixture

Currant bread, currant buns, Chelsea buns, Bath buns, hot cross buns, tea-cakes, malt bread, dinner rolls, doughnuts (cooked by frying).

FURTHER STUDY

THINGS TO DO

1 Using a basic scone mixture recipe, prepare a small quantity in the normal way. Repeat, replacing half the flour with cornflour.

H

Repeat, replacing all the flour with cornflour. Compare the results, and explain the differences.

2 Using equal quantities of plain flour in each case:

a add sufficient cold liquid to form a smooth paste, measuring the amount required and noting the time required.

b add the flour to the same amount of cold water and mix, noting the time required

c repeat *a*. using hot liquid instead of cold

d repeat *b*. using hot liquid instead of cold.

Repeat all four mixtures using cornflour instead of plain flour. What general rules for the mixing of flours and liquids can you form from the results?

3*a* Make a small quantity of short crust pastry (100 g of flour) and cost it exactly. Compare this with exactly the same weight of ready-made pastry. Repeat with bread dough and commercial roll-dough.

b Cook both pastries, using each for the same dish (e.g. cheese straws, jam tarts) and compare appearance, flavour and ease of use. Repeat comparison with bread rolls.

What conclusions can you draw?

4 Using a basic scone recipe, make a small quantity of the normal mixture and bake as directed.

Repeat with the following variations:

a omit raising agent altogether

b omit raising agent and replace plain with self-raising flour

c use bicarbonate of soda alone—omit cream of tartar

d use cream of tartar alone—omit bicarbonate of soda.

Compare and contrast:

a rising performance

b colour

c texture

d flavour.

Note your conclusions.

5 Make a small amount of scone mixture. Divide it into two equal parts. Cut out and cook one half immediately. Prepare the second half for cooking but allow it to stand for half an hour before cooking. Compare the finished results for

a rising performance

b texture

c colour

d flavour.

What have you proved?

6 Compare the costs of

a a home-made Victoria sandwich cake

b a similar cake made from a packet mix

c a similar cake purchased from a baker's shop.

Weigh each to compare value for money. Compare the keeping properties, colour, texture and flavour of each and tabulate all your results. What conclusions can you reach?

7 Make up two different sauces from packets of 'ready-mix'. Prepare similar quantities of home-made sauces of the same variety. Cost each one and compare

    a expense   *c* colours

    b time required for preparation   *d* flavours.

8 Carry out a morning's cooking showing the use of as many raising agents as possible.

9 Today is your baking morning. Prepare, cook and serve three separate dishes for use during the next few days. In all, use no more than 500 g flour and include a short crust pastry dish and a yeast mixture.

(A.E.B.)

QUESTIONS TO ANSWER

1 Write out the following statements, and complete them, using only the words in the right-hand column to fill in the blanks.

a Starch mixtures, i.e. those made from flour, have the property of thickening and setting due to the .... of starch.	carbon dioxide
b When mixtures are made with cornflour, although they may rise, they collapse again owing to the absence of .... in the flour.	bran
c The outer layers of wheat grains, called .... are removed during the preparation of flour, the more removed the whiter the flour.	salt
d When nutrients are removed with the husk and germ of the wheat grain, they are replaced artificially; this process is known as	proving
e The processes of breaking, sifting and sieving wheat grains is known as	lemon juice
f .... is added to all starch mixtures; it improves the flavour and, used in small quantities, helps to strengthen gluten and 'feed' yeast.	gelatinization
g The elasticity of gluten can be improved by the addition of	gluten
h Yeast is known as a 'living organism' and is capable of reproduction during which the gas .... is produced.	milling
i This is made possible by the action of .... which is halted in cold conditions.	fortification
j During bread-making, the dough is allowed to rest for a time to be 'blown-up' by the production of gas; this is called	enzymes

2 Give the recipe for a basic white sauce and suggest three variations. Say what dishes they would accompany or be used for.

What special care would you take to ensure good results in making the basic sauce?

3*a* Give *six* different uses for sauces in cookery, with an example in each case.

b Give the basic proportions of fat, flour and liquid for *three* different types of roux sauces. Give an example for the use of each type.

c Explain, with reasons, the following faults in a white roux sauce:

(*i*) a dull coating sauce

(*ii*) lumpiness

(*iii*) brown specks throughout the sauce

(*iv*) a sauce that is too thin and watery. (A.E.B.)

4 Describe the changes which take place to bring about the thickening of

a a white sauce

b an egg custard.

5 What is the value of sauces used to accompany main dishes? What sauce would you serve with the following:

a steamed sponge pudding

b grilled plaice fillet

c cauliflower

d roast lamb

e baked ham

f stewed gooseberries.

Give reasons for your choice.

6 What are the qualities of good short crust pastry? Explain why the following should be used when making short crust pastry:

a soft plain flour

b a mixture of margarine and lard

c cold water.

Give *five* general rules, with reasons, that should be observed when making pastry. (A.E.B.)

7 Show how the proportion and type of fat used in pastries affects

a the method of incorporating it into flour

b the heat of the oven

c the finished result.

8 For each of the following:

a short crust pastry

b either flaky or rough puff pastry

c suet pastry

give in tabulated form:

(*i*) the basic proportions of fat to flour

(*ii*) the name of fat or fats

(*iii*) the method of cooking with oven temperatures if applicable.
Write brief notes on the origin of

a margarine

b lard

c cooking oil

and discuss their use in cookery. (A.E.B.)

9 A housewife has the choice of buying cakes ready made, using commercial cake mixes or making her own cakes from basic ingredients. Give your opinion of the relative advantages of each way of obtaining cakes for the family.

10*a* What would be the quantities of other ingredients if you were given a 50 g (2 oz.) egg to make each of the following:

(*i*) pancake batter

(*ii*) a creamed mixture cake

(*iii*) a baked egg custard

(*iv*) a fatless sponge cake?

b Explain, giving *two* reasons in each case, what may have caused the following faults:

(*i*) a Victoria sandwich cake in which the texture is uneven and has large holes

(*ii*) a creamed mixture cake that has risen to a peak in the centre and has a badly cracked top

(*iii*) a curdled egg custard

(*iv*) hard lumps in the crumbs of a fatless sponge cake.

(A.E.B.)

11 State the types of fat used, the proportion of fat to flour and the method of incorporating them in *four* different mixtures. Give detailed instructions for the preparation of *one* type.

12 Give the basic proportions for the following types of cake mixtures: *a.* creamed; *b.* whisked; *c.* plain.

Give examples of one cake made by each method. (A.E.B.)

13 Yeast, under certain conditions, will give off carbon dioxide.

a Describe an experiment you have seen (or may have carried out to illustrate this statement.

b Explain how a knowledge of this action can help in bread-making.

c Give possible reasons for the following:

(*i*) a loaf is badly risen and has a close texture

(*ii*) a loaf is well risen and has large uneven holes. (A.E.B.)

14 What do you understand by a 'batter'? Suggest as many ways as you can of using a batter *a.* in savoury dishes, *b.* in sweet dishes.

15 From what sources do we obtain flour? Give as many types as possible and suggest ways in which each may be used.

Basic Recipes

(Where not otherwise stated, flour is measured in 100 g)

Dish	Proportions	Ingredients	Texture	Method of Incorporating Fat	Variations	Special Care	Storing
Batters Coating *a*	100 g flour to 125 ml milk	1 egg $\frac{1}{2}$ level tsp. salt	thick fluid setting to soft coating				
b	100 g flour to 250 ml milk	1 level tsp. B.P. $\frac{1}{2}$ level tsp. salt	as above				
Pancake or Yorkshire Pudding	100 g flour to 250 ml milk or milk and water	1 egg $\frac{1}{2}$ level tsp. salt	thick liquid setting to soft light, close texture		toad-in-the hole fruit in batter black-cap pudding		
Biscuits Rubbed-in	$\frac{1}{4}-\frac{1}{2}$ fat to flour and an equal quantity of sugar	sufficient milk/egg to mix to stiff dough pinch salt	very crisp when cold	rub into flour	almond coconut cinnamon cheese chocolate etc.	remove from oven while still soft and barely coloured	in airtight tins but *not* with cakes
Creamed	$\frac{1}{2}$ to equal weight of fat and sugar to flour	egg/milk pinch salt	see above	cream fat and sugar together		see above	
Melted	$\frac{1}{4}$ fat to flour, $\frac{1}{4}$ sugar to flour, $\frac{1}{2}$ syrup to flour	milk/egg pinch salt	see above	melt the fat, add the syrup or treacle and warm; pour into flour with liquid as required	ginger	see above	

Dish	Proportions	Ingredients	Texture	Method of Incorporating Fat	Variations	Special Care	Storing
Suet	¼–½ fat to flour	½ level tsp. salt 60 ml water 1 level tsp. B.P. suet	close, soft	grate or shred finely and mix well into flour	spotted dick meat puddings dumplings fruit puddings	serve hot	
Sauce Pouring *a*	25 g cornflour 500 ml milk		fluid	melted into liquid (if required)	custard powder	avoid lumpiness and under cooking	in screw-top jar in a cool place
b	25 g flour 25 g fat 500 ml liquid	pinch salt	fluid	blended into roux with flour	cheese, egg, anchovy, caper, onion, mustard, parsley, shrimp	see above	see above
Coating *a*	20 g cornflour 250 ml liquid		thick fluid	melted into liquid (if required)	as above	see above	see above
b	25 g flour 25 g fat 250 ml liquid	pinch salt	thick fluid	blended into roux with flour	as above	see above	see above
Panada	50 g flour 50 g fat 250 ml liquid	pinch salt	very thick binding fluid	blended into roux with flour		see above	see above
Scones	25 g fat 200 g flour	½ level tsp. salt 25 g sugar (if required) 125 ml liquid 4 level tsps B.P.	light, close	rubbing in	fruit wholemeal cheese potato oatmeal treacle	make soft, elastic dough do not cut too thin or too thick	in airtight container

11

RÉCHAUFFÉ COOKERY

One of the attributes of a good cook is imagination and in making use of left-over foods she has ample scope for exercising both economy and imagination. An extravagant cook will throw extra cooked food away, an unimaginative one simply warm it up or serve it cold, an efficient one will deal with it in such a way as to present an attractive, appetizing and nutritious dish.

Treatment of Left-over Foods
Place scraps of left-over dishes in smaller containers and cover them to protect from flies and dust.

Allow them to cool as quickly as possible. When *cold*, place in a refrigerator if possible.

Wrap bread and butter in greaseproof paper, foil or polythene and place in bread-bin.

Put away cakes and biscuits in separate airtight tins.

Preparation of Foods for Re-heating
Meat   Remove fat, gristle and skin. Shred or mince.
Fish   Remove skin and bones. Flake.
Potatoes, root vegetables   Sieve or mash.
Fruit   Remove stones and skins.
Sauces, gravies   Remove fat, sediment and skin. Make quite sure that liquids are fresh-smelling before using them.
Note   It is essential that foods to be réchaufféd should show no signs of souring, mould or fermentation. Further heat treatment may increase the effects of this contamination and cause a good deal of unpleasant digestive upset.

RULES FOR RE-HEATING FOOD

Food must be re-heated and not re-cooked
Some food values (e.g. vitamins) are reduced when foods are cooked and there are other changes which take place during the cooking of foods (e.g. the coagulation of proteins) which should not be repeated

if the food is to remain palatable and nutritious. The amount of heat applied during réchauffé cookery should therefore be sufficient to make the dish attractively hot but not enough to over-cook any of it.

It should be heated as quickly as possible and protected by a coating when necessary
Long, slow heating may overcook some of the food and this is why frying is such a popular method of re-heating it. It also adds flavour and crispness. Frying in itself, though, may over-cook the outside of the food and it should therefore be protected by coatings of egg and bread-crumbs, batter, etc. Pastry is often used to enclose already cooked ingredients and it is quickly cooked in a hot oven without over-cooking the contents. Potato coverings may also be used with cooked meats and fish for shepherd's pie, etc., but these must be cooked first and both ingredients re-heated together.

Foods to be re-heated should be used as soon as possible after first cooking, e.g.
   a potatoes are more easily mashed or sieved when warm than when cold
   b meat is more easily minced or shredded before it hardens on cooling
   c gravies, sauces, etc., are more easily used for blending while they are warm and liquid than when cold and solid.
   It is advisable, therefore, to make up left-over foods into suitable dishes as soon as possible after they have been removed from the table. This also simplifies the storage of the foods and all the washing-up can be done together.

Ingredients to be re-heated should be minced, flaked or otherwise finely divided
It is difficult to heat large, solid pieces of food right through without over-cooking the outside. Separating the food into small pieces means that the heat can more easily penetrate, and food value and flavour are not impaired.

All ingredients must be cooked before mixing
When two or more foods are to be combined to form a réchauffé dish it is important that both should be cooked beforehand (e.g. shepherd's pie—meat, potatoes and onions should all be cooked before being combined). Otherwise, the first cooking of one ingredient will entail the over-cooking of another.

Re-heated foods should be combined with some strong-flavoured ingredient
First cooking with subsequent cooling and re-heating may impair the

flavour of some foods. This loss should be compensated by the addition of strong flavours, like onion, celery, bacon, seasoning, which, besides improving the flavour of the dish, make it more attractive and therefore more easily digested.

Extra moisture should be added to réchauffé dishes and fresh gravy or sauce should be made if necessary
There is often some loss of moisture during the first cooking of food, and re-heating may increase this evaporation. Once-cooked foods do not absorb moisture completely and liquids added should be warm in order to make absorption easier. The use of coatings also reduces the rate of evaporation during re-heating.

Some crisp food should be served with re-heated dishes
Sieving, mashing, mincing, etc., all tend to make réchauffé dishes soft in texture, so they should be served with such accompaniments as crisp-breads, potato crisps, toast and biscuits.

Some fresh or freshly cooked foods should be served with all re-heated foods
There is bound to be some loss of food value in re-heated foods and to supplement their reduced value fresh foods should be served with them. The most usual losses are in vitamins and mineral elements and these can be replaced by serving fresh salads (green or fruit), and freshly cooked fruits and vegetables.

RÉCHAUFFÉ DISHES

Cooked Meat
Shepherd's pie, rissoles, Durham cutlets, galantine, meat in aspic, croquettes, meat flan, hash, curried meat, kromeskies, fritters, mince toast.

Cooked Fish
Russian fish pie, croquettes, cutlets, fish cakes, scallops, fish pie, fish flan, kedgeree.

Cooked Fruit
Fritters, fools, trifles, charlottes.

Other Dishes
Bread made into raspings, rusks, crumbs for coatings, bread and butter pudding, summer fruit pudding, fruit charlotte, cheese charlotte.
Vegetables used as 'Bubble and Squeak'.

12

THE HOSTESS

A meal may be perfectly cooked and attractively served and yet still be a failure, because the hostess has not studied the comfort of her guests. This must include not only their physical well-being but also their mental ease. Note that although in this chapter the people eating are referred to as 'guests' these rules should also apply to family meals.

PREPARING THE ROOM

1 Make sure that the room is warm and well ventilated.

2 See that it is not dusty or untidy, and that there are no dead flowers.

3 Arrange the table in such a position that none of the guests will be sitting in a draught or too close to the fire.

4 Make sure that chairs are a suitable height for sitting at the table and that there is sufficient room for each guest to eat without being bumped by his neighbour's elbow.

5 Try to keep cooking smells out of the dining-room.

PREPARING THE TABLE

1 Extend the table (if possible) when necessary to give adequate room for each guest.

2 Arrange the chairs so that no one is sitting uncomfortably near a table leg.

3 Make sure that the tablecloth or table mats are perfectly clean. Cloths should be placed evenly on the table, with a level over-hang at each side and with fold creases running along its length.

4 Use heat-resisting mats if hot plates and dishes are to be placed on a polished table-top.

5 Arrange cutlery as shown in the diagram, with the pieces to be used first on the outside.

6 Place a small plate on the left-hand side of the 'cover' (the correct name for each person's 'place'). A water glass should be placed at the top right-hand side of the cover, right way up. If the table is laid

for some time before the meal is served, the glasses may be upturned to prevent them from becoming dusty, but they should always be standing upright when the meal is served. The table napkin should be folded and placed on the side-plate. If preferred, it may be folded into a fancy shape and, if rolls are served, one may be placed inside each napkin. Otherwise, rolls or pieces of bread should be served in a basket, inside a folded napkin.

7 Make sure that there are sufficient serving spoons for every dish. The hostess will serve the main dish and the appropriate servers must be placed in front of her cover, as well as the necessary mats for the dishes. Servers for dishes to be handed round should be placed at the corners of the table.

8 Check that cruets are filled, and fill the water jug at the last possible moment with fresh water. Add ice if possible.

9 Use low vases and small flowers for decoration, so that the guests' view of the opposite side of the table is not obstructed.

10 Place sauce-boats on stands or small plates with spoons, to avoid drips on the cloth.

11 When using patterned china, see that the design is the same way up on each piece as it is placed on the table. When arranging cups and saucers place all the handles on the right-hand side and the tea-spoons with their handles in the same position. Tea-pot and coffee-pot handles should be arranged in the same way, ready to be held by a right-handed person.

SERVING THE MEAL

1 Do not come to the table with greasy or unwashed hands, untidy hair or wearing an apron, even if there are last-minute finishing touches to be carried out in the kitchen.

2 Make sure that there are warmed plates for the serving of hot dishes.

3 Serve soup from a tureen if necessary; otherwise, serve each portion individually in small warmed bowls or deep plates, covered if possible.

4 The hostess should serve the main dish on to plates placed in a pile at her cover. The ladies of the party are served first, beginning with the most important guest, gentlemen next, the hostess last.

5 Allow accompanying dishes to be passed round during the serving of the main dish, so that guests may help themselves before the food becomes cold.

6 Serve quickly but unhurriedly and make sure that guests have all they require with as little delay as possible.

7 Talk to the guests during the meal, but avoid arguments and controversial subjects which may make some feel uncomfortable and which certainly do not aid digestion.

1. Lunch table set for four persons

(MEAL TO CONSIST OF SOUP, MAIN DISH AND
VEGETABLES, SWEET, BISCUITS AND CHEESE)

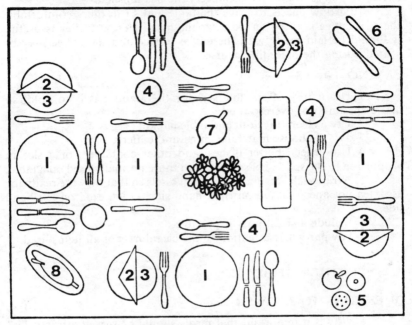

KEY 1. HEAT-RESISTING MATS   5. CRUET
2. TABLE NAPKINS   6. SERVING SPOONS
3. SIDE PLATES   7. WATER JUG
4. GLASSES   8. SAUCE BOAT & JUG

2. Coffee tray set for
two persons

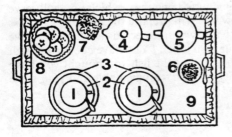

KEY 1. CUPS
2. SAUCERS
3. PLATES
4. MILK JUG
5. COFFEE-POT
6. SUGAR BOWL & SPOON
7. FLOWERS
8. BISCUITS
9. TRAYCLOTH

8 Offer guests second helpings when possible, but do not insist on their accepting them.

9 Remove all traces of one course before serving the next one, but do not start to do this until everyone has finished.

10 Allow guests to leave the table and sit in more comfortable chairs if coffee is to be served after the meal. Here a trolley is useful. It should be laid ready with the coffee service and the coffee may be heated during the preceding course.

LAYING TRAYS

1 Use a tray of suitable size for the amount it is to hold, so that dishes are not overcrowded.

2 Use a clean traycloth and table napkin.

3 Try to choose matching china and cutlery.

4 Use cruets, butter dishes, and other containers of a size in proportion to the space, i.e. smaller than those normally used on a table.

5 Arrange all serving dishes and vessels so that they are ready for use—tea-pot and milk jug on right-hand side, cruet, etc., on left-hand side.

6 Include a small posy if possible.

7 Pay particular attention to the cleanliness of all items used.

FURTHER STUDY

QUESTIONS TO ANSWER

1 Why is it important that meals should be served attractively? Illustrating your answer where possible, give detailed instructions for serving:

a a cooked breakfast for two people

b 'elevenses' for three people

c a three-course lunch for four.

2 How can a housewife make her guests feel welcome when they visit her for a meal?

3 What preparations would you make for two friends to come to visit you for a day? Give the menu for one meal which you will serve and draw a diagram to show how you will prepare the table.

4 How would you cope with two unexpected guests who arrive just as you are about to serve your own lunch? You have cooked enough vegetables to last you for two days and of the fish you bought you have only cooked half. You have plenty of fresh fruit available and your store cupboard is well stocked.

13

SHOPPING

GENERAL

In the preceding chapters hints have been given on how to buy specific foods but there are some general rules which will be of assistance when shopping for any foods:

a Allocate a definite percentage of the income to the purchase of food and try to keep within the limit. This will vary with the circumstances of the family, the amount of produce which is 'home-grown', eating habits, the amount of entertaining and the amount of time available for home cooking.

b Try to plan meals ahead so that the best use is made of foods purchased and money does not run out before the week is over. Remember that meat and fish are expensive items but that, with good meal planning they can be 'stretched' with nutritious accompaniments (see chapter 2).

c 'Shopping around' is often advised as a help to economical buying, but the time taken in doing so must be balanced against the amount of money saved. Make a careful list before setting out, bearing in mind the amount of cooked and uncooked food already in the house. Careful planning of shopping expeditions should make daily (or even more frequent) visits to shopping centres unnecessary. It is true that goods purchased in markets (as distinct from supermarkets) can often be a few pence cheaper than those in conventional shops; this is because the very nature of the market makes the overhead expense considerably less.

d Do not be attracted to 'special offers'. An apparent reduction *may* have been made on an inflated price!

e Do not be misled by attractive packing; the amount of the contents is what matters. A cellophane-wrapped pack of biscuits, for example, may be several pence cheaper than a similar weight of the same type of biscuit presented in a colourful cardboard packet.

f Read the labels and note the date, if shown on the packet, of either the expiry of 'freshness' or of packing.

g Compare weights for prices rather than prices of apparently similar-sized containers.

217

h Order dry goods (such as flour, sugar, cereals) in as large quantities as convenient. This is the cheaper way of buying them, and although they are in constant use, there is less danger of 'running out' at inconvenient times.

i Fruit, vegetables, meat and fish should be bought as fresh as possible, especially when no refrigerator is available. A home deep-freeze may, of course, be used to store these safely and with little change in food value if required.

j Buy from clean shops with closed fronts.

k Buy from shops which obviously have a rapid turnover, to avoid purchasing stale goods.

l Put away foods carefully as they are unpacked and make sure that tins, jars and packets are labelled.

m Keep a reserve supply of tinned, dried and frozen (if possible) foods for emergencies.

n Replace stocks of dry goods just before the last portion is used.

CONVENIENCE FOODS

There is now available to the housewife a very large variety of foods which have been so far prepared as to save her time and labour. These are referred to as 'convenience foods' and may range from the long-established tin of fruit, ready to use as it is or as an ingredient of a more elaborate dish, to a complete pre-cooked meal which only requires heating.

Examples of convenience foods

Canned: fruits, vegetables, soups, meat (for serving hot, e.g. stewed beef, or cut into slices for serving cold, e.g. ham, tongue, galantine); paté; custard sauce; puddings; pie fillings; milk; cream; baby foods.

Bottled: fruits; vegetables; shellfish; sauces.

Dehydrated: fruits; vegetables (particularly peas, beans, potatoes); instant tea and coffee; milk; soups; herbs; prepared dishes.

Frozen: prepared dishes; fruits; vegetables; sweets; cakes; pastries; fish; meat.

Freeze-dried: vegetables.

Prepared for 'instant' mixing: sauces; soups; cakes; whipped sweets.

Other items which save time and trouble: self-raising flour (to save adding baking powder to plain flour); jellies (including quick-setting ones); cornflour mixtures (custard powder, blancmange); pasta; stock cubes; whipped fats (for ease in creaming); spices/curry powder; flavouring essences; tea/coffee bags; powdered gelatine.

Use

a Many items take up less storage than their natural components.

b They can be stored and used for emergencies such as the arrival of unexpected guests; illness of the usual cook; weather conditions which do not encourage shopping expeditions.

c They may be used by the imaginative cook as ingredients which improve the quality of her meals and the range of her cookery repertory.

d They may be used to minimize the labour in feeding a family which is enjoying a camping, sailing or touring holiday.

e They are valuable to professional people who have little time or energy for cooking but still need to entertain frequently.

f They may be used to provide main dishes (or accompaniments —a recent addition provides these and requires the addition of the main ingredient) and to avoid taking trouble in preparing meals. This is not a wholly desirable use; it must be remembered that considerable service has been rendered in preparing these meals and this must be paid for. Extensive use of completely prepared dishes, therefore, is expensive, and, although a certain amount of cost is offset by the absence of waste, it is an extravagant general practice. Some fresh food should always be served in conjunction with prepared dishes.

g People from other countries may find a number of familiar foods/dishes available.

FOOD ADDITIVES

This term covers a wide variety of colourings, flavourings, preservatives, thickening agents and nutritive enrichments which may be added legally. These may be natural or synthetic in origin and are controlled very strictly under the laws relating to foods. They must conform to any or all of the following requirements:

a improve the attractiveness of the food without misleading the buyer

b improve the nutritive value of the food

c act as preservatives

d improve the flavour or texture without masking any deterioration of the food

while not

a disguising inferior quality of processing or preparation

b deceiving the consumer

c reducing the nutritive value of the food

d replacing a more economical method of processing.

Colourings, originally from natural sources (animal or vegetable pigments), are now often produced artificially. Natural sources include cochineal (from an insect), alkanet (from a vegetable)—red, saffron (from crocus), anatto (from anatto tree), turmeric (from a plant)—yellow, and caramel (from sugar)—brown.

Synthetic colourings are available in a large variety of colours and are very concentrated, permanent and pure. In this country, colour is not added to natural foods (except occasionally to the skins of citrus fruits which must be labelled 'colour added') or to milk or cream.

Pre-packed foods must be labelled with a declaration of the colouring agent among the ingredients.

Preservatives are chemical substances which prevent or retard the unpleasant changes in food (not including salt, sugar, vinegar, herbs, spices and alcohol, which are natural preservatives).

These must conform to the following requirements. They

a must not be injurious to health

b must not permit unfit raw materials to be used

c must not allow inferior or imperfect methods of processing to be used

d must be non-irritant

e must be effective

f must not inhibit digestion

g must not become toxic when eaten

h must not be used instead of high standards of hygiene

i must be readily identified for controlling purposes.

Emulsifiers are used to disperse oil evenly throughout a watery liquid. They are used in the manufacture of

a margarine, ice cream, mayonnaise

b cakes ⎫ to prevent them becoming stale quickly and to reduce

c bread ⎭ the amount of fat required.

Sweeteners   Natural ones are fruit sugars which have a low joule value. Chemical sweeteners are very much more concentrated but have no food value.

Flavourers were originally from leaves, stems, roots or fruits of plants. These can be synthesized in very concentrated forms

Herbs: sage; mint; basil; parsley; tarragon.

Spices: peppers; saffron; chillies; cayenne; paprika; horseradish; allspice; cinnamon; cloves; ginger; nutmeg; mace; vanilla; aniseed; caraway; coriander; cumin; dill; fennel; mustard.

Synthetics are more concentrated and less expensive than the natural forms and can be blended with them, e.g. fruit flavours, butter flavour.

The strong natural flavours of herbs and spices were used to mask the smell and flavour of deteriorating foods for many years before food preservation principles were understood and practised.

FURTHER STUDY

THINGS TO DO

1a Collect equal quantities (25 g) of as many brands of tea as you can. (Label each one carefully.) Note the price of each.

b Shake each one separately through a fine nylon sieve and weigh the amount of dust obtained from each. Calculate the price of the leaves as distinct from that of the whole sample.

c Compare the samples for the best value for money.

d Empty sufficient tea bags to produce 25 g of leaves. Calculate the cost and compare with results found in *b*. and *c*.

2*a* Open two packets of similar-type biscuits, one plain-wrapped and one packeted. Note the weights indicated on the packets.

b Count the biscuits in each packet and calculate the cost of each.

c Weigh the biscuits without the wrappings and compare with the weight shown on the packet.

d Weigh one biscuit from each packet and compare with *b*.

3*a* Find out how many glasses of fruit drink you can make from a bottle of fruit squash, using exactly the same quantity of concentrated squash and the same glass throughout. Calculate the cost of each glass.

b Fill the same glass from a bottle of non-concentrated fruit drink. Find out how many glasses you can obtain from the bottle and calculate the cost.

c Compare *a*. and *b*. for cost, colour and flavour.

4 With each of the following foods note the prices, and compare them, of the large and small sizes of packages. Note the weights of both sizes compared to the prices to find the better value: tinned peaches; baked beans; washing-up liquid; disinfectant; chocolate powder; ground coffee.

QUESTIONS TO ANSWER

1 Write out the following statements, and complete them, using only the words in the right-hand column to fill in the blanks.

a The time during which any food or food product remains safe for eating and palatable is referred to as its	saffron
	fructose
b A food additive with the function of dispersing oil evenly throughout a watery liquid is known as an	gravy browning
c The usual natural sweetener added to foods is	emulsifier
d Substances which resemble natural ones but are produced by chemical means are called	herbs
	shelf life
e A red colouring fluid produced from a crushed beetle is called	synthetics
f Yellow colouring which is produced from a species of well-known flower is	spices
g Flavourings which are produced in a concentrated fluid form are referred to as	cochineal
h A crystalline or liquid colouring made from caramelized sugar is used for	essences

i Aniseed, caraway, chillies and ginger are examples of ....

j Basil, tarragon and sage are examples of ....

2 How would you assess the standards of hygiene practised in shops selling food? Give reasons for your requirements.

3 What do you understand by the following:

a food additives	*d* 'contains preservatives'
b shelf life	*e* date stamp
c oven ready	*f* net weight?

4 'Convenience Foods' is now a very commonly understood term. Which do you consider to be the most useful of these commodities and which do you think should be avoided when housekeeping money is limited? Give your reasons.

GENERAL QUESTIONS

1 Write out the following statements, and complete them, using only the words in the right-hand column to fill in the blanks.

Section A

a Vitamin C, without which scurvy can develop, can be purchased commercially as	basting
	panada
b Sugar is to be found in milk as lactose; when attacked by bacteria this is broken down into ...., causing the flavour to be changed.	pepper
c Wheat grains contain a protein without which all the principles of the use of raising agents would be useless; this is	gelatine
	ascorbic acid
d A thickened sauce which is useful for binding together dry ingredients such as minced meat is called a	lactic acid
e A dish which has been sprinkled with breadcrumbs and browned under the grill immediately before serving is described as	junket
	pasta
f The occasional pouring of hot fat or syrup over food being cooked is known as	gluten
g An incomplete animal protein food which is used for its setting effect rather than its food value is	au gratin
h When milk is 'set' by the action of the enzyme added to it after it has been warmed with sugar, the dish is named	

i Flour paste, made from a special 'durum' wheat, is used to produce a large variety of ....

j The seasoning .... may be purchased in powder form (black, white or red) or as complete dried berries which may be used whole or ground as used.

Section B

    a A sweet sauce may be prepared from commercially-prepared coloured, sweetened corn-flour called ....

    b The enzyme which clots milk in the stomach and which is commercially prepared to produce a similar effect in the preparation of cheese and other milk dishes is ....

    c To .... can mean to whiten; in cookery it involves the short immersion of vegetables or nuts in boiling water to facilitate the removal of skins and to destroy surface bacteria.

    d The yellow, glossy outer film of the rind of a lemon or an orange is called the ....

    e A collection of herbs tied inside a piece of muslin and used while cooking soups, stews and stock and then removed is called a ....

    f A stew made of light-coloured meats and cooked and served in a thick white sauce is called a ....

    g A savoury jelly in which meat and vegetables may be set and served chilled is called ....

    h When fats deteriorate the fatty acids are broken down and unpleasant flavours are produced; they are said to have become ....

    i When foods are tossed in fat or cooked quickly in a frying pan they are described as ....

    j Pulses are nutritionally valuable seeds; beans and peas are available fresh, dried, frozen and tinned, but .... are usually used only in their dried form.

rancid

zest

lentils

rennin

blanch

sauté

aspic

custard powder

bouquet garni

fricassée

    2 Why is it sometimes necessary to re-heat cooked food? How would you ensure that these dishes remain palatable, attractive and safe to eat? Illustrate your answer with as many examples as possible.

    3 In the modern kitchen much use is made of aluminium foil and of paper. Suggest as many ways as possible in which the housewife finds these products useful.

    4 Write a paragraph on each of the following:

    a the advantages and disadvantages of shopping at a supermarket

    b points to be considered when re-heating foods

    c the actions and reactions which take place in the stomach.

(A.E.B.)

5 Write a paragraph on each of the following topics:
  a the planning of meals for an overweight teenager
  b the buying of a cooker of your own choice
  c the advantages and disadvantages of convenience foods.
(A.E.B.)
6 What are the most common accidents which happen in a kitchen and how can they be avoided? State how you would deal with *one* particular accident.

7 What do you understand by a 'beverage'? Give as many examples as you can and explain why they are valuable in the diet.

8 Certain faults are fairly common in some dishes. Which would you expect to find in the following examples and how could they be avoided?

a baked egg custard	*e* scones
b steamed sponge pudding	*f* rich fruit cake
c deep fried potato croquettes	*g* fruit salad
d stewed neck of lamb	*h* marmalade

9 Imagine that you are going to leave your kitchen in the charge of your two teenage daughters for a week. Compile a set of instructions which you can leave them so that you can be certain that it will remain hygienic and safe.

10 Write a paragraph on each of the following:
  a the enzyme action that takes place in bread-making
  b the advantages and disadvantages of 'bulk buying'
  c points to be considered when choosing saucepans for a cooker of your choice.
(A.E.B.)
11 Give reasons for the following practices:
  a the proving of a yeast mixture in a warm place before cooking
  b the soaking in water and the drying of chipped potatoes before frying
  c the rolling of a Swiss roll on sugared greaseproof paper on a damp cloth
  d the serving of finely-grated cheese in a salad
  e the stewing of tough meat.
(A.E.B.)
12 Write a paragraph on *three* of the following:
  a the prevention of food poisoning in the home
  b the economy of fuel in the kitchen
  c attractive presentation of all family meals
  d vegetarian cookery.
(A.E.B.)
13 Write a paragraph on *three* of the following:
  a kitchen hygiene
  b the attractive presentation of food
  c precautions to be observed when using left-over food
  d different types of fats and oils and their uses in cookery.
(A.E.B.)

14 Give detailed reasons for *each* of the following practices in cookery:

a stewing of shin of beef

b grating of cheese

c conservative cooking of green vegetables

d keeping milk cool, clean and covered

e not allowing an egg custard to boil.

15 Write a paragraph on the points to be considered when

a preparing a nutritionally balanced packed meal

b economizing on fuel and food in cookery

c purchasing *either* an electric *or* a gas cooker.

16*a* Describe *four* different ways in which food may become contaminated.

  b Describe precautions that should be taken by a housewife when purchasing and storing food.

  c Explain, with reasons, how you would store the following: (*i*) flour; (*ii*) milk; (*iii*) bread; (*iv*) root vegetables.   (A.E.B.)

17 Write a paragraph on the points to be considered when:

a preparing a nutritionally balanced packet meal

b economizing on fuel and food in cookery

c purchasing *either* an electric *or* a gas cooker.   (A.E.B.)

18 Why are the following processes necessary? (Include as many scientific principles as possible.)

a blanching vegetables before deep freezing

b covering a trifle placed in the refrigerator

c warming the milk to blood heat for making junket

d using warm ingredients for bread-making

e keeping milk cold in the bottle.

19 Suggest as many ways as possible in which a housewife may economize in time and movement by the arrangement of her kitchen furnishings.

20 What are the causes and possible results of food contamination? How could the contamination of food be prevented *a*. in the shop, *b*. in the home?   (C.U.B.)

21 Explain as fully as possible why

a biscuits are stored in an airtight tin and bread in a ventilated container

b mouldy jam need not be thrown away

c fresh dishes may be frozen but thawed ones should not be re-frozen

d oil remains liquid in cold weather while butter becomes too hard to spread

e lard is a better fat to use for frying than margarine or dripping

f food will remain hot in a vacuum flask

g soda is added to hot water for soaking greasy pans.

INDEX

absorption of: fats 52; meat 111;
mineral elements 59; nutrients 42;
proteins 45; sugar 49; vitamins 56;
water 62.
accelerated freeze drying 163.
accompaniments 149; beef 116;
lamb/mutton 118; pork 121; small
153; veal 120; sauces 179.
additives 219.
air as a raising agent 170, 179, 181,
182, 187, 194, 196.
albumen 68, 69, 72, 77, 100, 101, 109,
196.
alkanet 219.
almond(s) 191; biscuits 198, 206;
cake 193, 195, 207; paste 103.
amino acids 41, 45, 110.
ammonia 32.
apples 47, 60, 61, 70, 73, 130, 131,
135–7, 147, 151, 165, 166, 189.
apricots 57, 58, 131; dried 60, 129.
artichokes 132, 135.
asparagus 132, 134.
aubergine 132.

bacon 54, 55, 58, 59, 61, 68, 72, 74,
90, 212; choice 112; cooking 113;
cuts 122; production 112; rinds 156;
rolls 131; storage 14, 113; value 41,
113.
bacteria 31, 81–5, 89, 93, 124, 148,
162, 163.
baking 73; eggs 104; fish 123, 125;
fruit 137; pastry 189; vegetables 135.
baking powder 170–2, 181, 192.
baking tins 198.
balancing meals 140, 146, 148, 151, 153.
bananas 37, 47, 137, 147, 166.
basal metabolism 46.
batter 75, 86, 102, 137, 170, 176, 181,
182, 206.
beans 41, 43, 57, 58, 60, 129, 131, 132,
151, 163, 218.
beef 57, 58, 60, 61, 68, 107, 109, 110,
111; canned 218; cuts 116–7;
suet 188.
beef tea 62, 150.
beetroot 132, 133, 136, 143.
beverages 62.
bicarbonate of soda 134, 170, 171, 189,
190, 195.
binding: agent 102; sauce 180.
bins 6–7.
biotin 54.
biscuits 90, 147, 176, 178, 197, 198,
206, 212; buying 217; storage 14,
206, 210; value 41, 47.
blackberries 136.

blackcurrants 41, 55, 56, 61, 128.
blanching 165, 166, 191.
blancmange 176, 218.
blending method 180, 191.
body builders 40, 41, 147, 148.
boiling 68, 76, 188; bacon 113;
eggs 103; fish 123, 125; meat 108,
116–20; vegetables 134, 163.
bottling 131, 162, 163, 218.
braising 116–20.
bran 176, 177.
bread, 71, 90, 147, 173, 177, 178, 199,
212, 220; bin 14; brown 207; currant
201, 206; food values 44, 47, 54, 55,
57, 58, 61; storage 14, 207;
wholemeal 41.
breakfast 142, 145.
brisket 110, 117.
broccoli 132, 134.
broth 148, 158, 159.
brussels sprouts 44, 61, 128, 132.
buns 178, 193; Bath 207; currant 201.
butter 134, 146, 153, 164, 179, 191,
197; production 90; storage 36;
value 41, 44, 46, 50, 53, 55, 60.
buttermilk 89, 90.

cabbage 44, 61, 129, 130, 132, 135, 136,
151.
caffeine 68.
cakes 102, 147, 152, 176, 178, 179,
190–7, 206, 220; classification 190;
creamed mixture 90; fish 212;
frozen 218; ingredients 191;
'instant' 218; rich fruit 171, 172;
storage 14, 207, 208, 210; value 41,
206; varieties 207.
calcium 41, 44, 53, 55–9, 61, 62, 80,
86, 89, 95, 96, 100, 111, 123, 128, 141.
calcium carbonate 177.
canning 162, 163, 218.
caramelization 50, 84.
carbohydrate foods 48, 52, 90, 111.
carbohydrates 40, 46, 101; composition
47; in diet 50, 55, 60, 100; in fruit /
vegetables 129; in meals 140, 144, 146,
153; in milk 86; tables 41, 44.
carbon dioxide 63, 171, 172.
carotene 44, 53, 60, 63, 100, 128.
carrots 44, 49, 53, 55, 60, 69, 128,
130–3, 136, 143, 147, 151, 159.
casein 86, 96; -ogen 81.
casserole(s): cookery 70, 71; dishes 10.
cauliflower 60, 61, 132–5, 143, 152;
au gratin 179.
celery 132, 134, 136, 151, 159, 212.
cellulose 47, 48, 50, 69, 73, 129, 130,
134, 136.

alison McKenzie 4H.   1980-81